Assessment and Evaluation
in
Whole Language Programs

Assessment and Evaluation
in
Whole Language Programs

Edited by

Bill Harp
Northern Arizona University

Christopher-Gordon Publishers, Inc.

Norwood, MA

Dedication

To Rod Fielder and Fred Harp, who always believed.

Credit Lines

Chapter 1

Quote from "Questions We Ask of Ourselves and Our Students" from *The Reading Teacher*, Vol. 42, No. 8 (April 1989) used with permission.

Chapter 3

Figure 3.1, from "Reading Assessment: Time for a Change," from *The Reading Teacher*, Vol. 40, No. 8 (April 1987) used with permission.

Chapter 7

Excerpt from work of Lucas Albrighton used with permission.

Excerpt from work of Silas Bowler used with permission.

Excerpt from work of Daniel J. Eipper used with permission.

Chapter 11

Figure 11.3 used with permission of Lincoln County School District, Oregon.

Figure 11.4 used with permission of Carol Richman, Whole Language Team, Cuyamaca Model Education Center, CA.

Student work used with permission of Alexis Young, Breezy Guinn, Mike Jensen, and Jessica Griffy.

Christopher-Gordon Publishers, Inc.
480 Washington Street
Norwood, MA 02062

Printed in the United States of America

10 9 8 7 6 5 4 3 2 1   96 95 94 93 92 91

ISBN: 0-926842-06-4

Short Table of Contents

Long Table of Contents

Preface

The whole language movement is in a very real sense at a crossroads. While many educators at every level have embraced the basic tenets of whole language and support classroom instruction that is child-centered, meaning-focused, and holistic, the critics and traditional assessment and evaluation practices remain firmly entrenched. And how we deal with assessment and evaluation in the coming years will either confirm whole language or kill it.

Assessment and Evaluation in Whole Language Programs attempts to answer many of the critical questions being asked about the role of whole language in our schools. In pulling this volume together we called on some of the most talented educators working in the whole language arena, and gave them a challenge. We asked them to create a scholarly, yet practical work that not only examines the growing research base that supports whole language, but also offers practical and realistic suggestions for tackling the many thorny issues involved in the assessment and evaluation of students.

The book begins with an examination of the basic principles of whole language. Chapter One serves as an introduction to the movement for those new to whole language instruction. This chapter defines and illustrates whole language, explains characteristics of whole language instruction in light of a child-centered, developmental approach to literacy, and concludes by examining the philosophical/research base of whole language.

Chapters Two and Three examine past assessment and evaluation practices and offer guiding principles for future practice. John Bertrand offers valuable insights on assessment and evaluation by examining the traditional philosophy and methods of testing and evaluation through to present day needs. He calls for change that will bring assessment and evaluation in line with whole language learning processes. Bill Harp then offers twelve principles of assessment and evaluation that do not violate the basic principles of whole language instruction. The key here is that assessment and evaluation are viewed as very much a part of the teaching and learning process.

One of the greatest changes the whole language movement has brought to our view of literacy processes is in how we look at children's use of the reading process.

From seeing reading as a product that can be measured by grade scores on norm-referenced measures, we now look at how children use the reading process. In Chapter Four Dorothy Watson and Janice Henson offer practical suggestions for using miscue analysis in ways that lead to specific strategies for helping children. Their practical applications are extended in Chapter Five by Ward Cockrum and Maggie Castillo, who show how teachers can develop their own assessment and evaluation strategies.

Chapters Six through Nine, the heart of the book, focus on whole language assessment and evaluation in primary, intermediate, special education, and bilingual, multicultural settings. Jeanne Reardon invites you into her classroom where she and her students collaborate in the evaluation process. Here, assessment is the teacher's discovery and understanding of a child's learning from the child's perspective.

In Chapter Seven, Yvonne Siu-Runyan illustrates ways in which whole language instruction works in intermediate classrooms by focusing on dialoguing with students about their progress. She carefully shows how talking with students about their progress can be used in combination with anecdotal records and student portfolios.

Special education teachers who embrace whole language as the truly sensible way in which all children can be brought to literacy are constantly faced with the conflict between their beliefs in whole language instructional principles and mandated assessment and evaluation practices. In Chapter Eight, Hilary Sumner directly addresses this conflict and offers realistic suggestions for dealing with local, state, and federal guidelines.

In Chapter Nine, Dorothy King examines the complexities of multicultural classrooms and suggests that observation and analysis are critical to assessment and evaluation in these settings. She discusses the interactions of language, culture, and academic development and offers concrete examples of evaluation in real multicultural classrooms.

Whole language teachers recognize early on that old ways of keeping records do not fit into the classrooms they now wish to foster. In Chapter Ten Jean Church explores the purposes of record keeping, the kinds of records that should be kept, and what needs to be recorded.

No discussion of whole language assessment and evaluation is complete without including the principal's view and examining issues within the school and across the district. In Chapter Eleven, Ron Hutchison offers this perspective as he explores the issue of reporting progress to parents and communicating success to central administrators, school board members, and other interested parties.

Finally, we look to the future of assessment in whole language classroom. Jerome Harste and William Bintz assert that if education in this country is ever to be more than just a practice in mediocrity, literacy assessment in the future must look significantly different than it does today. This chapter will entertain and challenge, and may forever change how readers think about assessment and evaluation.

I'd like to take this opportunity to thank some of those persons who have contributed significantly to the success of this book. First, my sincere appreciation to each of the contributors who accepted the challenge and worked diligently to produce a truly fine manuscript. Next, my heart-felt thanks to Sue Canavan of Christopher-Gordon Publishers, who had the vision to get this project started and who has carefully guided its development. And finally, my thanks to the reviewers, Mona Matthews and Kate Kirby, whose thoughtful examination of the original material gave both guidance and encouragement.

B.H.
November 1990

Chapter 1

The Whole Language Movement

Bill Harp

The teacher is reading an enlarged text of *Greedy Cat* (1988) to a group of first graders. It is a wonderful New Zealand story about a greedy cat who looks in the shopping bag and eats whatever Mum has brought from the store. The predictable text follows a pattern of "Mum went shopping and bought some XXXX. Along came Greedy Cat. He looked in the shopping bag. Gobble, gobble, gobble, and that was the end of that." After the first episode the children are eagerly reading along with the teacher, usually needing support for only the names of the things Mum buys at the store.

The teacher reads ". . . and that was the end of that!" And asks, "What would you like to do with this story now?" The responses from the children are eagerly offered and extremely varied. One child suggests that they could write about Greedy Cat. Another adds that they could write about Greedy Cat. Some want to make shopping lists for their mother. One child quietly offers the possibility of reading the book to a partner or by one's self. When several children say that's what they want to do, the teacher poses the question of how they can arrange for everyone who might want to reread the book to get a turn. One child suggests a sign-up sheet and busily finds paper and paper clip to put the sign-up sheet on the cover of the big book. Another child suggests that they could make a game about Greedy Cat and he is instantly joined by two other classmates who want to do that, too.

The teacher then allows each child to choose how to respond to *Greedy Cat* and facilitates his or her other work. A few children return to activities they were engaged in before the reading of *Greedy Cat*, but most of them initiate one of the choices of activities suggested by the group.

Grant, Eric, and Julie have their heads together on the creation of a game. They make several trips to the game cupboard to get ideas for their game board. Olivia goes to the teacher with a writing problem. She wants to write "Greedy cat is too hungry." But she isn't sure which spelling of "to," "two," or "too" is right. The teacher seizes that moment to spend a little time with Olivia on a lesson on "too," and then enters an anecdotal note about Olivia's growth in her record book.

As children complete their chosen activities they share with each other and some move on to the library corner, activity centers, or to complete work started earlier. The teacher calls a group of six to the large table to engage in a guided reading activity with small copies of *Greedy Cat*.

In this classroom, as in other whole language classrooms, the children are viewed as experimenters—each hypothesizing and testing his or her theories. The teacher is the director of the laboratory. The teacher sets the stage for the children to explore, experiment, and grow. The teacher then observes carefully for ways to lead from behind by providing additional experiences that will take the children toward greater literacy.

What is Whole Language Instruction?

The scenario above gives us some insight into what is meant by whole language. Consider the important features of what happened in this classroom.

- Children were exposed to literature that confirmed what they know about how language works. The predictable text of *Greedy Cat* allowed even the emergent readers in the group to join in the reading, feel success, and find a way to respond to the selection.
- Whole language teachers think differently about readers' development and the nature of texts. In traditional classrooms the readability of *Greedy Cat* would have been determined and only children reading instructionally at that level would have been exposed to the text. Because whole language teachers think of readers developmentally, the same text can be used with all children, but the expectations for response from the children will vary. The emergent readers in the classroom benefitted from the shared reading of the text with the voice support of the teacher. Other children will be able to engage in guided reading activities with the text with limited support from the teacher and peers. Still others will be able to read the text independently.
- Whole language teachers engage in assessment as an ongoing part of instruction. The teacher noticed each child's participation in the shared reading of *Greedy Cat* and decided which children would benefit from a follow-up guided reading activity. The teacher made an instantaneous decision to

engage Olivia in a lesson on writing "to," "two," and "too." That objective was not planned in advance, but became important as Olivia exhibited a need for the instruction.

■ Whole language teachers empower children to make choices about what they learn and how they demonstrate that learning. Notice that the question at the end of the shared reading was, "What could we do with this story now?" This opened the situation to the wide variety of responses the children chose. Whole language teachers believe that literacy develops naturally through meaningful, functional use of language. The literacy activities the children chose were meaningful and functional to them.

■ Whole language teachers value risk-taking and see it as both a tool of evaluation and a form of growth for children. Again, Olivia is an example. She took a risk in spelling "too," and the teacher used that risk-taking as a tool of evaluation and as a way to help Olivia grow.

■ Whole language teachers create learning activities that are language rich, success-oriented, and carried out in a noncompetitive environment. In whole language classrooms the *process* is often of greater importance than the *product*.

■ Whole language teachers create environments in which children use print in a variety of forms for a variety of important purposes.

Other Characteristics of Whole Language Instruction

Whole language is not an approach to the teaching of reading and writing. It is not a method that can be spelled out in a teacher's guide with a defined set of instructional strategies. Instead, whole language is a mind set about instruction. It is a mind set that draws on what we know about the importance of child-centered instruction (Berglund, 1988).

Whole language instruction is not text or test driven. Instead, it is driven by what teachers know about the developmental nature of literacy and the development of children. Whole language teachers are knowledgeable about language and child development. They are knowledgeable about literature as well as other content fields. Whole language teachers arrange rich classroom environments that invite students to use language in meaningful, purposeful ways—and to take risks in doing so. Whole language teachers facilitate this growth in literacy by observing and interacting with children (TAWL, 1984).

Whole language instruction is a total literacy immersion program. Children read, read, read, and read. They write, write, write and write. They are exposed to whole selections of literature that confirm what they know about how language works. The focus is first and foremost on the creation of meaning. Only after children understand that reading and writing are meaning creating processes are they exposed to the subskills. And then, as they can benefit from that instruction.

Whole language instruction empowers both teachers and learners. It empowers teachers to be true professionals who plan and execute the best in instruction for children. Teachers are empowered to be accountable for their work through documentation in child development and research in instruction and literacy. Children are empowered to take responsibility and ownership for their learning. With choice comes responsibility. In the process children learn self-evaluation, self-confidence and self-appreciation.

Whole language teachers have very strong beliefs about language and how it is learned. Language is used to comprehend the meaning of others, to create meaning, and to share meaning. Language is used for real purposes and to solve real problems. Language is used to get things done, for interpersonal relations, to solve problems, to pretend and imagine, to explain to others, and to recreate past experiences (TAWL, 1984).

Whole language teachers use integrated, thematic units that build bridges between literacy events and a variety of subject areas. Thematic units are defined more broadly than traditional units. They have a focus or topic that cuts across subject matter areas. Themes are often developed during most of the school day. Only those subjects not covered in the theme are scheduled separately. Many literacy goals can best be achieved through thematic units. Interesting activities in which reading, writing, listening, and speaking are required in order to accomplish the content goals serve as dynamic methods for meeting literacy goals.

Whole language teachers operate from a well-defined philosophical base. The probable reason so many of them are so articulate about their beliefs is that they have had to carefully examine their beliefs and defend them. Whole language teachers are so knowledgeable because they keep reading, studying, and going to conferences so they can cope with the tough questions they get from parents, colleagues, and administrators (Goodman, 1989).

The Philosophical Bases of Whole Language

The philosophical bases of whole language are the beliefs teachers hold about how children learn, the role of the teacher, and the nature of curriculum.

How Children Learn

Much of what whole language teachers believe about the development of literacy is born of our understanding about how children learn oral language in natural, developmental ways. Strong parallels exist between learning oral language and learning literacy.

The Development of Language

The fundamental philosophical base for whole language is what we know about how children learn language. As parents, we have often been amazed at the wonder of language development while at the same time eternally grateful that it wasn't our job to *teach* language to our children. We sometimes forget that the process is not a magical one; children do have to learn to use language and it does take time and effort. Observations of young children learning language have produced several principles of language acquisition.

Language learning is self-generated. Learning to use language is controlled by the learner and does not require external motivation. Children in situations where language is used will learn to use it without reward for each word learned. Communication with significant others is enough to keep the child learning. The best motivation for learning oral language is the same as for learning to read and to write—to communicate with others.

Language learning is informal. Parents do not have language lessons for their children. They play with them, sing with them, make cookies with them, show them the world and supply words to label the environment. Language is learned through use in meaningful contexts, not through talking about it or analyzing it. Children learn langauge in the process of living in a social situation and participating in activities with others. They learn literacy in much the same way. This is not to suggest that children learning to read and write will never have instruction, but that instruction should be in a context that is meaningful to the learner. The instruction should be focused on accomplishing communication rather than isolating the forms of language.

Language learning is active. Children learn language as they actively engage in language with others. If a child says "cat" to an approaching cat the caregiver is likely to respond, "Yes, that is a cat." If the child said "Dog" the caregiver would likely say, "No, that is a cat." The child must actively take the label "cat" and decide what it is about this particular animal that makes it not a dog. Children are continually engaging in such active learning processes in learning to communicate. They need the same kind of active learning opportunities in developing literacy.

Language learning is a holistic process. Children learn about the forms and functions of language at the same time. They learn the phonetics (sounds), the pragmatics (rules for using language), the semantics (meanings), and the syntax (word order) all at once. No one would suggest that language be broken into artificial, discrete units to make it easier to learn. If we know that language is not learned by practicing its components outside the process of using it, then it follows that the learning of reading and writing must also be a holistic process that involves children in actual experiences that require reading and writing.

Language learning is variable. Each child has a unique set of experiences and a personal environment that differs somewhat from that of others. Even though children acquiring language pass through very predictable stages and most children in the world acquire language on a similar schedule, there are individual differences. The schedule varies somewhat for each person, but almost all will achieve competence in communicating and will have mastered most of the skills required for communication by the age of five or six.

The Development of Literacy

Whole language teachers draw on what we know about the development of oral language to undergird our beliefs about the teaching and learning of literacy. We believe that the key principles of language acquisition apply to the development of literacy.

Literacy learning is self-generated. From the time children first scribble a line and "read" it to themselves or someone else, we see the self-generating nature of literacy development. Children want to communicate in written form, and those efforts will grow in environments where adults respond favorably to their reading and writing efforts.

Literacy learning is informal. Much of the real learning about reading and writing occurs outside the context of formal lessons in school. As children write more accurately through successive approximations to adult writing, they receive feedback on their writing. This feedback is then used to confirm their growing beliefs about how writing works. The same is true of reading. Children who understand from the beginning that reading is creating meaning, work through successive approximations to become more and more accurate in their reading. In a sense, each reading activity becomes a lesson for the next reading activity.

Literacy learning is active. Children learn literacy best in situations where they are using reading and writing continually—both in dramatic play and in real communicative contexts. Children, in fact, learn to read and write as they read and write. Whole language teachers find ways to involve reading and writing in virtually all curriculum areas. It is not uncommon to walk into a whole language classroom and have a child greet you with "Do you want to see what I am writing?"

Literacy learning is a holistic process. Children learn about the forms and functions of reading and writing at the same time. Just as learning oral language began with a desire to communicate meaning, so writing and reading begin the same way. Reading and writing need not be learned (in fact, are more difficult to learn) by practicing their components outside the process of using them. Whole language teachers believe that literacy moves from wholes to parts. Children are exposed to whole stories, whole paragraphs, whole sentences before they are ever asked to deal with the component parts, the sounds and letters.

Literacy learning is variable. Each child develops at his or her own pace, but virtually all will achieve competence if the focus is on communication, that is, meaning. Children acquire mastery of literacy through repeated practice with frequent constructive feedback. The practice of reading and writing must always be in real communicative contexts—not forced, artificial situations.

Reading and writing are inverse processes. The writer begins with ideas and transforms those ideas into print to be shared and responded to by a reader. The reader begins with the print and ends with ideas that are similar to the ideas of the writer. A transaction occurs between the ideas of the writer. A transaction occurs between the ideas of the author and the ideas of the reader.

Reading is a very complex process. The reader's knowledge of how language works combined with the ability to draw on background experiences are crucial to using the reading process successfully. Children need opportunities to generate and test hypotheses about print, and to read printed material that is meaningful and predictable. Children also need teachers and parents who stress meaning more than mechanics.

Learning to write is very much like learning to speak and read. It is a developmental process that moves through observable stages. Classroom environments may be structured to foster writing development. In such classrooms oral language is encouraged and celebrated, children engage in activities that invite thinking, talking, reading, and writing, and literature is shared frequently. In such classrooms children value each other's work and the teachers value the work of children.

Composition is not a single act, but a sequence of activities that is described as a process. This process involves prewriting activities, rough drafting, revision, editing, final drafting, and presentation. The process is more important than any one writing piece. Working through the process frequently with positive feedback from others results in improved writing.

The Role of the Teacher

The best definition of whole language teachers has been offered by Ken Goodman (1986) when he wrote:

> They believe in kids, respect them as learners, cherish them in all their diversity, and treat them with love and dignity. That's a lot better than regarding children as empty pots that need filling, as blobs of clay that need molding, or worse, as evil little troublemakers forever battling teachers. Whole language teachers believe that school exists for kids, not that kids are to be filled and molded by behavior modification or assertive discipline into look-alike, act-alike, Barbie and Ken dolls.
>
> Whole language teachers believe there is something special about human learning and human language. They believe all children have language and the ability to learn language, and they reject negative, elitist, racist views of linguistic purity that would limit children to arbitrary "proper" language. Instead, they view their role as helping children to expand on the marvelous language they already use. They expect them to learn and they are there to help them do it. (p. 25)

Teacher as Learner

The role of the whole language teacher is foremost one of learner. Teaching from a strong philosophical and research base about the primacy of language requires constant study, reflection, and planning. Whole language teachers know that the more they know about language and learning, the better teachers they will be. They know that when they keep language whole and meaningful, it will be easier for children to learn because it makes sense. Trust is an important part of the role of the whole language teacher. Whole language teachers trust that all of their children will be capable language learners. Just as parents trust that children will learn oral language, so teachers trust that children will become literate. Whole language teachers surround their students with print the same way parents surround young children with conversation. In both instances the significant adults *trust* that learning will occur.

Teacher as Facilitator

Part of the whole language teacher's role is that of facilitator. The teacher's job is to create a language rich classroom environment in which children are encouraged to explore, to experiment, and to take risks. Teachers arrange time so that it is flexible enough to permit children long periods of time for reading, writing, exploring, and pursuing personal interests. Some critics of whole language are aghast that the whole language teacher admittedly cannot specify all of the instructional objectives for a day *in advance*. Certainly, the whole language teacher is *responsible* for the learning of the children, but in a child-centered classroom the teacher *structures* the environment so that children can take the lead. And it isn't always possible to know in advance where the lead will take the children and the teacher!

Teacher as Observer and Evaluator

Whole language teachers are observers and evaluators. In traditional programs where the focus of instruction is texts, materials, and a prepackaged curriculum the evaluation is primarily in the form of tests—a kind of product evaluation. In whole language classrooms the focus is on children, their interests, their need to use language, the ways in which they use language as they explore, experiment, and communicate. Here the evaluation is primarily process-oriented. Teachers use samples of children's work to assess the ways in which children are growing in their use of the reading and writing processes. In whole language classrooms teachers more often ask questions intended to challenge children than give answers.

The Nature of Curriculum

The curriculum is everything we want children to know, do, or feel as a result of their educational experience. One of the truly distinguishing traits of whole language classrooms is the curriculum. Whole language curriculum is characterized by ownership on the part of children, choice for children, and activities and materials that are authentic.

Ownership

Whole language teachers believe that the more learning in school can be like learning out of school, the more effective and enjoyable that learning will be. Gordon Wells (1986) encapsulated this belief in his book about children learning language and using language to learn. He said,

> From observation outside school, we know that children are innately predisposed to make sense of their experience, to pose problems for themselves, and actively to search for and achieve solutions. There is every reason to believe, therefore, that, given the opportunity, they will continue to bring these characteristics to bear inside the school as well, provided that the tasks that they engage in are ones that they have been able to make their own. All of us, adults and children alike, function most effectively when we are working on a task or problem to which we have a personal commitment, either because the goal is one that we are determined to achieve . . . or because the activity is one that we find intrinsically satisfying, or both. (p. 120)

In order for children to have ownership of their learning they must have choice and direction in that learning. Through joint teacher/student planning each day whole language teachers find ways to give children responsibility for deciding what tasks to undertake and how to get them done. The teacher then supports that effort through careful observation, questioning, guiding, and inviting. In effect, the curriculum is then negotiated between teacher and pupil, with the teacher always having ultimate responsibility.

When children have ownership of the curriculum teachers discover that many management and motivation problems disappear. When children have agreed to the day's agenda they behave responsibly, moving from one important task to another with little guidance from the teacher. In fact, children in this environment ask for the teacher's help only when all other resources have been exhausted. Consequently, teachers are freed from many of the mundane classroom management tasks and can give much greater attention to individual children. Creating this kind of classroom environment takes a great deal of hard work and imagination on the part of the teacher. It requires experimentation, too. There is no magic formula. The organization of time, space, and resources is an important element. Whole language classrooms are usually organized around flexible activity centers.

The classroom contains a rich assortment of objects and creatures for children to study, chart, graph, and write about. Children have ready access to the myriad of materials necessary to accomplish the tasks (Bird, 1987).

Choice for Children

Remember the episode with *Greedy Cat* in which the teacher finished reading the book and then asked the children what they could do with the book after that? In this situation the teacher was opening up the range of activities to the imaginations and interests of the children. In whole language classrooms children have choice in the literature they will read and in the topics they will write about. This is not to say that in all situations they will have choice, but in every situation in which it makes sense for children to have choices they will have them. Whole language teachers challenge themselves not to teach as they were taught, but to draw on the best educational thinking in designing instruction.

Authentic Materials and Activities

In the April 1989 issue of *The Reading Teacher* Becky Reimer and Leslie Warshow published the individual narratives of experienced teachers attempting to resolve issues around whole language. JoAnne Swindle poignantly described her struggle with the meaning of reading ability. Swindle wrote:

> Little Bridget in my kindergarten class three years ago forced me to rethink what I valued as markers of reading ability. Bridget passed all my skills assessment and also all the readiness tests I could find. I could hand her any book in my classroom and she would proceed to sound out each word and blend it into something that sounded like a word.
>
> She made me feel very uneasy, though, because she seemed to only go through the motions of reading without really understanding why she was reading or what she was reading. I felt insecure about recommending her for 1st grade but I had no hard data to justify my feelings. Back then, I thought reading consisted of skills for learners to learn and that my role, as a kindergarten teacher, was to teach one sound a week and by mid-February begin to introduce one word at a time for the students to learn to sound out. By mid-March I introduced my students to reading very carefully controlled sentences.
>
> I was in a quandry, though. Bridget met all my criteria but yet I still knew she wasn't a reader. I sat down with her one day with a book and asked her to read it. She methodically proceeded to sound out each word. I stopped her at one point and asked her about what she had read up until that point. She shrugged her shoulders. I closed the book and asked her what she thought this book was about. She shrugged her shoulders.
>
> I was screaming inside. This child didn't have the foggiest idea about the purposes for print and I hadn't helped her make any of those connections. I had only been asking my students about the sound of particular letters and how they could

sound out the words I gave them. I wonder what they thought were the purposes of what I was doing with these letters, sound blending, and words. I never thought about asking them for what it meant to them. I had actually discouraged them from bringing books to school that didn't fit my carefully controlled reading scheme of letters, sound blending and CVC words.

For the past two years I have been consciously trying to orchestrate my curriculum so that reading and writing have real life connections. I start the year with questions which will help me learn about what they know and how they think about reading and writing and also help them to begin to think about the bigger picture for reading and writing: Why do people need to read/write? What is reading/ writing for? How do you think you will learn to read/write? What could you do if you knew how to read/write? What do you already know about reading/writing?

I no longer assume that reading is only skills. I support my kindergarten children by reading books to them and allowing them free reading time for choosing books. (p. 597).

What do whole language teachers mean by authentic texts? The best way to answer that question is to look at the language in texts that are labeled preprimer by one of the basal publishers. One that readily comes to mind went something similar to the following:

Sam and Sally went to the lake.
"Good morning, Frog," said Sam.
"Good morning, Frog," said Sally.
Sam and Sally went down to the lake.
"Duck, Frog," said Sam.
"Good, Frog," said Sally.

Like so many stories controlled for vocabulary and certain phonic elements, the story above is incomprehensible. Whole language teachers reject giving children such texts that fail to confirm what they know about how language works. Children know that stories are supposed to be understandable. They know that language works to create meaning. They expect the same things from print that they expect from oral language. Whole language teachers make sure that the texts they give children confirm what children know about how language works. When basal authors write meaningless stories such as the one above there is no recognition that readers bring a great deal of knowledge to the reading act.

Ken Goodman (1986) has asserted that language learning in school should be as easy as it is out of school. He posited that:

Language is easy to learn when:	**Language is hard to learn when:**
It's real and natural.	It's artificial.
It's whole.	It's broken into bits and pieces.
It's sensible.	It's nonsense.
It's interesting.	It's dull and uninteresting.
It's relevant.	It's irrelevant to the learner.
It belongs to the learner.	It belongs to somebody else.
It's part of a real event.	It's out of context.
It has social utility.	It has no social value.
It has purpose for the learner.	It has no discernible purpose.
The learner chooses to use it.	It's imposed by someone else.
It's accessible to the learner.	It's inaccessible.
The learner has power to use it.	The learner is powerless. (p. 8)

Teachers must make an initial curriculum choice. They choose a fixed curriculum and demand that learners adjust to it, or they start where learners are and build the curriculum around the needs and interests of the learners. Whole language teachers have chosen the latter. Critics who suggest that such curricular changes can't be made are well served when reminded that curriculum has changed dramatically over the history of American public education. It hasn't always been what it is—and it can still change.

The Research Bases of Whole Language

The true research base for whole language is the vast body of research that informs us regarding how students learn, how students learn to read and write, and what constitutes effective instructional strategies in literacy.

The whole language teacher's assertion that children must be active learners and that learning must be based on students' experiences is based on the work of Bateson (1972), Dewey (1938), and Eisner (1982) to name just a few. The work of these researchers reveals that children's learning needs to be reality-based rather than abstract and removed from experience. Whole language teachers use this body of work to justify the belief that literacy is best learned in a whole, meaningful context.

Our knowledge of language development is at the center of the whole language curriculum. We know that literacy develops in parallel lines to oral language development. Just as children move from producing very immature oral language to highly-developed oral language, so they move from scribbles to complete texts. We appreciate the importance of adult models and adult interaction in both oral language and literacy acquisition. The research base on which these beliefs are founded is made up, in part, by the work of Courtney Cazden (1986), Carol Chomsky (1969 and 1972), Jerome Harste (1984), and Lev Vygotsky (1986).

Reading and writing are processes that have much in common. Both readers and writers begin the process by using previous knowledge about the topic, the way language works, and about our alphabetic writing system. Both readers and writers bring certain expectations to the task. These expectations are based on previous reading and writing experiences, knowledge about the purposes of reading and writing, and knowledge about audiences (Butler and Turbill, 1984). Teachers who understand the development of language, reading, and writing provide activities that involve the children in all these processes. They know that these experiences must also be relevant to the children. Taylor et al. (1986) describes the characteristics of classrooms that implement a whole language view of reading instruction. These characteristics include: multiple and varied stimuli for reading, multiple and varied stimuli for writing, accessible and functional display of children's language products, integrative print, explicit classroom routines, and child-centered activities and instruction.

Whole language classrooms contain many books, directions, schedules, messages, and other materials for reading. Such classrooms stress functional reasons for writing such as message centers, sign-up lists, and well stocked writing centers. Print is used to take care of such tasks as attendance taking. Classroom chores and materials produced by the children are used for on going activities. Teachers also use print in typical projects such as hatching eggs so that their students can keep records, check off activities, produce charts, and use reference materials. The daily classroom routines are real opportunities for using print to keep records, make and record choices, and keep track of how many participants are involved in an activity at one time. Finally, the print is child-centered in that most of it is produced by children and reflects their activities and interests.

The research base that informs whole language teachers about the reading process rests, in part, on the work of Marie Clay (1979), Kenneth Goodman (1970 and 1984), Frank Smith (1989), David Rumelhart (1984), Yetta Goodman (1980 and 1983), and William Teale and Elizabeth Sulzby (1986).

The research base that informs whole language teachers about the writing process rests, in part, on the work of Donald Graves (1975 and 1983), Nancy Shanklin (1982), Lucy Calkins (1986), and Marie Clay (1982).

The research base on which whole language teachers build their views of how literacy develops includes the work of Carol Chomsky (1972), Marie Clay (1982), Dolores Durkin (1966), Carol Edelsky (1982), Don Holdaway (1979), Elizabeth Sulzby (1985), and Constance Weaver (1982).

The whole language research base is moving in a new direction. There is a small, growing body of research that looks at the effectiveness of whole language instruction or compares whole language instruction with traditional instruction. Such research is riddled with possibilities for error and misinterpretation, and whole language teachers do not look to this research to justify their work. However, it may be instructive to examine some of the work reported to date.

Hans Grundin (1985) revisited the data reported by Bond and Dykstra (1967) in the USOE First Grade Studies. While there were not true whole language classrooms in the studies, Grundin concluded that those approaches that came closest to being whole language actually produced the best results of the various approaches compared.

Donald Graves and Virginia Stuart (1985) report the results of a two year extensive study of the writing of 16 children. Major findings included that children write more and produce better writing when they are given control of topics and are encouraged to use their own developmental spelling. Children in the study learned to revise their writing and to assist each other in revision. They discovered that every child in the study had behavioral characteristics in the writing process that applied to that child alone. This led the researchers to conclude that children need a waiting, responsive type of teaching.

Lois Bird (1987) reports that when a resource teacher established a psycholinguistic reading laboratory in which children read and discussed fine children's literature daily, reading grade scores on the California Test of Basic Skills increased dramatically. In one year, fourth, fifth and sixth graders made between 13 and 21 months growth in reading in a nine month period.

Norman Smith was Principal of Fair Oaks school at the time the school moved from traditional instruction to whole language (Bird, 1989). He reports that interesting changes occurred after the move to whole language. First, student attendance increased. Second, the whole atmosphere of the school improved. He tells the story of one parent who came to Back to School Night to investigate why his daughter was suddenly so positive about school. After a year of whole language, third grade bilingual students began to achieve at nearly the same level on both the CTBS Español and the CTBS English test in the spring. Finally, Smith reports that historically only 10 to 20 percent of Fair Oaks students passed the Redwood City District sixth grade writing proficiency test each fall. After three years of students being immersed in process writing, the passing rate increased to 82 percent.

Carbo (1988) in theorizing that whole language instruction just might dramatically improve literacy levels in the United States, refers to a study done in the Portland, Oregon Public Schools. In a study of 18,126 students, the Portland public schools reported significantly higher reading achievement after one year of implementing a whole language program, compared to achievement during the previous five years when typical basal reader instruction was used.

A word of caution is in order in looking at this newer research base that compare the effectiveness of whole language instruction with other modes of instruction. Typically the comparison is based on norm-referenced test performance which whole language teachers do not value. It is paradoxical that even when measures that whole language teachers reject are used, whole language instruction is superior to traditional instruction.

References

Bateson, G. (1972). Effects of conscious purpose on human adaptation. In G. Bateson (Ed.), *Steps to an ecology of mind*. New York: Bantam Books.

Berglund, R. (1988, December, 1989, January). Whole language: A swing of the pendulum or a whole new pendulum? *Reading Today*, p. 18.

Bird, L. (1989). *Becoming a whole language school: The Fair Oaks story*. Katonah, NY: Richard C. Owen.

Bird, L. (1987). *What is whole language?* Paper presented at Whole Language Conference II, Lethbridge, Alberta, Canada.

Bond, G.L. & Dykstra, R. (1967). The cooperative research program in first-grade reading instruction. *Reading Research Quarterly, 2*, 5–142.

Butler, A., & Turbill, J. (1984). *Towards a reading-writing classroom*. Rozell, New South Wales: Primary English Teaching Association.

Calkins, L. (1986). *The art of teaching writing*. Portsmouth, NH: Heinemann Educational Books.

Cazden, C. (1986). Classroom discourse. In M.L. Wittrock (Ed.), *Handbook of research on teaching* (3rd ed.). New York: Macmillan.

Chomsky, C. (1972). Stages in language development and reading exposure. *Harvard Educational Review, 42*, 1–33.

Chomsky, C. (1969). *The acquisition of syntax from 5–10*. Cambridge, MA: MIT Press.

Clay, M. (1982). *Observing young readers*. Portsmouth, NH: Heinemann Educational Books.

Clay, M. (1979). *Reading: The patterning of complex behavior*. Portsmouth, NH: Heinemann Educational Books.

Clay, M. (1982). *What did I write? Beginning writing behavior*. Exeter, NH: Heinemann Educational Books.

Cowley, J. (1988). *Greedy cat*. Wellington, New Zealand: School Publications Branch, Department of Education.

Dewey, J. (1938). *Experience and education*. New York: Macmillan.

Durkin, D. (1966). *Children who read early: Two longitudinal studies*. New York: Teachers College Press.

Edelsky, C. (1983). Segmentation and punctuation: Developmental data from young writers in a bilingual program. *Research in the Teaching of English, 17*, 135–156.

Eisner, E. (1982). *Cognition and curriculum*. New York: Longman.

Goodman, K.S. (1989, Spring). Do whole language teachers have to suffer? *Teachers Networking—The Whole Language Newsletter, 9*, 3. Katonah, NY: Richard C. Owen.

Goodman, K. (1970). Behind the eye: What happens in reading. In K. Goodman & O. Niles (Eds.), *Reading: Process and program*. (pp. 3–38). Urbana, IL: National Council of Teacher of English.

Goodman, K. (1984). Unity in reading. In A. Purves & O. Niles (Eds.), *Becoming readers in a complex society.* 83rd yearbook of the National Society of the Study of Education: Part I. Chicago, IL: University of Chicago Press.

Goodman, K. (1986). *What's whole in whole language?* Portsmouth, NH: Heinemann Educational Books.

Goodman, Y. (1983). Language, cognitive development and reading behavior. *Claremont Reading Conference Yearbook* (pp. 10–16). Claremont, CA: Claremont Graduate School.

Goodman, Y. (1980). The roots of literacy. *Claremont Reading Conference Yearbook* (pp. 1–32). Claremont, CA: Claremont Graduate School.

Graves, D. (1975). An examination of the writing processes of seven year old children. *Research in the Teaching of English, 9,* 227–241.

Graves, D. (1983). *Writing: Teachers and children at work.* Portsmouth, NH: Heinemann Educational Books.

Graves, D. & Stuart, V. (1985). *Write from the start: Tapping your child's natural writing ability.* New York: New American Library.

Grundin, H.U. (1985). A commission of selective readers: A critique of *Becoming a nation of readers. The Reading Teacher, 39,* 262–266.

Holdaway, D. (1979). *The foundations of literacy.* Portsmouth, NH: Heinemann Educational Books.

Harste, J., Woodward, V. & Burke, C. (1984). Examining our assumptions: A transactional view of literacy and learning. *Research in the Teaching of English, 18,* 84–108.

Reimer, B.L. & Warshow, L. (1989). Questions we ask of ourselves and our students. *The Reading Teacher, 42,* (8), 596–606.

Rumelhart, D. (1989). Understanding understanding. In James Flood (Ed.), *Understanding reading comprehension.* Newark, DE: International Reading Association.

Shanklin, N. (1982). *Relating reading and writing: Developing a transactional model of the writing process.* Monographs in Teaching and Learning. Bloomington, IN: Indiana University School of Education.

Smith, Frank. (1989). *Understanding reading* (4th ed.). New York: Holt, Rinehart and Winston.

Sulzby, E. (1985). Children's emergent reading of favorite story books: A developmental study. *Reading Research Quarterly, 20,* 458–481.

Taylor, N., Blum, I.H. & Logsdon, D.M. (1986). The development of written language awareness: Environmental aspects and program characteristics. *Reading Research Quarterly, 21,* 132–149.

Teale, W.H. & Sulzby, E. (1986). Introduction. In W. Teale & E. Sulzby (Eds.), *Emergent literacy: Writing and reading.* Norwood, NJ: Ablex.

Tucsonans Applying Whole Language (TAWL). (1984). *A kid-watching guide: Evaluation for whole language classrooms.* Tucson, AZ: Arizona Center for Research and Development, University of Arizona.

Vygotsky, Lev. (1986). *Thought and language.* Cambridge, MA: MIT Press. (Original work published 1934)

Weaver, C. (1982). Welcoming errors as signs of growth. *Language Arts, 59,* 438–444.

Wells, G. (1986). *The meaning makers: Children learning language and using language to learn.* Portsmouth, NH: Heinemann Educational Books.

Chapter 2

Student Assessment and Evaluation

John E. Bertrand

This chapter addresses the history of traditional evaluation and assessment in an attempt to chronicle how we have arrived at the present state of affairs. We'll look at the philosophy of traditional evaluation, along with the assumptions on which traditional assessment and evaluation have been based. We'll then identify and contrast the philosophy and assumptions on which whole language evaluation rests with those of traditional forms. The chapter concludes with a review of sources of data and insight for the whole language teacher.

Distinction Between Assessment and Evaluation

Evaluation usually refers to the process where a teacher collects, analyzes, and interprets data to determine the extent to which students are achieving instructional objectives (Gronlund, 1985). Assessment is the gathering of data, usually quantitative in nature and based on testing, that provide the information for evaluation to take place. Though technically one is a subset of the other, assessment and evaluation are terms that have often been used interchangeably in traditional classrooms. The measurement of student knowledge or performance is usually accomplished by quantifying some aspect of student output through testing and separating students into categories based on scores. This has led to a blurring of the distinctions between evaluation and assessment or testing (Gronlund,

1985; Mager, 1973). In classrooms, it is nearly always the scores that pupils generate in testing that are used exclusively to evaluate students.

Background

Testing is a very old concept. In the Old Testament, Jephthah (Judg. 12:5) ordered that all those who approached the Jordan fords unable to pronounce the word "shibboleth" should be killed. By doing so, he distinguished between his own men and those of the enemy, who could not say the sound "sh." Thus, those who came with the password pronounced as "sibboleth" failed a very effective, early, criterion-referenced achievement test and received immediate feedback (Micheels & Karnes, 1950). The ancient Chinese used an examination that tested knowledge of the classics to determine who would be admitted to civil service (Phillips, 1968), and students were given performance tests on spelling, composition, grammar, and handwriting as early as Colonial times in the United States (Hodges, 1977).

Students in the United States have always been asked to provide evidence of their learning in structured ways, either by recitation or in writing. Even at beginning levels of schooling, kindergarten and below, the belief that learning can and should be tested has not historically been given much challenge. Teachers have always been expected to give grades and to differentiate between students based on periodic checks of performance and these checks of performance have been and are nearly always based on tests of some sort.

The controversies surrounding testing as the principal means of assessment and evaluation have centered around the types of testing to be used, not whether or not testing should exist. Phillips (1968) reported a study conducted in 1900 wherein copies of the same geometry paper were shown to 116 teachers for grading. The teachers' marks ranged from 28 to 92, leading to criticisms of teachers' ability to grade accurately and objectively. Hulten (1925) gave 28 English teachers a paper to grade and found that 15 of the teachers who passed the paper the first time failed it when asked to grade it again two months later. Furthermore, 11 of those who initially failed it passed the paper on the second grading opportunity. These and other similar reports helped popularize demands for more objective forms of testing.

In this country, calls for testing not open to interpretations by teachers are as old as public education. Horace Mann himself suggested the use of written examinations as early as 1845, calling for large numbers of questions and the standardization of answers. By 1878, the Regents' Examinations were in place in New York. The College Entrance Examination Board was organized in 1900 to provide questions used by about 1000 colleges as part of entrance requirements.

Nearly as soon as they were in common use, standardized tests began to be criticized. Many people of the day felt that they were undemocratic, and those in the growing scientific movement in education were unhappy with the tests' validity and reliability. As a result, what Micheels and Karnes (1950) called the "Testing Movement in eduction" was born. They reported that the first standardized tests born out of the statistical work begun by Thorndike and his students came into being in the field of arithmetic in 1908 and in handwriting in 1910. By 1928, over 1300 published tests were in existence, with statistically calculated validity and reliability. By 1944, over 60 million standardized tests were administered to over 20 million people. Today, of course, it is virtually impossible to take part in schooling at any level without submitting to periodic standardized tests.

Closely related to the development of statistically reliable standardized tests was the rise of state and private testing bureaus, whose function it was to prepare and distribute tests. By the end of World War I, over 100 test bureaus were in operation. In the late 20s, state-wide testing was introduced. The University of Iowa Every-Pupil Scholarship Testing Program, begun in 1929, was one of the first. By 1939, 26 states had similar projects. Coincident to and to some extent because of the development of modern style tests, the statistical concepts and techniques necessary to handle such a huge mass of data were invented. Today, every state in the US maintains departments of educational testing.

It is important to remember that traditional teacher-made tests and standardized tests vary only in degree of rigor and statistical control. The intent of both is the same, to measure quantitatively a student's attainment of the information and skills specified by the curriculum. In fact, several books urge teachers to use statistical methods to insure the validity and reliability of teacher-made tests (Gronlund, 1985; Phillips, 1968; Storey, 1970). It is this reliance on quantification that has made testing and evaluation nearly synonymous.

Standardized Testing

In practice, traditional evaluation has evolved as a dual system. Teacher-made tests are usually used to provide grades, while results of standardized tests are used to make or assist in making larger decisions about the pupil, the school, and even the school system. Standardized achievement tests usually share a number of common attributes. For instance, nearly all of them fall into one of two classifications: norm referenced or criterion referenced.

Norm-referenced tests are intended to provide a measure of performance that is interpretable in terms of an individual's relative standing in some known group (Gronlund, 1985). Usually, the comparison group is large (such as all the 12th grade students in a state), and the norms for the test have been established using a large sample representative of that group. Thus, we might say that a student scoring at the 76th percentile in mathematics earned a score that exceeded 76 percent of the students in the comparison group.

Norm-referenced tests usually share the following characteristics: They cover a large domain, with a few items measuring each learning task. They are used to discriminate between students for the purpose of rank ordering. They are designed to include items of average difficulty and avoid easy items, in an effort to stimulate a wide range of scores. Interpretation of a score requires a clearly defined population whose norms are well described.

Criterion-referenced tests, on the other hand, usually attempt to provide a measure of performance that is interpretable in terms of clearly defined and relatively narrow domains of learning. That is, specific skills and knowledges are tested, to which the test giver knows for certain the student has been exposed. These tests are intended to identify strengths and weaknesses in individual students in terms of knowledge and task performance. They are used primarily to test relative mastery and require, for interpretation, a clearly stated level of desired performance. This level of performance may be stated in terms of time, number correct, or a combination of requirements. An example might be: "The students in the third grade at Countwell School will be able to correctly identify at least eight out of ten correct answers on a multiple choice test covering 'Helpers in our Community' each Friday during Social Studies class."

Both criterion and normed tests use the same kinds of questions, and both require a relevant sample of items representing the domain. The quality of the items is judged by the same standards of validity and reliability, and both are usually constructed so that the scores are amenable to statistical manipulation and interpretation.

The Philosophy of Traditional Testing and Evaluation

The above description of traditional testing practices rests on a set of assumptions that had, according to Micheels and Karnes, already taken on the status of articles of faith when their book was published in 1950. The most basic of these assumptions is: "Anything that exists at all exists in some quantity, and anything that exists in some quantity is capable of being measured" (p. 2). They went on to say that achievement certainly exists, both as a concept and as a quantity; and therefore, achievement can be measured. The problem, according to Micheels and Karnes (1950) is only in developing instruments that discriminate sufficiently well to rank pupils. They said, "Our present instruments for measuring achievement are crude in comparison with the various electronic devices used in physical measurements, but definite improvements are being made continuously. In the years ahead, we shall be able to place more and more faith in the results of such tests" (p. 19).

Little has changed since the 50s among authorities who accept traditional assumptions about testing and evaluation [Bloom, Madaus, and Hasting (1981); Gronlund (1985); Mager (1973); Payne (1974); Storey (1970)]. All of them generally accept the same set of purposes for evaluation and the same set of assumptions, that is, that objective assessment (testing) is the most appropriate and reliable means of arriving at an evaluation of student performance.

Little seems to have changed in classrooms, either. Tests are still by far the tool of choice used in grading, and most tests are of the traditional types. Implicit in traditional tests is another, less well articulated set of assumptions that is, nonetheless, quite powerful. This set follows a logical progression that might be stated as follows: Knowledge of facts is the most important goal in grading and evaluation, and this knowledge can be broken down into its component parts. These individual facts can be tested using traditional methods. These traditional methods are valid and reliable in producing a profile of the student's learning. This profile is all that is appropriate to know about a student when assigning a grade.

This logical progression, long accepted, is now being questioned. Simple observation in most public school classrooms leads to the conclusion that too few students know how to engage in acts of synthesis and higher order analysis. Glasser (1990) reports that the situation has reached crisis proportions, with less than ten percent of present high school students able to deal with even simple tasks of integrative learning, such as summarizing a 1000 word theme or calculating the cost of a family meal from a menu. Rather, the average test in public school classes reflects the type of lower order thinking most students are comfortable with (Shanker, 1990). It is fill in the blank, true-false, multiple choice, or some other "objective" measure that reflects lower order thinking. Critics often point to the lack of context or purpose in this process for students as the reason for many of the present ills in education (Glasser, 1990).

Another assumption on which traditional testing rests is that teachers should not be allowed to depend on their own judgment in evaluating students. Because there did not historically exist a research based theory of language and learning, teacher assigned grades therefore varied enormously (Hulten, 1925; Phillips, 1968). Only in the last 25 or 30 years has a coherent, research based theory of language and learning been developed. For this reason, teachers have been urged over the decades to engage in "objective" testing that does not allow them much professional participation in the process of evaluation. Storey (1970) puts it as simply as possible: "The most valid and reliable data available to the classroom teacher is that resulting from his own well designed, item-analyzed, multiple choice tests" (p. xiv). Storey (1970) stated that these tests yielded student achievement profiles that were easy to produce and revealed all that was needed in evaluation of performance. Implicit in his statement is that teachers' judgments are not valid and reliable enough to produce student achievement profiles.

Embedded in the notion of "objective" testing is the assumption that the outcome of instruction is learning and that learning is testable in some objective fashion. The results of these tests are supposed to provide the type of information that allows the teacher to grade student performance. For these reasons, assessment and evaluation have become synonymous, and teachers have found themselves removed farther and farther from the evaluation process. The reality today is that school personnel make life altering judgments about children with little or no input from those who know the children best, teachers and parents, much less the children themselves. Instead, team meetings of school personnel consider grades, standardized test scores, and behavior as the criteria for the labelling and placement of children.

In many places, standardized tests have become the curriculum. The paramount consideration in what is taught in many schools is aimed at good test scores (accompanied by the assumption that good scores accurately reflect real learning), and the paramount consideration in evaluation and assessment is to produce numbers by which children can be ranked, labelled, and compared (Smith, 1986; Stice & Call, 1987).

Calls for Change

For several reasons, however, the status quo is changing. First, many educators are dissatisfied with present evaluation/assessment methods as a means for arriving at any true understanding of how well a student can perform. If, in fact, the original assumption underpinning standardized testing, that is, that all students in any given referenced group begin as potential equals, is being violated by teaching to the test, then standardized testing is losing its ability to differentiate between students either individually or in groups with validity and reliability (Stice & Call, 1987).

Some believe that failure of standardized tests to differentiate between students fairly on the basis of what they really know is both undemocratic and potentially racist. Evangelauf (1990), citing a report entitled "From Gatekeeper to Gateway: Transforming Testing in America," quoted Bernard R. Gifford, Chairman of the National Commission on Testing and Public Policy.

There is ample evidence that the testing enterprise has in many instances gone haywire and is driving our educational system in the wrong direction. . .Current testing, predominantly multiple choice in format, is over-relied on, lacks adequate public accountability, sometimes leads to unfairness in the allocation of opportunities, and too often undermines social policies. . . (p. Al)

It may be seen from the above that more recent judgments of standardized testing are not generally accepting as they have been in the past.

Second, the definition of what constitutes education is changing. It is no longer enough, for instance, for workers to be merely able to read simple directions. They must be capable of higher level kinds of comprehension and synthesis (Mikulecky, 1987). Inability to function in these ways carries a strong risk of unemployment. Bertrand (1987) found that as companies struggled for survival, they tended to lay off up to two-thirds of their workers and gain added productivity from those remaining through the use of robotics and computerization. The employees who retained their jobs were ones who had the literacy skills that allowed them to be trained quickly in radically new ways.

This is a relatively new phenomenon. Shanker (1990) reports the situation as good news and bad news. The good news is that ". . .everybody has mastered the basics. Students can read basic material, and they can add, subtract, multiply, and divide whole numbers. But from there on, the news is all bad" (p. 346). 50 years ago, for everyone to read and do basic math would have been more than a single bright spot in an otherwise dismal picture; it would have been victory itself. As society has become more complex, the requirements for basic participation have risen. Thus, traditional evaluations and types of evaluating are now being discarded because they are obsolete. We are now faced with finding new ways to determine what pupils can and cannot do that reflect the kinds of learning people need to prosper today.

Lastly, as schools and classrooms are restructured and as philosophies of what constitutes appropriate instruction change, new means to evaluate learning are called for. Standardized tests, designed to assess learning, are being charged with doing no more than labelling learners. Many are calling for site-based management with empowerment to parents and teachers (Cawelti, 1989; Finn, 1987) as a way to establish meaningful evaluation without the constraints of what they see as a bankrupt assessment process.

Rethinking Evaluation

As we have seen, traditional evaluation has evolved from 1) time honored practices; 2) a view of desirable educational outcomes as products (knowledge of facts); 3) the desire to make evaluation objective; 4) a belief that it is good to discriminate and separate learners as early as the elementary level; and 5) a belief in the accuracy and reliability of scientific measurement. Smith (1983) points out another aspect of the development of present day schooling that has served as an additional spur to evaluation and which is spun together with objective assessment. He comments on the fact that classrooms today appear to be driven more by programs than by the judgments and expectations of teachers, and that students and teachers alike are often the victims of curricula that do not fit their needs or context. He says:

> Programs appear in a number of educational guises—as sets of materials, workbooks, activity kits, guidelines, manuals, record sheets, objectives, television series, and computer-based instructional sequences. The history of instructional programs is probably as long as that of education itself, but they began proliferating during the present century as experts in other fields (such as linguistics, psychology, computer science, and test construction) and other external agents increasingly asserted views about what and how teachers should teach. The assumption that programs could achieve educational ends beyond the capacity of autonomous teachers grew rapidly in North America with the educational panic that followed Sputnik in 1957 and the coincidental development of management systems and operational techniques for the solution of such logistical problems as sending people to the moon. . . . Despite their manifold variety in education, programs have a number of common elements, the most critical being that they transfer instructional decision making from the teacher (and children) in the classroom to procedures laid down by people removed from the teaching situation by time and distance. (pp. 108–109)

Smith (1983) goes on to say that such programs, removed as they are from the instructional setting, are by necessity based on fact and subskill knowledge and the expectation that children will by their very natures synthesize the facts and subskills into working practices of reading, writing, and problem solving. Smith (1983) strongly disagrees with this assumption and the sorts of evaluation that are supplied with programs, such as, tests of the ability to perform some feat of memory, or mastery of a subskill.

Smith (1983) makes an extremely important point. When knowledge is seen as facts and success for the student as the ability to make only lower level, recognition style use of those facts, then the types of assessment and related evaluations we have today are a logical outcome of these curricula. For instance, when using traditional basal instructional modes for reading instruction, it is common to assign children worksheets that drill identification of phonic letter patterns and protocols. Such worksheets have no way to provide a context that allows children to have a purpose for their work (other than receiving a grade or going out for recess). Usually, these tasks do not even relate to the story in the basal reader. To make the circle complete, schools often then test these subskills on standardized tests of what are called basic skills.

When prepackaged programs are the driving factors in curricula and the focus is surface level identification of facts, then the unconnected, no context, (and to the children utterly meaningless) sort of assessment previously described can seem logical and reasonable to those who authored the materials. For example, the authors of the basal readers may know that the skill being addressed is recognition of three ways to spell words with the long "a" sound. They know that the story contains long "a" words, four each with three different spellings, repeated five times throughout the text. The fact that the children never make the connection or that the connection is meaningless to children does not seem to matter (Goodman, Shannon, Freeman, & Murphy, 1987). After all, the authors and publishers of the series will never see the students or teachers and must therefore construct assessments that are unconnected with anything else going on in the class. Prepackaged, program driven curricula are increasingly coming under fire for failing to meet the needs of children. Influential commentators (Glasser, 1990; Finn, 1990; Shanker, 1990) are calling for schools that empower teachers and students and that give them context and meaning in daily activities. Their feeling is that evaluation needs to be contextually meaningful and under the control of teachers and students.

Whole Language Evaluation Philosophy

There are wide differences between whole language and traditional evaluation. Just as traditional evaluation is based on a philosophy and a set of assumptions, so is whole language evaluation. Before it was a curriculum or means of instruction, whole language was a philosophy about how children learn most effectively and easily, with its origins in the progressive era and humanism in education (Goodman, 1989b). As an instructional paradigm, it draws from a more recent research base in socio-psycholinguistics.

Some of the main tenets of whole language include:

1. Whole language teachers believe that language is integrative, that it cannot be broken down into fragments and retain meaning.
2. Whole language teachers define teaching in terms of learning and learners.
3. Whole language teachers want children to become efficient users of language and structure the classroom to help them do so.
4. Whole language classroom activities focus on meaningful events for children and the authentic learning of language in context; they do not focus on language itself.
5. Whole language learners are encouraged to use language in all its manifold ways, to take risks in using language for their own purposes.

6. Whole language teachers structure classrooms to facilitate the use of a variety of oral and written forms of language. (Goodman, 1986; Watson, 1987)

Because whole language classrooms are structured around authentic literacy events for children, each takes on the distinctive forms and activities brought to the situation by the teacher and the children. What actually happens in classrooms is therefore extremely varied, though whole language teachers, by definition, integrate language and content. For example, whole language teachers tend to agree that spoken and written language forms are only superficially different and that the process of learning each is the same (Cambourne, 1988). As a logical extension of this point, whole language teachers try to create and nurture the natural conditions which make language learning both possible and easy. They do not become prisoners of a prepackaged curriculum dictating their every move, but rather constantly try to conceive of innovative ways to make learners responsible for their own learning, recognizing that all people must have ownership of their learning and have their own purposes for learning in order to participate with enthusiasm and carryover (Cambourne, 1988).

The logical extension of this principle is that evaluation should be a natural outcome of the process of creating meaning, used by the learner to improve performance and by the teacher to gauge the student's overall progress. Evaluation conceived in this way is not the learner's ability to score at a certain level of mastery on a number of criteria. This distinction is at the heart of the difference between whole language and traditional evaluation. Whole language teachers assume that children learn best by doing and that the outcomes of these linguistic, intellectual endeavors are often visible in the processes of creating responses to the environment set up in the classroom. Traditional teachers assume that children learn best by being directed to attend to explicit treatments of factual curricula, and they evaluate accordingly.

An example will help clarify this distinction. One curricular goal of a traditional teacher may be to instruct the children in writing thank you letters. The teacher therefore would usually conduct a lesson on the proper ways to write a personal letter, emphasizing form, punctuation, and syntax. She or he would then usually require several practice letters, using assigned topics. At the end of the unit, the teacher would test the children's ability to perform on a criterion-referenced test by grading their performances in emulating as closely as possible the approved form of writing a thank you letter. Children could then be assigned a grade, allowing winners (As) and losers (Fs) to be identified, and those who fell in between to be differentiated by Ds, Cs, and Bs. In addition, the grading process is said to allow diagnosis (Bloom et al., 1981; Gronlund, 1985; Storey, 1970). For consistent failures over a wide scale of tasks, the diagnosis is often banishment (at least from the child's point of view) to a special class set up to deal with children who cannot make the grade.

The whole language teacher, by contrast, sees letter writing as one of a myriad of functions for language and is reluctant to assign writing for which the student sees no purpose. In this class, children write letters for their own purposes. For example, let us suppose that a child has read four books by Eric Carle. In response to his or her enthusiasm for the books, a teacher might suggest letting the author know how much the child likes his books, a "thank you" for the pleasure the books have given. "You know, I have heard that Eric Carle tries to answer all the letters he gets from children. Would you like to write him and tell him how much you liked his books?" If the child answers positively, he or she might then ask, "What do you need to know to be able to do that?" This might include looking at other letters, collecting books together to refer to, and talking about what to say with friends or the teacher. The teacher meanwhile can be satisfied that this activity fits within the parameters of desirable language development and be happy at seeing a child busy on a task that is personally meaningful and exciting.

Later, he or she would evaluate the letter with the writer using information gained from a variety of sources: a peer conference in which the letter is shared with others for their responses; a one on one conference with the writer to help the learner think through the process; the writer's own comments that reveal level of metacognitive awareness of the purposes of the letter; and finally the writing process itself of draft, criticism, reconception, rewriting, and so on, addressing syntax and spelling at appropriate times.

The teacher would look at this process from two points of view. First, from the child's point of view, does the feedback they collaboratively develop give the child support and encourage improvement? Second, from the teacher's point of view, does the evaluation illuminate the child's internal processes and provide evidence of the child's intentions, interests, strengths, weaknesses, and growth? Evaluation in the whole language classroom also enables the teacher to guide future development of the child by providing information and insight for informed judgments of the child's progress relative, not to others, but to the child.

Ken Goodman (1986) put it very well.

> . . .whole language teachers are concerned with helping learners build underlying competence. They have no interest in getting them to behave in predetermined ways in class and on tests. For example, spelling competence is not a matter of memorizing words for the Friday spelling test, but a matter of first trying out words as they are needed in writing and then learning the limits of invented spelling against social convention.
>
> The basic competence of children who can comprehend when they read English is not reflected in tests of word recognition or phonics "skills." Moreover, pupils can give right answers on tests for wrong reasons, and wrong answers for right reasons. Whole language teachers know that the language miscues pupils make

often show their underlying competence, the strengths they are developing and
testing the limits of. (p. 41)

Just as the whole language classroom centers on process, rather than product,
so does whole language evaluation. Learners (students and teachers as learners)
engage in an ongoing process of evaluation of their own work and that of others,
generating feedback that leads to improvement and development. This process,
like everything else in the whole language classroom, is in a state of constant
change and adjustment to reflect new knowledge and abilities as they develop.

Sources of Insight for Children and Teachers

What Yetta Goodman (1989a) calls the "double agenda of evaluation" is the underlying issue in all whole language evaluation. Students are learning, and they need
feedback that gives them the means to evaluate their own work and to use that
work for their own purposes. Simultaneously, teachers are learning through
reflecting, teaching, conferencing, consulting, facilitating, and demonstrating.
Good evaluation of students allows teachers to gauge what students might be ready
to learn next and to shape the curriculum of the classroom to support the child's
interests as well as the teacher's own purposes. At the same time, a teacher's
evaluation of his or her own performance allows opportunities for professional
learning and growth.

Goodman (1989a) sees this double agenda as teachers involved in evaluation
of language development, cognitive development, and curriculum in a continuous, ongoing, integral process. Simultaneously, students are learning about their
world, answering their own questions, solving their problems, and evaluating
their own learning. Not incidentally, language is the medium in which this process
is conducted. Therefore, children are learning language even as they are involved
in evaluating their own work and that of others.

For the teacher, this means having knowledge of how children learn, how they
learn language, and how they use language in learning. It also means having
knowledge of how individual children learn, what specific children are doing
(or not doing), and how specific children are developing. Theory, research, and
observational reflection form the knowledge base that provides teachers with
a general framework and the specific information they need to guide their transactions with children (Bird, 1989). Theory and experience lead to a vision of
what good learning looks and sounds like, and the teacher uses this vision to
constantly facilitate the structure and experiences children have.

This point is important. Whole language classrooms are often described as
being child driven. Teachers in whole language classrooms believe that children

must have a great deal of choice in terms of what subject matter will be addressed, and they provide a variety of options for activities in which the children may engage. This is by no means a *laissez-faire* process of management. Whole language teachers use an interaction of informed, intentional decision making with reflection, observation, and process evaluation to structure classroom experiences for optimum learning. The whole language teacher's ability to create an environment which "hooks the learner and inspires children to own their own curiosity, intelligence, and learning may be hard to describe, but it is there" (Edelsky, Draper, & Smith, 1983). Such an interaction is the process of synthesis that brings beliefs, goals, observation, reflection, theory, and practice together to produce classroom programs that truly reflect the ideas of whole language. The curriculum pivots around continual feedback to the teacher of how the children's efforts and his or her own are going. Evaluation of children and self is what makes the continually renewing process of whole language instruction possible.

As with language itself, it is the simultaneous nature of all the above that has made whole language curriculum and instruction so difficult to develop. Yetta Goodman (1989a) describes it as a three dimensional interaction between three axes: 1) interaction, observation, and analysis; 2) formal and informal ways of interacting, observing, and analyzing; and 3) incidental and intrinsic modes of interaction, observation, and analysis. In the course of a day or a week, the typical whole language teacher does interact, observe, and analyze on most or all of these axes, using information, experience, knowledge, and vision to arrive at an informed judgment of each child's development.

This sounds like a difficult task for the teacher, and it is. However, it is the soul of the whole language classroom. A teacher who is not able to judge what is going on in the class must invent instruction with no basis for judging its effectiveness or follow a prepackaged plan of some sort. Only a realistic and informed analysis of what is happening leads to realistic and informed guidance of what will happen next. Only with true feedback can the teacher match what is happening with a vision of what should be.

Sources of Data for the Whole Language Teacher

Whole language teachers evaluate all the time and constantly use the results to guide and plan for what happens in class curriculum and instruction. Traditional teachers take only periodic checks of how children are doing and usually require blocks of valuable time to both give tests and provide feedback to children. A whole language teacher who constantly works collaboratively with children also has the intimate knowledge of each child to inform and guide the evaluation of that child. The traditional teacher, hemmed in by objective measures, finds that he or she is eventually involved in a process that becomes dehumanizing in that it insulates him or her from intellectual intimacy with the students.

Engaging children in discussion (either in groups or individually), facilitating children's work, and planning and evaluating with children is how most whole language teachers spend the day. Traditional teachers tend to spend their time orchestrating classroom events, directing children through activities, moving children and materials through time and space, and correcting children's behavior and their academic work (Stice, Thompson & Bertrand, in press). Please notice the distinction here. Traditional teachers spend little time dealing with individuals or small groups in collaborative endeavors. Because of the way traditional classrooms are structured, with a reliance on separate subjects and subject related blocks of time, there is little time for the kinds of observation, interaction, and analysis in which whole language teachers engage.

Yetta Goodman (1989a) offers the example of a child apparently lost in thought. From this, the teacher may conclude that the child is concentrating or he or she may decide the child is daydreaming. Goodman (1989a) says about this scenario "Of course, the professional verifies such observational judgments through interacting, by engaging the student in conversation or asking a question, or through more formal evaluation, if warranted" (p. 9). It is easy to visualize this as a positive interchange between student and teacher, the teacher leaning down and saying, "Hi, what are you thinking?" It is equally easy to visualize this same interchange in a traditional classroom wherein students have a directed task given them for each minute of the class and part of the teacher's job is to demand and ensure on task compliance. Since a large part of the teacher's role is to be enforcer of task and warden of time, there will exist a buffer that makes collaboration with students more difficult. Real personal knowledge and real intellectual intimacy with students tends not to exist to nearly the same extent in such programs. Students always know that there will be a test at the end and that they will be in an adversarial position relative to other students and the teacher.

Summary

Testing has existed as a means of opening or denying opportunities for many years. In the 20th century, two movements have emerged in traditional classrooms. First, teachers have relinquished, for a number of reasons, most claims to the use of judgment and qualitative evaluation of students in favor of measures based on objective testing methods. Second, standardized tests, both norm- and criterion-referenced, have made huge gains in importance as they relate to the evaluation of both individuals and groups of students. However, both these movements have come under examination and attack recently.

Whole language teachers, by contrast, embrace the idea of process evaluation based on their own observations, judgments, knowledge of how children learn, and interactions with the children. They usually find standardized tests inappropriate to the goals and ambitions they have for children. These teachers typically spend more time and effort in evaluation than traditional teachers, because evaluation of student performance and teacher performance is the linchpin of the whole language classroom. In the traditional classroom, curriculum is usually program driven, and therefore is set in advance with little attention to the individual interests and abilities of students. The whole language classroom is defined by the teacher's ability to marry theory and practice, constantly reflecting on and responding to the learner, as well as reflecting on and altering teaching as necessary. Evaluation is one of the most essential components of the whole language classroom. Without thoughtful, informed, and collaborative evaluation, whole language classrooms have no rudder to provide direction.

References

Barnes, D., Britton, J., & Rosen, H. (1969). *Language, the learner, and the school.* Middlesex, England: Penguin.

Bertrand, J. (1987). The changing corporate concepts of literacy. In D. Lumpkin (Ed.), *Changing conceptions of reading: Literacy learning instruction.* Muncie, IN: Seventh Yearbook of the American Reading Forum.

Bird, L. (1989). The art of teaching: Evaluation and revision. In K. Goodman, Y. Goodman, & W. Hood (Eds.), *The whole language evaluation book.* Portsmouth, NH: Heinemann Educational Books.

Bloom, B., Madaus, G., & Hastings, J.T. (1981). *Evaluation to improve learning.* New York: McGraw-Hill Book Company.

Cambourne, B. (1988). *The whole story: Natural learning and the acquisition of literacy in the classroom.* Auckland, NZ: Ashton Scholastic.

Cawelti, G. (1989). Key elements of site-based management. *Educational Leadership, 46*(8), 46.

Clay, M. (1990). Research current: What is and what might be in evaluation. *Language Arts, 67*(3), 288–298.

Edelsky, C., Draper, K., & Smith, K. (1983). Hookin' 'em in at the start of school in a 'whole language' classroom. *Anthropology and Education Quarterly, 14*(4), 257–281.

Evangelauf, J. (1990). Reliance on multiple-choice tests said to harm minorities and hinder reform; panel seeks a new regulatory agency. *The Chronicle of Higher Education, XXXVI*(37), A1.

Finn, Jr., C (1990), The biggest reform of all. *Phi Delta Kappan, 71*(8), 584–592.

Finn, Jr., C. (1987). A call for radical change in educational delivery. *Education Digest, 52*(1), 2.

Glasser, W. (1990). The quality school. *Phi Delta Kappan, 71*(6), pp. 425–435.

Goodman, K., Shannon, P., Freeman, Y., & Murphy S. (1987). *Report on basal readers*. Katonah, NY: Richard C. Owen Publishers.

Goodman, K. (1986). *What's whole in whole language?* Portsmouth, NH: Heinemann Educational Books.

Goodman, Y. (1989a) Evaluation of students. In K. Goodman, Y. Goodman, & W. Hood (Eds.), *The whole language evaluation book*. Portsmouth, NH: Heinemann Educational Books.

Goodman, Y. (1989b). Roots of the whole language movement. *Elementary Education Journal, 90*(2), 113–127.

Goodman, Y. (1985). Kidwatching: Observing children in the classroom. In A. Jagger & M.T. Smith-Burke (Eds.), *Observing the language learner*. Newark, DE: International Reading Association.

Gronlund, N. (1985). *Measurement and evaluation in teaching* (5th edition). New York: Macmillan Publishing Company.

Hodges, R. (1977). In Adam's fall: A brief history of spelling instruction in the United States. In H. Robinsin (Ed.), *Reading and writing instruction in the United States: Historical trends* (pp. 1–16). Newark, DE: International Reading Association.

Hulten, C. (1925). The personal element in teachers' marks. *Journal of Educational Research, 12*, 49–55.

Mager, R. (1973). *Measuring instructional intent*. Belmont, CA: Fearon Pitman Publishers, Inc.

McKenna, M. & Robinson, R. (1980). *An introduction to the cloze procedure*. Newark, DE: International Reading Association.

Michaels W. & Karnes, M.R. (1950). *Measuring educational achievement*. New York: McGraw-Hill Book Company.

Mikulecky, L. (1987). The status of literacy in our society. A paper presented at Reading Symposium on Factors Related to Reading Performance IV, Milwaukee, WI: The University of Wisconsin at Milwaukee.

Payne, D. (1974). *The assessment of learning: Cognitive and affective*. Lexington, MA: D.C. Heath and Company.

Phillips, R. (1968). *Evaluation in education*. Columbus, OH: Charles E. Merrill Publishing Company.

Shanker, A. (1990). A proposal for using incentives to restructure our public schools. *Phi Delta Kappan, 71*(5), 345–357.

Smith, F. (1986). *Insult to intelligence*. New York: Arbor House.

Smith, F. (1983). *Essays into literacy*. Exeter, NH: Heinemann Educational Books.

Stice C. & Call, T. (1987). The test may have become the curriculum. *Tennessee Reading Teacher, 2*, 11–16.

Stice, C., Thompson, D., & Bertrand, J. (monograph in press). *Emergent literacy in two contrasting classrooms: Building models of practice toward a theory of practice.* Nashville, TN: Tennessee State University Press.

Storey, A. (1970). *The measurement of classroom learning.* Chicago: SRA.

Watson, D. (1989). Defining and describing whole language. *The Elementary School Journal, 90*(2), 129–141.

Weaver, C. (1988). *Reading process and practice.* Portsmouth, NH: Heinemann Educational Books.

Chapter 3

Principles of Assessment and Evaluation in Whole Language Classrooms

Bill Harp

The whole language movement has swept the nation. While it is difficult to identify an exact number, some estimates place at 20 percent the number of classrooms in which teachers are applying the principles of whole language instruction. Whole language instruction is well established. We are in the midst of an instructional revolution in literacy. Whole language is now a commonly known term in every school district. Whole language principles are in forming educational policy across Canada and in many states (Goodman 1989/1990). Now there is a critical need to take the next step. The next step is identifying ways to engage in assessment and evaluation activities without violating the principles of whole language instruction. This chapter specifies twelve principles of assessment and evaluation that do not violate the basic tenets of whole language. These principles can be used to guide our practice in the future.

Assessment and evaluation in whole language classrooms requires a new look at the purposes of evaluation. Dorothy Watson set the tone for evaluation in the future at a Whole Language Special Interest Group meeting. She said that we must ask ourselves who evaluation is for. The answer in whole language classrooms is that evaluation is first for students so that they may watch and understand their own progress. Second, evaluation is for teachers. Third, it is for the school, to let administrators, other teachers, and parents know how a child is doing. Finally, evaluation is for the general public and legislators (Berglund, 1987). Traditional practice has not put the child's recognition of his or her progress first as the reason for evaluation.

Just as whole language instruction has demanded a fresh new look at teaching and learning, so it now demands a fresh new look at assessment and evaluation. Clearly, many of the old practices born of the testing movement of the 40s will no longer serve the needs of whole language teachers. Whole language teachers reject assessment and evaluation strategies based in tradition and turn instead to a set of principles that guide their work.

Principle One: Assessment and Evaluation Strategies Must Honor the Wholeness of Language

We know that children learn to read and write in the same developmental ways that they learn to speak. Our use of language is always driven by a need and desire to communicate. Assessment strategies that attempt to determine what children know and need to learn next and evaluation strategies that measure the effectiveness of instruction must honor the communicative nature of language in all of its forms. Teachers assess what children know about language as they watch children use language in real communicative situations—writing stories and poems, writing lists of plans in activity centers, writing self-evaluations, keeping reading logs, and writing in journals. Teachers watch children read for pleasure, for information and for self selected purposes. Reading ability is evaluated as children respond in a variety of ways to whole texts, not to fill in the blank activities following the reading of a short, excerpted piece.

Principle Two: Reading and Writing are Viewed as Processes

Teachers with ten or more years of teaching experience remember well the reading skills checklist that they were asked to complete on a regular basis. The extensive lists of reading subskills were to be kept as each skill was tested, taught, mastered, and in some instances retaught and retested. Many school districts created sets of such tests and ways in which these data could be recorded on computer. Management by objective, it was called. Each objective specified a behavior related to a subskill e.g. "Given ten unfamiliar words, children will be able to decode initial consonant *d* with 80 percent accuracy." Countless hours were spent creating the tests, administering the tests, and recording the data. When the system worked as intended a group of teachers could agree that Tuesday morning was skills time, each teacher would select a skill or set of skills to be taught during skill time, and the computer would produce a list of the children across several classrooms who had failed the pretest on those particular skills.

We now know that such skills-based instruction ignores what we know about literacy development. Reading and writing are now viewed as processes, rather than accumulations of small skills. How children are handling the processes is the teacher's focus rather then the acquisition of discrete skills. In whole language classrooms children are asked to respond first to the largest units of meaning, whole selections, and only after truly meaningful experiences with whole selections are they asked to respond to smaller pieces such as paragraphs, sentences, words and letter-sound relationships.

In viewing reading as a process we know that readers predict that they will read, sample all of the possible cues on the printed page only to the extent necessary to confirm or reject the predictions, and then confirm or reject, predict again, and resample (Goodman, 1967). This view of the reading process causes us to focus on the behaviors of readers as they move from beginning readers to developing readers to mature readers. At each stage we are concerned with observing and recording the behaviors that give evidence of their use of the process rather than their ability to apply a given subskill. Concern for grade scores or instructional reading level is giving way to concern for increased use of semantic cues or the ability to monitor one's own comprehension, for example. This movement is leading to greater reliance on miscue analysis and the development of checklists for processes rather than for skills.

Miscue analysis helps us understand whether a reader is attempting to construct meaning or is simply decoding sound-symbol relationships. For example, if the text word is *house* and the child reads "horse" without noticing the loss of meaning, we can infer that this reader relies much more heavily on graphophonic cues than on semantic cues. If a meaningful word substitution is made, we can infer that the reader relies most heavily on semantic and syntactic cues. By doing a series of miscue analyses across time, we can observe a child's progress toward becoming an increasingly meaning constructing reader. These observations give us insight into how the reader is using the reading process.

Similarly, we are moving toward process evaluation in writing. We now understand that marking a writing piece a B+ does not help the student become a better writer. Instead, we examine how the child uses the writing process from prewriting activities to first draft, second draft, editing conferences, rewriting copy, revision conference, self-editing, and publication. By collecting work samples at each of these stages and keeping anecdotal records of our observations of each child in each stage of the process we are able to truly assess and evaluate writing progress. Turbill (1985) says that evaluation in writing is looking at how things are going and making a judgment about how to keep things moving in a way that meets the needs of the child and teacher. She describes four components of evaluation in writing:

1. The most significant evaluation record is in the teacher's head. There is nothing wrong with the terms *impressionistic* and *subjective*.
2. Each teacher supplements the subjective evaluation with some kind of anecdotal record book or profile of day by day observations.
3. Periodically teachers go through each child's writing folder to look for patterns emerging over time.
4. The writing folder includes a page completed by the child entitled "Things I Have Learned." These components guide the evaluation of writing as a process.

Principle Three: Teacher Intuition is a Valuable Assessment and Evaluation Tool

One of the teacher's greatest responsibilities is decision making. Teachers make about ten instructionally significant decisions per hour (Berliner, 1984). One of the most important sources of decision making data is the teacher's intuition. Yet, in this age of accountability teachers have been encouraged—forced—to discredit their intuition as less valid and reliable than test data. Whole language teachers appreciate the importance of intuition in assessment and evaluation. The things we know intuitively we know without rational, logical explanation of how we know them—we just know them. Our critics insist that we must be accountable for student learning. They insist that we must document student learning gain in a variety of ways—virtually all of them through testing. Certainly teachers must be accountable for student learning. But such accountability does not always have to exist through testing. Teacher intuition that a child knows something is as valid a way of accounting for that knowledge as is testing. This assumes, of course, that teacher intuition is based on careful observation and knowledge of a child's learning.

Principle Four: Teacher Observation is at the Center of Assessment and Evaluation

Yetta Goodman (1978) talks about the importance of the teacher as "kid watcher." It is only through careful watching of children in authentic literacy events that we can bring our intuition as teachers to bear on planning appropriate learning experiences. Informal observations, knowledge about how children become literate, and teacher intuition about why children perform in certain ways form the basis of instructional decisions far more than do test scores (Shavelson and Stern, 1981).

The inexperienced observer (or one with lack of knowledge about literacy development) could look at the scribbles of an emergent writer and see only scribbles. The experienced observer will look at the same piece of writing and see indications of the child's development of hypotheses about the nature of writing, an understanding of the form of a letter, the development of important concepts about print, and a strong literacy set. The experienced observer will not only have spent time watching the writing being created, but probably will have engaged the child in conversation about the writing which will lead to more insightful observation (Johnston, 1987).

In the same way, the untrained observer will listen to a child read and hear only mistakes while the experienced observer who is knowledgeable about the reading process will hear much more. This observer will hear self-correction when meaning is lost, prediction, an emerging sensitivity to the creation of meaning while reading. Teacher interaction with the student is important here because the teacher can gain insight into the ways in which the reader constructs meaning and can intervene to provide support and suggestions. This model of evaluation in reading has been called dynamic assessment (Campione and Brown, 1985).

Teacher observation of children at work is at the heart of the assessment and evaluation strategies. Central to good observation is a teacher knowledgeable about both child development and literacy processes. At a recent whole language meeting a teacher anonymously wrote the following on the board:

I used to teach children and evaluate their progress.
But now I kid watch, facilitate the learning of children,
And try to discover why learners do what they do.
I have learned to celebrate children's strengths as language users.

Principle Five: Assessment and Evaluation in Reading Must Reflect What We Know About the Reading Process

We know that reading is an interactive process in which the background experiences, knowledge, theories (schemata) of the reader interact with the ideas of the author to create meaning. The meaning that is created in this transaction is not exactly the same as that originally intended by the author. In fact, three texts exist in the reading process: the text in the head of the author, the text on the printed page, and the text created in the head of the reader as a result of this interactive process (May, 1990). Assessment and evaluation in reading must acknowledge the interactive nature of the process. This interactive view of the reading process began long ago with Rumelhart's (1977) model of word recognition, and yet assessment and evaluation in reading have not reflected this interactive view.

How can assessment and evaluation in reading reflect this interactive view of reading? The Wisconsin Reading Association has provided some answers to this question in a publication entitled *Toward an Ecological Assessment of Reading Progress* (1990). The Assocation suggests that assessment and evaluation in reading must consider the factors which influence comprehension. Each of the factors is discussed below.

Prior Knowledge

The knowledge the reader brings to the reading act greatly influences comprehension. Prior knowledge can be assessed in reading tests by giving a multiple choice test that measures prior knowledge, by having children write predictions before they read, or by asking children to write about topics central to comprehension of the passage. When testing individuals, teachers can engage children in conversation about prior knowledge. The assessment of prior knowledge is useful in interpreting performance on a comprehension test.

Text Structure

Narrative selections which conform to a predictable text structure—problem-events-resolution, are more easily remembered than are texts with no discernable structure. Problems in comprehension can be caused by the lack of text structure. Children's knowledge of the various text structures used in expository writing aid in comprehension. Knowledge of text structure should be considered when assessing comprehension. We need to be sure that children understand text structure and we need to determine that texts used in tests have an identifiable structures.

Like text structure, it is also important for readers to understand story grammar. Children's understanding of story grammar and the ability to track one's developing understanding of the plot of a story is crucial to comprehension.

Reading Strategies

Metacognition is an awareness and understanding of one's learning process. Applied to reading this ability is termed metacomprehension. One's ability to monitor comprehension and take corrective actions is crucial in an interactive view of the reading process. Comprehension increases when children are taught what to do when comprehension fails. In individual assessment students should be asked to demonstrate what strategies they would use in a given reading situation. The degree to which readers ask themselves, "Do I understand? Does this make sense? How can I get help?" and the consequent corrective action is crucial to good comprehension.

Interests and Attitudes

The degree of interest in a topic and the attitude the reader has towards the reading task will influence comprehension. Our understanding of a reader's comprehension ability will be enlightened by knowing the interest and attitude the reader brings to the task.

Others have been working to identify process oriented ways to handle assessment and evaluation in reading. Valencia and Pearson (1987) reported several formats they are using to "reshape statewide assessment of reading." These innovative formats include the following.

Summary Selection

Students read three or four summaries of a selection written by other students. They select the one they think is best. In an alternative version they are asked to identify the reasons for their selection.

Metacognitive Judgments

Students are asked to think about a way they might have to use a selection after they have read it. An example would be asking readers to think about retelling the selection to a variety of audiences. They rate the helpfulness of several different retellings for each audience.

Question Selection

From a group of 20 questions students select the 10 they think will best help a peer understand important ideas in a selection.

Multiple Acceptable Responses

In recognition of the fact that interpretive and evaluative questions have multiple acceptable responses (despite what norm-referenced test makers would have us believe) students are asked to participate in a group discussion of all responses they find plausible.

Prior Knowledge

Students predict (yes/no/maybe) whether certain ideas are likely to be included in a discussion of a specified topic. In another version students are asked to assess the degree to which they think certain terms would be related to a topic.

Figure 3.1 is a set of contrasts between new views of the reading process and current practices in assessing reading offered by Valencia and Pearson (1987, p. 731).

Figure 3.1   A Set of Contrasts between New Views of Reading and Current Practices in Assessing Reading

New views of the reading process tell us that. . .	Yet when we assess reading comprehension, we. . .
Prior knowledge is an important determinant of reading comprehension.	Mask any relationship between prior knowledge and reading comprehension by using lots of short passages on lots of topics.
A complete story or text has structural and topical integrity.	Use short texts that seldom approximate the structural and topical integrity of an authentic text.
Inference is an essential part of the process of comprehending units as small as sentences.	Rely on literal comprehension test items.
The diversity in prior knowledge across individuals as well as the varied causal relations in human experiences invite many possible inferences to fit a text or question.	Use multiple choice items with only one correct answer, even when many of the responses might, under certain conditions, be plausbile.
The ability to vary reading strategies to fit the text and the situation is one hallmark of an expert reader.	Seldom assess how and when students vary the strategies they use during normal reading, studying, or when the going gets tough.
The ability to synthesize information from various parts of the text and different texts is hallmark of an expert reader.	Rarely go beyond finding the main idea of a paragraph or passage.
The ability to ask good questions of text, as well as to answer them, is hallmark of an expert reader.	Seldom ask students to create or select questions about a selection they may have just read.
All aspects of a reader's experience, including habits that arise from school and home, influence reading comprehension.	Rarely view information on reading habits and attitudes as being as important information about performance.
Reading involves the orchestration of many skills that complement one another in a variety of ways.	Use tests that fragment reading into isolated skills and report performance on each.
Skilled readers are fluent; their word identification is sufficiently automatic to allow most cognitive resources to be used for comprehension.	Rarely consider fluency as an index of skilled reading.
Learning from text involves the restructuring, application, and flexible use of knowledge in new situations.	Often ask readers to respond to the text's declarative knowledge rather than to apply it to near and far transfer tasks.

From Valencia, Sheila and P. David Pearson. "Reading Assessment: Time for a Change." *The Reading Teacher*. vol. 40, no. 8 (April 1987), pp. 726–732.

Another reading assessment strategy that is proving helpful is the process interview (Paratore and Indrisano, 1987). The process is intended to examine how a child views the reading process. The interview includes questions such as:

■ How do you choose something to read?
■ How do you get ready to read?
■ When you come to a word you can't read, what do you do?
■ When you have a question you can't answer, what do you do?

- What do you do to help remember what you have read?
- How do you check your reading?
- If a young child asked you how to read, what would you tell him or her to do?

Principle Six: Assessment and Evaluation in Writing Must Reflect What We Know About the Writing Process

The first purpose of assessment and evaluation in writing is to inform the child of his or her progress in using the writing process. In traditional classrooms the *product* of writing has been the focal point. Often students are given a piece of their work evaluated by the teacher with only a grade on the paper. Such evaluation does not help children understand how to make the writing better. In whole language classrooms the focal point of assessment and evaluation in writing is the child's growth in using the writing *process*. Consider the differences between a writing program that celebrates the process of writing rather than the product of writing.

If assessment and evaluation are to be consistent with what we know about the writing process, children must be given feedback on and be asked to self-evaluate their performance at each stage of the process. Thus teachers and students will take critical looks at the prewriting stage where children are thinking, observing, researching, and selecting a topic. They will then examine the rough draft writing stage where the work may be tentative, exploratory, and idea focused rather than mechanics focused. The revision/response stage of the process would be evaluated in terms of the child's ability to see the need to make changes, willingness to make changes, the ability to check for meaning, and the ability to accept the responses of others to his or her writing. The editing stage would be evaluated for the child's ability to self-edit, peer-edit, adult-edit and focus on the mechanics. The final draft or publication would be evaluated for careful proofreading, quality of presentation, and appropriateness for the intended audience.

Figure 3.2   Process v. Product Writing

When we write as a Process	When we write for a Product
The writing is student centered.	The writing is teacher centered.
The teacher's role is to model and coach.	The teacher's role is to assign and grade.
We write for many audiences.	The teacher is the primary audience.
The process is evaluated.	The product is graded.
The editing group or editing committee is the primary responder.	The teacher is the primary responder.
We write many, ever improving drafts.	We write one linear draft.
The entire process of thinking, writing, revising, editing, and publishing is done in class.	A draft is done in class

Principle Seven: Norm Referenced Achievement Testing is of No Help to the Whole Language Teacher

Norm-referenced tests exist to measure virtually every human trait we can imagine. Since World War II we have seen a growing and persistent use of norm-referenced tests in American schools. Whole language teachers recognize the discrepancy between norm-referenced testing and the instructional outcomes we hold important. In fact, norm-referenced test data are essentially useless to us.

Vito Perrone, Director of Teacher Education Programs at Harvard University says of norm-referenced tests,

> While these tests have come to affect Americans of all ages, in all fields, intelligence and achievement tests come down most heavily on the young, those between the ages of 3 and 21. Although problematic for young people of all ages and levels of schooling, they are particularly deleterious for children in preschools and primary grades. For it is in these early years that children's growth is so uneven, so idiosyncratic, that large numbers of skills needed for success in school are in such fluid acquisitional stages. (1990, p. 1)

Perrone goes on to say,

> I cry when I read about young children "held back" on the basis of a test, or placed in one or another of the schooling tracks that support various judgments about children's potential. And I wonder about those who believe that testing young children and then making placement, promotion, or retention decisions on the basis of such testing leads to any constructive end. (1990, p. 1)

The most destructive influence of norm-referenced testing is found in the daily reading activities of children. Reading curriculum has been designed to assure that children do well on the tests. So the activities in which children engage in the name of reading instruction look much more like the tests (fill in the blanks, draw a line from the d to the picture of the dog, and so forth), than like authentic reading and authentic writing activities (Edelsky and Smith, 1984). In classrooms where real communicative experiences are of primary importance, teaching to the test is counterproductive. The time spent in test-like activities robs time from the much more important experiences of real reading and real writing.

A vicious circle exists in the production of basal readers. In a test-driven curriculum mentality, the circle begins with norm-referenced tests, the tests influence the design of the basal, workbooks, and accompanying tests, and ends with the norm-referenced tests. (Goodman, Shannon, Freeman & Murphy, 1988). Whole language teachers are committed to breaking this circle with the kinds of assessment and evaluation described in the principles discussed here.

The test items on norm-referenced tests do not look like the real reading experiences children have in whole language classrooms. In Miriam Cohen's book entitled *First Grade Takes A Test* (19xx) a child found none of the answers to the questions posed by the test makers acceptable and decided to write in a response "so the test people would know." The test items are at odds with what children have come to expect of authentic texts. Children are accustomed to reading whole texts, not short paragraphs, and to respond to these texts in a variety of ways— positing a variety of possible answers to inferential and evaluative questions. A fifth grade teacher recently reported one child's response to a norm-referenced test that she was taking. After reading a selection the child said to the teacher, "Can't we just discuss it?"

Another destructive influence of norm-referenced testing is the appearance of scientific credibility. Teachers have been led to believe that grade scores and percentile rankings are scientific, and therefore more valid than their professional judgment (Harman, 1990). Yet, such standardized tests are designed so that half of the children will score below grade level.

> Therefore, tests cannot simply evaluate what children have learned because then everyone might do well. Some questions must be hard enough—or obscure enough—to guarantee that only a few children will get them right. That is, they must tap what has not been learned. So then schools must begin teaching to those questions, and the vicious spiral of alignment, premature teaching, and drilling whirls on. (p. 114–115)

Whole language teachers are committed to breaking the vicious spiral Harman describes. This will be done by rejecting norm-referenced testing for other assessment and evaluation measures that recognize the developmental nature of literacy.

Principle Eight: Assessment and Evaluation Instruments are Varied and Literacy is Assessed in a Variety of Contexts

Testing is only one form of assessment and evaluation. In addition to appropriate tests, whole language teachers use work samples—recordings of children's readings, samples of children's writing, observations of children in the library corner, and at work in other settings. Teachers watch for indications of growth in the use of the reading process in movement from emergent reading behaviors to developing reading behaviors to maturing reading behaviors. They observe and record ways in which children interact with print, listen to stories, use literacy acts in dramatic play, and make use of environmental print.

Principle Nine: Assessment and Evaluation are Integral Parts of Instruction

Our traditionally strong reliance on tests as *the* acceptable form of assessment and evaluation has caused us to think of assessing and evaluating as things teachers do before and after teaching rather than as integral parts of the teaching act. Whole language teachers recognize that the best assessment occurs while teaching. Teachers are continually on the look out for indications of children's strengths and signs of what the child needs to learn or be challenged with next. At the same time, teachers realize that evaluation is best done by watching performance on tasks that involve children in literacy acts that have real communicative purpose rather than a test given after the instruction. Because whole language teachers are open to the needs and interests of children, a lesson can take an unpredicted turn, responding to the desires of the students. Just as an instructional objective could not have been written for this new direction in learning, neither could a test have been created in advance. But the lesson most certainly will be evaluated based on the teacher's observations of the processes and products used and created in the act of learning.

Principle Ten: Assessment and Evaluation Strategies are Developmentally and Culturally Appropriate

Whole language teachers believe that children learn to read and write in the same developmental way they learn to speak. Learning activities that honor the developmental nature of literacy focus first on meaning and give children many, many opportunities to practice literacy in ever-increasingly accurate approximations of adult reading and writing. Tests which are designed so that half of the children will be below average are based on the assumption that half of the children will not perform as well as the other half. Yet we know that this is not true in literacy development. Further, when teachers are told to use tests which place one-half of the class below average they are forced to drill children on small bits of information that may be included on the test. This drill is contrary to the ways we know children develop literacy.

Cultural diversity is increasingly a consideration in our classroom. For children whose native language is not American English, five principles should guide our instruction—and therefore our assessment and evaluation. (Ovando, 1989)

1. Language development in the home language as well as in English has positive effects on academic achievement.
2. Language proficiency includes proficiency in academic tasks as well as in basic conversation.

3. A child with limited English proficiency should be able to perfom a certain type of academic task in his or her home language before being expected to perform the task in English.
4. Acquisition of English language skills must be provided in contexts in which the student understands what is being said.
5. The social status implicitly ascribed to students and their languages affects student performance.

It follows from these principles of teaching and learning that assessment and evaluation strategies with culturally diverse students must occur first in their home languages. Such strategies should be sensitive to cultural norms that may differ from those of majority children. For example, in some Native American cultures eye contact and competition are not acceptable. Teachers who do not understand this could form inaccurate conclusions about such students.

Principle Eleven: Assessment and Evaluation Occur Continuously

Collecting work samples periodically for a writing portfolio, recording an oral reading episode for miscue analysis, and making entries in an anecdotal record are examples of important *periodic* assessment and evaluation activities. These strategies form an important part of the teacher's overall assessment and evaluation plan, but minute by minute assessment and evaluation are the heart of the strategy. Teachers are constantly observing children and their work to make mental notes about the latest achievement and the next challenge. The Wisconsin State Reading Association (1990, pp. 54–55) has identified characteristics of expert evaluators that help teachers define what good observation means. The seven characteristics are discussed below.

1. *The expert evaluator recognizes patterns.* When listening to children read, the expert hears patterns, for example, in miscues that lead to an understanding of the cueing systems on which the reader primarily relies.
2. *Expert evaluators have procedural knowledge.* They know how to elicit certain literacy behaviors from children so that they can then be observed, recorded, and filed in some way.
3. *The expert in informal assessment is a listener.* Expert observers hear children's growing abilities in literacy.
4. *Expert evaluators empower learners with responsibility for self-evaluation.* This is a critical aspect of continuous assessment and evaluation.
5. *Expert evaluators are advocates rather then adversaries of students.* The teacher sits beside the child focusing on process, treating the child and the work with the greatest respect.

6. *An expert evaluator's assessment is timely and immediately influences instruction.* The teacher is both teacher and evaluator at once. Evaluation is therefore efficient. This first-hand information is more helpful in planning than second-hand information gained from tests.

7. *Expert evaluators emphasize process and what the child can do.*

Principle Twelve: Assessment and Evaluation Must Reveal Children's Strengths

Whole language teachers reject the clinical, medical model of educational assessment. In this model one looks for what is wrong with the child, and then writes a prescription to fix it. The child-centered nature of whole language instruction demands that we look first at the strengths of children—what they know, how they can use what they know to learn, and what they can teach us. We also firmly believe that children do not have to be forced or threatened by tests in order to get them to learn. Children are natural learners in environments that seriously invite learning. Their strengths show in such environments. Teachers have found the following strategies helpful in identifying the strengths of children:

1. Make five minutes available to spend with a child. Let the child guide the discussion and discover what you can.
2. Watch the child's social interactions. What communicative strengths does the child have and how are they used?
3. Have children write self-evaluation letters to the teacher or to the parent. Here the child has an opportunity to identify his or her perceived strengths as well as area for growth.
4. Permit children to identify their next learning step. When conferring with children, ask first what are the child's goals for future learning. Then negotiate goals shared by the child and the teacher and finally indicate goals that the teacher has for the child. This "Yours, Ours, and Mine" approach to goal setting permits the child to take the lead and yet recognizes the teacher's responsibility in instructional planning.

Summary

The implementation of these principles of assessment and evaluation will necessitate a dramatic change from traditional practice. We will have to come to grips with the fact that current tests do not test what we value in reading education (Bussis and Chittenden, 1987). Assessment and evaluation in whole language will move us away from test and text driven measures to student centered observation.

We will accept only assessment and evaluation measures that keep language whole and fulfill children's expectations for how language works.

References

Berglund, R.L. (1988, December 1989, January). Whole language: A swing of the pendulum or a whole new pendulum?" *Reading Today*, p. 18.

Berliner, D.C. (1984). Making the right changes in pre-service teacher education. *Phi Delta Kappan, 66*, (2), 94–96.

Bussis, A. & Chittenden, E.C. (1987). Research currents: what the reading tests neglect. *Language Arts, 64*, (3), 302–308.

Campione, J.C. & Brown A.L. (1985). *Dynamic assessment: One approch and some initial data.* (Technical Report No. 361). Urbana, IL: Center for the Study of Reading.

Edelsky, C. & Smith, K. (1984). Is that writing—or are those marks just a figment of your curriculum? *Language Arts, 61*, 24–32.

Goodman, D. (1989). The whole language umbrella. *Teachers Networking—The Whole Language Newsletter, 9*, 9–11, Katonah, NY: Richard C. Owen Publishers.

Goodman, K. (1967). Reading: A psycholinguistic guessing game. *Journal of the Reading Specialist. 6*, 126–135.

Goodman, K.S., Shannon, P., Freeman, Y., & Murphy S. (1988). *Report Card on Basal Readers.* Katonah, NY: Richard C. Owen Publishers.

Goodman, Y. (1978) Kid watching: An alternative to testing. *National Elementary School Principal, 57*, 41–45.

Harman, S. (1990). Negative effects of achievement testing in literacy development. In Constance Kamii (Ed.), *Achievement testing in the early grades: The games grown-ups play.* Washington, DC: National Association for the Education of Young Children.

Johnston, P. (1987). Teachers as evaluation experts. *The Reading Teacher. 40*, (8), 744–748.

May, F.B. (1986). *Reading as communication: An interactive approach.* (2nd Ed.). Columbus, OH: Merrill Publishing Company.

Ovando, C. (1989). Language diversity and education." In J.A. Banks & C.A. Banks (Eds.), *Multicultural education: Issues and perspectives.* Boston, MA: Allyn and Bacon.

Paratore, J.R. & Indrisano, R. (1987). Intervention assessment of reading comprehension. *The Reading Teacher. 40*, (8), 778–783.

Perrone, V. (1990). How did we get here? In Constance Kamii (Ed.), *Achievement testing in the early grades: The games grown-ups play.* Washington, DC: National Association for the Education of Young Children.

Rumelhart, D. (1977). Toward an interactive model of reading. In S. Dornic (Ed.), *Attention and performance VI.* Hillsdale, NJ: Erlbaum.

Shavelson, R. & Stern, P. (1981). Research on teachers' pedagogical thoughts, judgments, decisions and behavior. *Review of Educational Research. 41*, pp. 455–498.

Turbill, Jan, (Ed.). (1985). *No better way to teach writing!* New South Wales, Australia: Primary English Teaching Association.

Valencia, S. & Pearson, P.D. (1987). Reading assessment: Time for a change. *The Reading Teacher. 40*, (8), 726-732.

Wisconsin State Reading Association. (1990). *Toward an ecological assessment of reading progress.* Schofield, Wisconsin: WSRA.

Chapter 4

Reading Evaluation— Miscue Analysis

Dorothy Watson and Janice Henson

Introduction

> I don't know what to do with or for Ted. He is in the fourth grade and can't even read the first-grade basal! I've looked at all his test scores—the CTBS, and Informal Reading Inventory, the basal end-of-level test, and the state achievement test; I still don't know what to do with Ted. I'm desperate and ready for suggestions anyone has to offer.

To educators who have voiced similar concerns, the authors suggest whole language evaluation that includes its most formal technique—reading miscue analysis.

In this chapter we offer a rationale for the use of miscue analysis, tell a bit about the background of the instrument, present one form of the Reading Miscue Inventory (RMI), and perhaps most importantly, show how miscue analysis can lead to specific strategies within a whole language curriculum.

Why Reading Miscue Analysis?

Ted's teacher presents a problem that we feel *only miscue analysis as part of whole language evaluation can address.* It can help in at least three ways.

First, miscue analysis provides information about language and about the reading process. Without such information, Ted's teacher is vulnerable: ". . .I'm desperate and ready for suggestions anyone has to offer." The feeling of desperation may stem from her lack of knowledge about the reading process and about the ways in which language cues support readers in their effort to construct meaning. With information about the natural reading strategies of *sampling* from text and from background experience, *predicting* what is coming up in the text, *confirming* when the reading makes sense and sounds okay, and *integrating* new information with old, the teacher can knowledgeably study Ted's reading. She can also evaluate materials and methods of reading instruction and make decisions consistent with solid information about how language and the reading process work together.

Secondly, miscue analysis provides information about Ted's in-process reading, his beliefs about reading and reading instruction, and about his comprehension. Through *marking and coding* the reading, teachers can judge the proficiency and efficiency with which readers are handling text. The *Burke Reading Interview*, as well as *Reflection on Reading* (self-evaluation) are two parts of the inventory that let the teacher in on what students think about (1) themselves as readers, (2) reading instruction, and (3) their performance on the material they have just read. The student's *retelling* reflects the reader's comprehension of the text.

Finally, miscue analysis enables the teacher to create a curriculum in which students' strengths are valued and used, while their needs are clearly addressed. Miscue analysis points the way to strategies and suggests materials that will help students become more proficient readers.

What is Miscue Analysis?

The term "miscue" is used in billiards when the cue stick slips off the ball, and in the theater it refers to an actor answering a wrong cue or missing one. Ken Goodman saw some parallels to reading, and made use of the term in his 1964 research, and later in 1973 when he developed the Goodman Taxonomy of Reading Miscues. Goodman rejected the idea that teachers can "get a window on the reading process" by looking at paper and pencil test scores, so he proposed an interesting alternative. He asked children to read aloud a story that they had never read before and then to tell what they remembered of it. As students read, they deviated from the text; Goodman called these unexpected responses "miscues." It's important that he didn't call them errors or mistakes; to do so would have meant that the reader was totally responsible (guilty) for the deviation. As Goodman investigated children's miscues, he realized that the miscues were not equal in terms of how they changed the text. In fact, some miscues didn't cause any change meaning or in syntax, while others destroyed both.

Over the years, many educators helped themselves to Goodman's work, adapting it to their own settings. In 1987, Yetta Goodman, Carolyn Burke and Dorothy Watson built on Goodman and Burke's original *Reading Miscue Inventory* (1972) in order to provide four different miscue analysis procedures. Their work, *Reading Miscue Inventory: Alternative Procedures* (1988), is the basis for the suggestions given in this chapter.

Alternative Procedures of Miscue Analysis

There are four miscue analysis procedures. One (Procedure III) is introduced in this chapter. Procedure I is the most complex and time-consuming option; it offers intensive information about a reader's individual miscues in relationship to all other miscues. Procedure I is recommended for teacher eduction courses in which there is a focus on miscue analysis and for some research studies. Procedure II assesses miscues within the structure of the sentence. This option is often used by reading teachers or special education teachers who need numbers, profiles, and forms for student records. Procedures II and III provide in-depth information about a student's reading and are similar in their focus. Procedure IV is an informal analysis to be used with students during individual reading conferences.

No matter which procedure is chosen, after doing even one miscue analysis, teachers say they never again listen to students read in the same way. We agree with their assessment, and invite you to investigate this whole language evaluation procedure.

Procedure III is only **introduced** here. An intensive study of miscue analysis requires more information than can be provided in a single chapter; therefore the authors suggest that teachers read *Reading Miscue Analysis: Alternative Procedures*, as well as some of the other works cited at the end of this chapter.

Preparing for Miscue Analysis

Selecting Students

Select a student for miscue analysis who presents a challenge to you—one who is a real puzzle. Ted is a prime candidate. He is not the least proficient reader in class, but he is the most baffling: "I don't know what to do with or for Ted." Your most troubled reader may produce a discouraging amount of complex miscues and therefore be overwhelming for anyone using the procedure for the first time. Save this reader for a time when you have gained more experience.

Selecting the Story

Although the length of the story used for miscue analysis depends to some extent on the age of the reader, there must be a complete text with a beginning, middle, and end. The story should be new to the reader, but not the major concepts it contains. It must be written in a way that supports readers in their attempt to make meaning. Since a **minimum** of 25 miscues is needed to give a description of a reader's strategies, the story must be slightly difficult for the student. Teachers usually collect two or three stories that are, in conventional terms, one or two years beyond the grade level indicated by the student's reading test scores. Some teachers use the best stories out of basal readers; this provides a grade level that is understood by skills-oriented educators and parents. Reading time usually takes 15 to 20 minutes, depending on the age and proficiency of the reader.

Preparing the Typescript

The student reads directly from the original source or from a very good black and white copy. If a copy is used, the passage should look as much like the original text as possible. Specifically, the length of lines and pages, the spelling, and any special tables, charts or pictures must be identical to the original text. This gives the teacher information about the influence of the physical text and format on the reader.

The teacher needs a typescript of the text. Three spaces between each line is sufficient room for *recording* miscues on this typescript; a wide right margin allows space for *coding* miscues and jotting brief notations. The last line of each original page is indicated on the typescript by a solid horizontal line. This format helps the teacher determine if turning the page influences the reader. The line and page number of the original text is typed along the left margin of the typescript; for example, line 4 of page 1 of the original text is typed "0104," line 18 of page 11 is typed "1118."

Taping the Reading Session

In addition to collecting all the materials and having the tape recorder in good working order, the teacher arranges suitable tables and chairs, proper lighting, and a reasonably quiet location. A neck microphone is preferable, but if not available, place the mike on a stand or cloth with the mike directed toward the reader and away from any background noises.

The reader and the teacher sit either side by side or across from each other. As the student reads, the teacher marks as many miscues as possible on the typescript. If the student is bothered by the marking, the teacher should discontinue marking until the pupil becomes absorbed in the reading. Since the session is audio-or videotaped, the teacher need not worry about getting all the information on the typescript. Marking the self-analysis of miscues is facilitated by the teacher's familiarity with the story.

Beginning the Reading

Teachers briefly explain to students that they are taping them in order to learn more about their reading. Before a severely nonproficient student sees the story, the teacher might say, "I'd like you to read this story called 'Space Pet,' " or "This story is about something you might be doing this summer—camping."

Students are asked to read the story aloud and to read as if they are by themselves. They are told they won't receive any help and that when they are finished the teacher will take the book and ask them to retell the story in their own words. To assure readers that the procedure won't last all day, teachers let students see exactly how long the story is. Ted's teacher gave the following instructions:

> Ted, thanks for agreeing to read this morning. I think we can find out a lot about your reading. Have you ever read this story or heard it before? (Ted looks at the story and shakes his head no.) It's six pages long. (Ted checks the number of pages.) Please read aloud; I'm going to record your reading. When you come to something you don't know, do whatever you would do if you were reading all by yourself. I won't interrupt you. (This lets Ted know that he isn't going to receive help.) When you're finished, I'll take the book and then ask you to tell me the story in your own words. Any questions?

Reading Miscue Inventory: Procedure III

The remainder of this chapter introduces Procedure III, the option that is used most often by classroom teachers.

The components of the RMI should not be viewed as parts of a formula. Teachers and researchers must decide the focus of their evaluation and use the components accordingly. We believe, however, that the following will provide abundant information for the teacher who is faced with a problem reader:

1. Initial interview
2. Oral reading
3. Retelling: unaided, aided, cued
4. Reflection on reading
5. Analysis of miscues: marking, coding, profile
6. Curriculum planning

Initial Interview

The instrument most often used to initiate the RMI is the Burke Reading Interview, but teachers may want to devise their own set of interview questions. Examples from the Burke Interview are provided below and the entire interview follows this chapter. No matter what form it takes, the purpose of the interview is to find out how students feel about themselves as readers and about the reading process. Question one of the interview helps teachers learn how students handle difficult text. This example from Karen, a third grader, illustrates the kind of information obtainable (T = Teacher, K = Karen).

T: When you're reading and you come to something you don't know, what do you do? (Burke Q1)

K: . . . its's pretty fun to me when you read and you say blank or something and you go back and you try to figure out what the word is. It's like a mystery to me.

No interview should be seen as a script to be followed slavishly. Many times, follow-up questions need to be asked: (C = Connie)

T: When you're reading and you have some trouble, or you come to something that gives you a problem, what do you do? (Burke Q1)

C: Tell the teacher.

T: What do you tell her?

C: I tell her I have a problem with my reading.

T: Let's say the teacher wasn't there and you had a problem with reading. What would you do?

C: I'd go find her and tell her what I need.

T: Do you ever do anything else when you have a problem?

C: When I'm at home I tell my parents. And when my dad and mom's. . . my sister. . .I ask her about it.

These answers to follow-up questions suggest that Connie has one major strategy to fall back on when she has trouble reading: She usually relies on help from others. It is important to find out if Connie expects the teacher to give her similar help in this situation.

Questions may be added to any interview. This question about family literacy provided information about Mike, a fifth-grade boy in a remedial reading class.

T: Who reads at your house, Mike?

M: No one, hardly.

T: Nobody.

M: Just my uncle.

T: Does he live with you?

M: Yeah.

T: What does he read?

M: Car books or something, you know, how to fix your engine or some-thing . . . and like getting parts for his motorcycle or something, just reading.

The influence of reading in this family became evident when Mike was asked about the kind of things he liked to read:

M: Like, I don't like stories that much, but I like, like how to build things or something, or 'struction, how to take things apart or something.

Carol's views of reading practices are revealed in these interview questions.

T: Would you like it if your mom (still) read to you?

C: Yeah, to bring good memories back.

T: What kind of good memories?

C: How fun it was when she read to me...

T: What do you like about how reading is taught?

C: Teacher reading to you.

T: How do you feel about that?

C: It reminds me of when my mom read to me, when I was a kid.

Carol has a less positive response to another instructional method:

T: Which do you like best, silent reading or oral reading?

C: Silent reading.

T: Why is that?

C: Because I like reading to myself... because... I'm embarrassed to read books.

T: You're embarrassed to read books out loud?

C: Most of the time.

T: Why is that?

C: 'Cause I miss words and the class laughs at me.

Oral Reading

Unaided oral reading provides a "window on the reading process." The reader is allowed to work through the text without help or interference. This not only reveals in-process comprehending (see below), but it provides information about the student's view of instruction. When third grader Sarah read "Zoo Doctor," she kept hesitating, waiting for her teacher to supply unknown words. When she wasn't given the expected help, she said, "My teacher last year said to skip it. Do you want me to skip it?" Sarah didn't trust the strategies she had been taught and needed confirmation that they were okay. When she found out that she could rely on strategies that moved her along in the text, she began to read the story with relative ease and with comprehension. If the teacher had supplied unknown words or corrected Sarah's miscues, none of this information would have come to light.

Checking oral reading against the retelling of the story helps teachers check alternative approaches to instruction. Mitch, a fifth grader, remembered very little of the story, "First Kill." Without the oral reading, his teacher might conclude that Mitch had problems reading the words in the text. This wasn't the case. Listening to Mitch read orally revealed that he was excellent at "recoding," going from print to sound. What he didn't do well was invest himself in the reading, which became evident when he was unable to retell the story. Without that commitment to the text, Mitch was unable to monitor his meaning construction process. Mitch actually skipped entire paragraphs without changing his speed or without correcting himself.

Retelling

Comprehension or lack of it can never be based on reading performance alone; therefore, retelling is a vital part of miscue analysis.

Unaided retelling consists of readers retelling the story in whatever way they prefer. Unaided retelling is introduced simply with, "Tell me all you remember about the story." With this prompt, some students willingly recreate the story, often including plot, characters, and underlying theme. If encouragement is needed, the teacher can provide non-content related prompts such as, "Tell me more" or "What else do you remember?"

In *aided retelling*, the teacher picks up on anything the reader has mentioned during the unaided retelling. Here the teacher must be careful not to put words in the student's mouth. Sam, a third grader, said during the unaided retelling, "And he saw something bad. And he, he saw something coming out of Mrs. Miller's window, and the fire truck came, and it took the house somewhere. . . that's all I know of." The teacher aided the retelling with, " . . . you say the fire truck came and took the house. Tell me more about that."

Misconceptions can be cleared up during aided retelling, as when Sherry, a fifth grader, read "Zoo Doctor" and substituted the word *indigestion* for *injection*. On the second encounter with the word she substituted a non-word. She never said *injection*. During the retelling, however, she discussed the elephant getting a shot and the danger of the needle breaking off if the elephant moved. Sherry obviously understood the author's intended meaning.

Cued retelling is a way of telling readers that there is more in the story to be told; for example, in one story, five animals helped the princess escape the evil knight. Sally tells in great detail what three of the animals did. When it was obvious that she was not going to tell more, the teacher said, "Sally, you mentioned how the dog, the kangaroo, and the cat helped the princess. Were there any other animals that helped her?" Such a question obviously cues the reader that there were other animals and that it is important to report that information.

Reflection on Reading

This procedure involves self-evaluation and self-reporting. Students often have reading problems that are difficult to pinpoint and to understand. When teachers need more information or need to confirm information they have gained from the miscue analysis and retelling, it makes sense that the students themselves should be consulted. After the cued retelling, the teacher asks the student to reflect on the reading by posing questions such as:

How do you think you did with your reading?
How do you think you did on your retelling of the story?
When did the reading go well? (Return the book to the student.)
Where did you have trouble? (Student may point to a specific word or mention a confusing concept.)
Why did you leave out this word?
Do you remember what you said for this word? What do you think it means?
Did the pictures help or bother you?

To help reflect on her reading, Kate's teacher asked her about specific miscues. Kate, a third grader, liked to read, but her oral reading was particularly dysfluent. She often made miscues that seriously affected the meaning of the story. Kate's teacher expected her to have just as much trouble with the retelling, but such was not the case. In her retelling, Kate included most of the major elements of the story, and was correct on many of the details. To help understand this apparent discrepancy, Kate was asked to comment on some of her miscues. Here a more complete picture emerged. Below we see how Kate attempted to bring her knowledge of language into the meaning making process in order to work through an unfamilar concept. She actively tried to construct meaning even though she didn't know the word. Kate read a sentence about filling a water *trough*, for which she substitutes the word *through*. She was asked to respond to her miscue (Italics ours):

T: What does that mean, "I filled the water *through* twice?"

K: That, well, I don't know if that's the true word, but like, *"through* twice," I thought that was because he poured it in, but now I just noticed that, 'cause when it [goes] *through* when you, like, when you go *through* a hoop it just goin' straight *through*, but I know you don't pour water *through* it.

T: So what do think about that?

K: That *maybe that it could be a different word*, or that maybe there's a word like it, like homophones, or there's another one, but it's the opposite of homophones, maybe it's one of those, like the word's the same, if they're spelled the same but they mean different.

At other times, Kate was able to come up with the author's intended meaning, even though it wasn't apparent from her oral reading.

T: Would you read this paragraph?

K: While they *whipped* the medicine and water from their faces, the (inaudible) were figured out what to do next. (Text word is *wiped*.)

T: What does it mean, "They *whipped* the medicine"?

K: Like they, I was thinking that maybe they shoved it in, or they gave it to her really fast and then, she. . .threw it out, the water really fast, too. And then she *wipe*, they *wiped* their faces from it. They *wiped* their faces from the, see, from their face, they *wiped* the medicine and water from their faces, well. . .

T: Oh, so *whipped* means what?

K: That maybe they *wiped* their face, they *wipe* all their clothes off.

When information from the student's reflection on reading is added to the other RMI information, a more complete picture of the reader is constructed. In Kate's case, she did far better on retelling than anyone expected considering the large number of miscues she made. This would indicate that her active approach to constructing meaning was paying off.

Analysis of Miscues

Understanding any cognitive process is difficult. We can't see into the mind, and so must rely on the very best observable information available. Reliable evidence for understanding and reading process comes from an analysis of a reader's miscues. In this analysis the teacher looks for patterns that tell something about readers' use of the cues of language and the strategies they use to process written material.

The first step in analysis is to mark the typescript. Some marking can be done as the reading takes place, but even so it is necessary to listen to the recording to confirm exactly what the student did. Tapes of readings can also be used to show the longitudinal development of students.

Most of the RMI marking is very straightforward. Substitutions are written above the word in the text.

Something was wrong inside those four tons of ~~flesh~~ fresh and ~~bone~~ bones.

Read: Something was wrong inside those four tons of fresh and bones.

Omissions are circled:

He reached through the bars to lay a hand on ~~the~~ elephant's trunk.

Read: He reached through the bars to lay a hand on elephant's trunk.

Repetitions of a word are marked with an "R" and a line under the repeated text:

®
As Jim left the hospital with a box . . .

Read: As Jim Jim left the hospital with a box of cones. . .

The same notation is used when a miscue is repeated:

About sixteen million units of penicillin. . .

Read: About six six million units of penicillin. . .

Multiple repetitions are indicated with lines below the repeated text. Each line represent a repetition:

When there was no more smoke the firemen. . .

Read: When there was no more smoke the the the firemen. . .

Insertions are marked with a caret:

What's the matter, old girl? the zoo doctor asked.

Read: What's the matter old girl? said the zoo doctor asked.

Corrections are marked with a "C" and a line under the text that is read. The line should stop at the end of the last word spoken before the correction.

He reached through the bars to lay. . .

Read: He reached those the bars, through the bars to lay. . .

. . .and she isn't going to like it.

Read: . . .and she said isn't going to like, she isn't going to like it.

Don't talk to her, Doc, the keeper said.

Read: Don't talk to her, Doc, said the keeper, the keeper said.

Unsuccessful attempts to correct are marked with "UC." (Non-words are marked with a $.)

The zoo has no scale big enough to weigh Sudana.

Read: The zoo had no $sooks $scisee big enough to weigh Sudana.

I filled her trough twice.

Read: I filled her water twice, through twice.

. . .down the length of her rough leg. . .

Read: . . .down the length of through her though her leg. . .

Occasionally a reader will say the correct word and then replace it with a miscue. This is called abandoning the correct response and is labeled "AC."

. . .they figured out what to do next.

Read: . . .they figured out what to, what do, we do next.

Some miscues are complex and difficult to mark. If you are unsure of a marking, it is best to write out in the margin what the reader said and number each attempt. In all cases, the criteria to use when marking are: accuracy, clarity, and efficiency. In other words, your marking must accurately reflect what the reader did, should be possible for others to interpret, and should be relatively easy to record.

Coding

The purpose of coding is to facilitate the analysis of miscues. An important assumption of miscue analysis, based on extensive research, is that all miscues are not equal. A simple counting of errors does not provide usable information, but through an analysis of miscues teachers can learn how the student handled the cues of language and what strategies were used.

At the most basic level, miscues are analyzed in terms of their syntactic and semantic acceptability. In other words, if a miscue is made, does the sentence result in something that sounds like English (syntax check), does it make sense (semantics check), and does the miscue change the meaning of the story? An additional question gives information about the graphic (letter) similarity between any substitution and the text item for which the word is substituted. Four questions are asked in this RMI procedure:

Is the sentence, as finally read by the student, syntactically acceptable in the reader's dialect and within the context of the story?

Is the sentence, as finally read by the student, semantically acceptable in the reader's dialect and within the context of the entire story?

Does the sentence, as finally read by the student, change the meaning of the story? (Question 3 is coded only if Questions 1 and 2 are coded yes [Y]).

How much does the miscue look like the text item?

The questions are answered by reading the sentence as the reader left it. Consider Kate's sentence:

The sulfa would have to be weighed out; sixty grams of sulfa were used for every

thousand pounds of elephant.

Read: Her suffle would have to be weight out; sixty grams where used of very thousand pounds of elephant.

The answers to the RMI questions:

1. Is the sentence syntactically acceptable?   No
2. Is the sentence semantically acceptable?   No
3. Is there a meaning change?   Yes

Not all miscues result in such a dramatic change in syntax and semantics. The highest level miscue is one that does not substantially change either syntax or semantics:

Susan
Sudana was sick.

The sentence is coded as both syntactically and semantically acceptable. The substitution of "Susan" for "Sudana" does not change either the grammar or the meaning of the sentence. This sentence would be coded: "Y" (syntax), "Y" (semantics). In this case, the reader read "Susan" for "Sudana" throughout the story; therefore there was no change of meaning either at the sentence or story level and the miscue is marked "N" (no meaning change).

The following sentence is very different.

fresh
Something was wrong inside those four tons of flesh and bones.

Read: Something was wrong inside those four tons of fresh and bones.

This sentence is coded "N" (syntax) and "N" (semantics) because it is not grammatically acceptable to say, "Something was wrong inside those four tons of fresh and bones," and the resulting sentence does not make sense. There is a change of meaning at both the sentence and story level and is therefore marked "Y" (meaning change).

A sentence can be syntactically acceptable, but not be a meaningful sentence. This most often happens when there is a substitution of a non-word (marked with a $):

ears   her $thrit and   through
He slipped his hand under her ear, down the length of her rough leg and back along her body.

Read: He slipped his hand under her ears, down her $thrit and through her leg and back along her body.

The non-word "thrit" has the characteristics of an English noun, making it an acceptable placeholder in the sentence. Despite the many miscues, Kate followed the rules of English syntax.

Occasionally miscues will partially change the meaning, either of the sentence or of the story, as in this example:

said   came
He saw Mrs. Miller come home from the store.

Read: He said Mrs. Miller came home from the store.

To code graphic similarity, the marking of "H" (for a great deal of similarity), "S" (for some similarity), and "N" (for no letter similarity) is placed on the typescript in a circle directly above the word-level substitutions.

The right margin of the typescript serves as a coding form for the first three questions. The summary of the RMI can be presented as follows:

Syntactic Acceptability	__Y__%__N__%
Semantic Acceptability	__Y__%__N__%
Meaning Change	__Y__%__P (Partial Change)__%__N__%
Graphic Similarity	__H__%__S__%__N__%

To compute the first three questions, count the number of sentences coded and divide that number into each raw score. To determine percentages of the graphic similarity, divide each "H," "S," and "N" count by the number of coded word-level substitutions.

Management Issues

Although miscue analysis is time consuming, it can be incorporated into the whole language classroom. It is interesting, but unnecessary to analyze the reading of students who are progressing and enjoying their literacy. Select the students for miscue analysis whose strengths and weakness are a puzzlement to you and possibly to themselves, students such as Ted.

Scheduling the data collection must not require a major revamping of the class schedule. One 30 minute block for the reading and retelling, 15 minutes for the Burke Reading Interview and possibly a 15 minute follow-up interview will be needed. Teachers might ask a student teacher or aide to take on class responsibilities while they work with a reader. If no such help is available call in a trusted parent volunteer, or make arrangements with another teacher to schedule an activity that involves both classes (of course, reciprocate with a later, multiclass activity. Perhaps older students can read, tell stories or sing with your class; they might present a project they have been working on, or work individually with students on a math or science concept, or on your students' research projects. That should take care of the 30 minute block of time needed.

The reading interview and any follow-up needed to clarify a student's answer might be worked in during regular conferencing time. If conference time isn't available, search your schedule for those times when students can do just fine without your supervision. The rule of thumb might be, "What am I doing for students that they could do for themselves?"

The analysis of the data must be done when the teacher has time to study the reading phenomena. It isn't possible to say how long it will take to mark and code the miscues, and analyze the retelling and reflection-on-reading; it depends largely on the reader's responses. Normally the process can be done in an evening.

Application to Curriculum Planning

The major purpose of reading evaluation is curriculum planning. Miscue analysis is especially suited for classroom application because it provides a great deal of indepth information; this information must be analyzed before it can shape the curriculum for Ted or any other reader. One method of analysis is to look for trends or patterns that present the complete reader. These patterns often emerge as questions, like the following. Answer these questions in light of all available data.

1. How do the readers feel about themselves as readers? How do they feel about reading?
2. What strategies do they see as legitimate? Do they know when a strategy is not working? Do they have alternatives?
3. How well do their strategies work? How compatible is their meaning construction with the original text? What conditions facilitate meaning construction? Which ones hinder it?
4. How do the readers define literacy? What do they see as the main purposes of reading and writing?
5. What is the role of literacy in the family?
6. What instructional procedures do the readers perceive as facilitating learning? Which ones have an adverse effect?

Answer these questions in light of an analysis of miscues:

1. What percentage of sentences make sense within the context of the story?
2. Do the readers correct miscues? What type of miscues are usually corrected? What type of miscues are usually left uncorrected?
3. Do the readers substitute words that look or sound like the words in the text?

4. If the readers substitute blank or non-words, how are they used?
5. What kinds of words are most often miscued on? Are they usually function words or content words?
6. Do the readers have many regressions? Do the regressions result in corrections?
7. Do the readers attempt to "sound-out" words? Are there multiple attempts at a word? Are the readers usually able to produce the intended word?
8. Do the readers omit sections of the text? Are these omissions noted by the readers?
9. Do the readers change the punctuation? Do these changes result in meaningful sentences or non-sense?
10. For all of the above, were there trends? Did the trends change as the reading progressed?

A case study is presented here to illustrate the kind of information obtainable from a Miscue Analysis and to illustrate how that information can inform the curriculum.

Case Study

Sue is a fourth-grader in a class that uses basal readers exclusively. She is in the low reading group, and is reluctant to read, resisting the teacher's every attempt to get her to do so. With the exception of workbook assignments, Sue often doesn't complete her homework. She does not volunteer answers to questions, and when asked for answers, she is often incorrect. Her oral reading is not fluent. She makes many miscues, and usually waits for the teacher to supply the correct word. She frequently causes behavior problems and spends much of her time sitting in the hall.

Her teacher sees Sue's behavior as incomprehensible. End of level reading tests suggest remedial activities, but none of them appear to work. In fact, Sue's attitude and reading performance get steadily worse. Miscue Analysis provides Sue's teacher with information that suggests a reading program to capitalize on her strengths and to meet her needs.

Interview

From the interview, several important concepts emerge. As can be seen from this dialogue, Sue's early training with reading stressed perfection.

T: How did you learn to read? (Burke Q8)
S: By my mom setting me on the couch and telling me to read this book.
T: What did your mom do. . .?

S: She. . .would read a page and then. . . I would have to listen so I would know the words when I came to them, so when she was done reading, I had to read the page and then if I messed up I would have to read it over until I got it right.

Almost all of Sue's reading instruction in school supports the idea that reading should be flawless. Despite the fact that she lists several strategies for dealing with unknown text (sounding out, using context, skipping words, saying "blank"), she doesn't truly think good readers ever use such strategies. Sue believes good readers can always effortlessly say the correct word.

T: What would you like to do better as a reader? (Burke Q9)

S: Know the word and you wouldn't have to stop all the time.

T: You say you wouldn't have to stop. What do you have to stop for?

S: Words that I don't know.

T: But why do you have to stop?

S: Well, sometimes I'll stop to try to sound it out, and I can't sound it out. . .

Because of her belief that reading must be perfect, Sue feels she must stop to sound out any unknown word. She knows this breaks up the flow of her reading, but she doesn't think she has a choice. Her stress on letter perfect reading interferes with her ability to concentrate on meaning.

T: What is your biggest problem with reading?

S: I don't understand the books mostly.

T: Why do you think that is?

S: Well, I don't read. I try the words so hard that I just don't get them out right, and they come up wrong.

By asking her questions about instruction, the teacher gains information about successful and unsuccessful teaching strategies. For example, when Sue's teacher introduces new words before a lesson, it establishes a mind set that is restricting and deepens her fear of the unknown.

T: What are the hardest things for you to read?

S: Books like we have in the fourth grade. . . like *Weavers*. . . and sometimes we have to read *Gateways*.

T: Why are your reading books hard to read?

S: Because they have new words that, that you don't know.

T: How do you know they have new words?

S: Well, sometimes she tells us to go ahead and look through the book, and the story that we're gonna read next, go ahead and just skim through it. And you see all these words in there that you don't know.

Basal reading assignments given as homework are also counterproductive. Rather than reading the stories, Sue asks someone at home to read them to her. Also according to Sue, the homework assignment doesn't leave any time to read for pleasure and only increases her aversion to reading. Sue sums up her feelings in this way: "I have a lot of trouble reading and...usually I let my mom or dad read the story to me and...when they read it to me, I'll just listen and I won't look at the words to see what they are."

There are instructional activities that work well with Sue. She likes to write because "People say I have a good imagination." She also likes to use her imagination in other ways.

T: What do you like best about reading class?

S: When you can visualize pictures and draw them.

T: What does that have to do with reading?

S: We'll read the stories and the pictures that they don't have in there, we get to visualize them and draw them.

T: Why is this your favorite thing?

S: Well, because I like drawing, and then I can see the picture, and then I can read the part over...

There are times when Sue does enjoy reading and is able to respond to the reading, as is shown in this dialogue:

T: Why don't you read much?

S: I don't like to read.

T: Have you ever liked to read?

S: Well, sometimes I'll get a spooky book, and I like to, I like to get (unintelligible) books...I have it here right now. There's a whole bunch of books. I had one...for the summer, and his little sister said that she had a doll, and she said that the doll said that there was a ghost in the window...(She continues telling the story.)

Sue also recognizes the importance of motivation in reading:

T: Is there anything you like reading about?

S: Well...it's like you like that book and then...you're interested in it, so you want to read it, so you try the best you can to...get the...words right so you can understand what it's about.

From the interview the teacher can get a great deal of information on how to help Sue, but in order to gear instruction to her needs, she must know how Sue handles unknown written material without assistance. In other words, what strategies does she actually use?

Oral Reading

Sue's reading is somewhat hesitant, but not dysfluent. There are no pauses longer than two seconds, and she only occasionally repeats the first letter of a word. She does not skip any portion of the story longer than a word, and her phrasing matches the punctuation of the story.

Retelling

From the retelling we learn that Sue is a better reader than she thinks she is. She understands most of the major points of the story. She has one misconception at the end that may be related to a lack of prior knowledge.

Reflection on Reading

One of Sue's most telling comments comes when she is asked how she feels about her reading. She answers that she hasn't done well because of the number of times she stopped. This statement is significant because there were no noticeable pauses. What she interprets as stopping was not perceived as such by her teacher. When asked why she stopped, she said it was to sound out words quickly. This is another indication that she expects reading to be flawless.

Analysis of Miscues

Trends in the miscue data provide more information about Sue's reading. Sue often corrects her miscues. This indicates that she is monitoring the reading based on her knowledge of syntax and semantics, as in these two examples:

We had a little trouble hiding her. . .

Sue recognizes that *table* does not make sense in the entire sentence, and she corrects the miscue to make the sentence meaningful.

But we liked her too much to take a chance. . .

Read: But we knew, we, but we liked her too much to take a chance. . .

The commoness of the phrase "we knew" compels Sue to substitute the word "knew" for "liked." These two words have no resemblance phonetically and, except for the letters "k" and "e," have no resemblance orthographically. The substitution of "knew" for "liked" in the sentence does not change the meaning substantially. Nevertheless, Sue notices the difference and corrects her miscue.

A second trend is revealed by Sue's treatment of unknown multisyllabic words. Usually she substitutes the word "blank" for the text word. There is only one instance in which she supplies the correct word; the remainder of the "blanks" are left uncorrected.

This tendency to use "blank" as an uninflected placeholder, rather than substituting a word that makes sense, is another indication of Sue's reluctance to take risks. In this example she sustitutes "blank" for "divided."

blank

But we found it easier to think of time as being divided into day and night.

She does not add a past tense inflection ("ed") to the placeholder ("blank"). She also doesn't substitute a reasonable word, such as "broken." She doesn't go back after finishing the sentence in an attempt to substitute a meaningful word for "blank." For all intents and purposes, the placeholder "blank" is simply a way to skip the word.

Applications

Only by looking at the whole picture can we get an idea of how to help Sue. We know that she feels reading must be perfect and flawless. She doesn't meet her own expectations. She doesn't have confidence in her own abilities, and so she avoids reading. Requiring skill sheets, comprehension drills, and multiple readings does nothing but encourage these negative feelings.

Despite this, Sue is able to read for meaning. She even enjoys reading and responds with a "lived through experience" if the book is one she chooses. She likes to write and visualize scenes that are evoked by the stories she reads and writes. These are encouraging signs and things to capitalize on.

There are many strategies for Sue's teacher to consider. Her major goal should be the creation of a classroom where risk-taking is maximized, risk is minimized, and literacy learning is meaningful. Such a classroom has several characteristics.

Students are encouraged to take linguistic risks. When this happens, miscues occur. When Sue's miscues do not change the meaning of the text, they should be ignored. All deviations from the text are seen as opportunities for students to learn new reading strategies and to use the appropriate strategies they already know. Strategy teaching, however, should only be done after the reader has worked through the text without assistance.

Students have many opportunities to experience reading and writing as ways of communicating. Sue needs to see herself as an author. In order to do this, she must write every day, but the writing must be authentic. Grammar drills or writing in response to story-starters will not make students feel like authors. Authentic writing satisfies some felt need: To tell a story or to communicate an idea. This can only happen if students have control of topic and genre and if there are opportunities for students to share their work.

The writing must be risk free. Risk is diminished when students are allowed to concentrate on ideas and intentions rather than perfection in their first drafts. Later in the writing process, students work on conventions such as spelling, grammar, and handwriting.

The classroom should be organized in a way that invites self-initiated learning and promotes a community of learners. This can only happen if students are allowed to interact with each other. Interactive, student-centered learning can take place without sacrificing classroom order if the classroom is thought of as a teaching/learning strategy. Materials need to be easily available and as varied as possible. Students must understand the guidelines for class organization and be involved in establishing rules within their classroom community. Above all, the classroom must be built on mutual trust among all learners, including the teacher.

Students need choice not only in what they read, but in the total curriculum. A reading strategy that allows students a certain measure of choice is literature study in literature discussion groups. This strategy, with its emphasis on cooperation and meaning making rather than "one right answer," could be especially helpful with Sue because of her lack of confidence in her own abilities as a reader.

Literature discussion groups are formed based on a common interest in a book, thereby tapping into Sue's increased motivation to read books she likes. Several times a week the groups meet for discussion. Topics of discussion are free ranging, but certain themes usually emerge. As the students and teacher discuss these themes, they learn how to work through reading problems. They find out that good reading is not necessarily flawless reading, and that there can be many different interpretations of a text. The groups may plan projects in order to re-experience their literature. Participation in projects offers Sue an excellent opportunity to use her imagination and artistic abilities. Through these groups and other student-centered activities, the classroom becomes a community in which students learn from each other and discover their own strengths. Sue needs such a classroom to help her feel the joy of literacy.

Conclusion

This chapter is an introduction to a Reading Miscue Analysis procedure that provides teachers with immediate and accessible information about the reading abilities and needs of students. The authors encourage teachers to pursue the study of this whole language evaluation instrument by delving into the references and resources listed below. We hope, too, that teachers will investigate the informative qualities of the Reading Miscue Inventory—by using the inventory, along with the reading interview and other suggestions given above, to gather information about a student who poses curricular questions and uncertainties. We feel such a comprehensive study will provide an abundance of data on which a strong and appropriate reading program can be built.

Note: Excerpts are from interviews that were done as part of a Weldon Spring Grant, University of Missouri, 1987–88.

Bibliography and References

Theory and Research

Gollasch, F.W. (Ed.). (1982). *Language and literacy: The selected writings of Kenneth S. Goodman* (Vols. 1 and 2). Boston: Routledge and Kegan Paul.

Goodman, K. (1969). Analysis of reading miscues: Applied psycholinguistics. *Reading Research Quarterly, 5*(1), 652–658.

Goodman, K. (1984). Unity in reading. In A.C. Purvis and O. Niles (Eds.), *Becoming readers in a complex society*. Chicago: University of Chicago Press.

Goodman, K. (1985). *What's whole in whole language?* Toronto: Scholastic.

Goodman, Y. Kidwatching: An alternative to testing. *Journal of National Elementary Principals, 57*(4), 41–45.

Goodman, Y. & Burke, C. (1972). *Reading miscue inventory manual: Procedures for diagnosis and evaluation*. New York: Richard C. Owen.

Marek, A., Goodman, K., & Babcock, P. (1985). *Annotated miscue analysis bibliography* (Occasional paper No. 16). Tucson: University of Arizona.

Whole Language Curriculum and Instruction

Buchanan, E. (Ed.). (1980). *For the love of reading*. Winnipeg: CEL Group.

Cochrane, O., *et al.* (1984). *Reading, writing, and caring*. Winnipeg: CEL Group.

Edelsky, C., & Smith, K. (1984). Is that writing—or are those marks just a figment of your curriculum? *Language Arts, 61*(1), 24–32.

Gilles, C. (1990). Collaborative literacy strategies: "We don't need a circle to have a group." In K. Short & K. Mitchell-Pierce (Eds.), *Talking about books: Creating literature communities*. Portsmouth, NH: Heinemann.

Gilles, C. (1989). Reading, writing, thinking and learning: Using literature discussion groups. *English Journal, 78*(1), 38–41.

Gilles, C., & VanDover, M. (1988). The power of collaboration. In J. Golub (Ed.), *Classroom practices in teaching English 1988: Focus on collaborative learning* Urbana, IL: National Council of Teachers of English.

Gilles, C., Bixby, M., Crowley, P., Crenshaw, S., Henrichs, M., Pyle, D., & Waters, F. (1987). *Strategies that make sense for secondary students*. New York: Richard C. Owen.

Goodman, Y., & Burke, C. (1980). *Reading strategies: Focus on comprehension*. New York: Richard C. Owen.

Goodman, Y., & Watson, D. (1977). A reading program to live with: Focus on comprehension. *Language Arts, 54*(8), 868–879.

Harste, J., Woodward, V., & Burke, C. (1984). *Language stories and literacy lessons*. Exeter, NH: Heinemann Educational Books.

Newman, J. (1986). *Whole language: Translating theory into practice*. Exeter, NH: Heinemann Educational Books.

Rhodes, L. (1981). I can read! Predictable books as resources for reading and writing instruction. *Reading Teacher, 34*(5), 511–518.

Watson, D. (Ed.). (1987). *Ideas and insights: Language arts for elementary children*. Urbana, IL: National Council of Teachers of English.

Watson, D., Burke, C., & Harste, J. (1988). *Whole language: Inquiring voices*. Toronto: Scholastic.

Chapter 5

Whole Language Assessment and Evaluation Strategies

Ward A. Cockrum and Maggie Castillo

This chapter covers whole language assessment and evaluation strategies of developmental checklists, interview sheets, journals and logs, writing portfolios, and holistic scoring. We describe format, purpose, and use of each of the strategies and provide sources of published examples of instruments and suggestions for the development of your own instruments. We begin the chapter by discussing the power of observation because these whole lanuage assessment and evaluation strategies are based on observation. The chapter concludes with a rationale for marking report cards based on the data gathered using whole language assessment and evaluation strategies.

Power of Observation

Observation is the primary method of gathering data for evaluation in a whole language classroom. Goodman stated "whole language teachers are constant kid watchers" (1986, p. 41). This observation or kid watching can take many forms. It can be as informal as watching the child play games on the playground to using a checklist while conducting an interview with the child. Regardless of the structure of the observation, using observations for assessment and evaluation should not be undervalued. Observation can be very powerful in developing a complete picture of a child's literacy development.

Observation as the basis of evaluation requires active participation on the part of the teacher in the child's language acts. Standardized tests or even teacher made tests place the responsibility for evaluation in the instrument. This can result in a teacher being upset with a child's score on an exam because the teacher "knows" the child performs at a much higher level in class. A whole language kid watcher trusts his or her evaluation of a child because he or she is a part of the child's language use. Whole language teachers are as involved in the child's language development as parents are with a child learning to talk.

Observation as the basis of evaluation requires ongoing kid watching. The evaluation of the child's literacy development needs to be based on many observations in many contexts at many different times. The power of using observations to evaluate a child is directly related to the amount of observation used to form the evaluation. Too few observations are just as dangerous as one time testing to evaluate a child's language development.

A good kid watcher is always looking for what the child can do. The total language development picture the teacher is attempting to build is based on what he or she has observed the child do, not on what he or she has not seen. It is assumed that any abilities the child has not demonstrated are ones which will develop in the future. For instance, inaccuracy in language use is a sign that the child is in the process of developing that ability. Those abilities not visible may require a change in the instructional approach so that the child has an opportunity to develop them. But, never should a child be made to feel that he or she is lacking or deficient, instead he or she should always feel that he or she is a capable learner.

Observation makes the evaluation process less stressful for the child and the teacher. The focus on what the child can do and the continuous nature of observation helps to limit stress in the evaluation. Observation does not generate negative behavior because the child is not placed in a powerless situation. When observation is used as a basis for evaluation, the learner's view is important to the observer and the observer needs to communicate on a one to one basis with the child to be sure the observations are accurate reflections of the child's ability.

When observations are used in evalution of a child's literacy development, self-evaluation is possible. The child can look at his or her own work and tell the teacher what he or she is attempting to do. The child can see from models provided in the classroom what is needed to reach the standard of the model. The child can keep examples of and notes about his or her own work in portfolios, which then become part of the observation-evaluation process.

Observation also is a powerful method of evaluation because the teacher is in the role of a learner. As a teacher uses observation strategies to determine the child's literacy development, he or she becomes more knowledgeable about literacy development. The teacher becomes an expert in the way literacy develops in the classroom. He or she doesn't wait for the results of a test to report if achievement in literacy has occurred. He or she knows, because he or she is a part of the literacy community in that classroom.

The most powerful aspect of using observation as the basis of evaluation is that it can reflect the 'real world.' Society has expectations as to the literacy abilities of people graduating from the 12th grade. They are frequently disappointed. Business people complain about recent graduates' lack of ability to do as simple a task as correctly filling out a job application. Parents decry the lack of interest in reading in their children. College professors tell us students come to them ill prepared in the area of written communication. Some of these problems may be attributed to the method used to determine a student's literacy development. When only multiple choice questions or fragments of language are used to determine success in language development, educators and students can be misled. Job applications don't have multiple choice responses, high school English teachers can't follow students to college to find their spelling errors for them. A more valid view of a 12th grader's literacy development can be obtained by observing his or her actual reading and writing. What children do in their own reading and writing in school is a more accurate reflection of what they will do in their own reading and writing out of school. This issue is essential to the value of whole language assessment and evaluation. Many times whole language instruction is attacked on the basis of standardized test results. Such results are however, "inappropriate for judging whole language programs," (Goodman, 1986, p. 42). The true test of the success of whole language programs will be in the total literacy development of students as they enter the world after formal education.

Strategies for Observing Literacy Development

Several strategies have been developed to provide structure to the observation done for evaluation and assessment purposes. Two strategies, developmental checklists and interviews, are in the form of instruments; two others, writing portfolios and journals and logs, are a way of organizing student-produced work. Each of these strategies have use for both instruction and evaluation and can be modified to use for self-evaluation.

Developmental Checklists

The developmental checklist is the most frequently used method of guiding observations for whole language assessment and evaluation. The term "developmental" has two meanings, both of which can be applied to these checklists. One refers to the maturation of the child and implies that certain stages of language development occur as the child grows older. This type of development can be seen in very young children and some checklists in the kindergarten and first grade are based on stages of maturation.

However, most checklists used in whole language assessment and evaluation are based on the view that development in language ability occurs because the child had been provided the opportunity to use language. The checklists based on this view of development help the teacher see how effective the classroom environment has been in allowing the children to develop their language ability.

Format of Developmental Checklists

Developmental checklists usually contain a list of the language traits for which the teacher is watching and some system to mark the occurrence or quality of the traits when they are observed. An example of a checklist to evaluate a kindergartener's awareness of environmental print, titled 'What Can I Read', is shown in Figure 5.1.

Purpose of Developmental Checklists

Checklists are used in whole language assessment and evaluation to keep the observer focused, to provide a method of recording observations that requires a minimum of writing and to provide consistency from one observation to the next. In addition they can be customized to match the instructional focus of a given teacher.

Uses of Developmental Checklists

The number of specific uses for developmental checklists may be unlimited, since any literacy event can have a checklist designed to facilitate the observation and evaluation of that event.

The editing stage of the writing process provides a nice example of the use of developmental checklists. The mechanical aspects of writing (use of capitals, use of punctuation, and so forth) are put on a checklist. Levels of attainment of the use of those mechanics (present, absent, or not observed) are also put on the checklist. The teacher can then look at a sample of the child's writing while using the checklist to record observations. The teacher can document changes in the student's use of writing mechanics by repeating the use of the checklist at a later date. The teacher can also evaluate the effect of the learning environment on the student's use of the mechanics of writing.

The same checklist can be part of classroom instruction. The student can fill out the checklist prior to an editing conference with the teacher. The teacher and the student can then determine those concepts related to writing mechanics which the student has not yet attained. Letting students self-evaluate their writing allows them to develop independence. Students become responsible for finding and fixing their own errors.

Figure 5.1 Sample Developmental Checklist

What Can I Read?

Name _____

Date _____

Level of Attainment

I. **Most Common**	NR	NC	C	NL	DC
Butterfinger	☐	☐	☐	☐	☐
Cheerios	☐	☐	☐	☐	☐
Corn Flakes	☐	☐	☐	☐	☐
Lunchables	☐	☐	☐	☐	☐
Mayonnaise	☐	☐	☐	☐	☐
Pizza	☐	☐	☐	☐	☐
Salt	☐	☐	☐	☐	☐
Spaghetti	☐	☐	☐	☐	☐
II. **Next Most Common**					
Burger King	☐	☐	☐	☐	☐
K-Mart	☐	☐	☐	☐	☐
McDonald's	☐	☐	☐	☐	☐
Pizza Hut	☐	☐	☐	☐	☐
Jack in the Box	☐	☐	☐	☐	☐
Safeway	☐	☐	☐	☐	☐
Taco Bell	☐	☐	☐	☐	☐
III. **Least Common**					
TV Guide	☐	☐	☐	☐	☐
IGA	☐	☐	☐	☐	☐
Ranger Rick	☐	☐	☐	☐	☐
Daily Sun	☐	☐	☐	☐	☐
Newsweek	☐	☐	☐	☐	☐
Time	☐	☐	☐	☐	☐

NR = No Response
NC = No Contextualization, response does not fit context, e.g., says Jello when shown candy bar wrapper
 C = Contextualization, response does fit context, e.g., says candy bar when shown candy bar wrapper
NL = Names Letters, response fits context and indicates some sound symbol recognition
DC = Decontextualization, able to read product name when written on index card

(The three categories of product names were established by asking children to bring in things they could read at home. Category one contains those products that 10 or more students brought, category two–5 to 10, category three–less than 5.)

Several authors have included examples of developmental checklists that could be used for evaluating writing. One appropriate for the early elementary grades can be found in Marie Clay's book, *What Did I Write?* (1975). Two that seem to be useful in the upper elementary grades appear in *Now We Want to Write* by Jan Turbill (1984) and *Spell by Writing* by Wendy Bean and Chrystine Bouffler (1987). And Evelyn Lerman (1984) designed a writing checklist for grades seven and eight.

Checklists for the assessment and evaluation of other language uses are also available. A selected listing is included here:

The Concepts About Print Test in *The Early Detection of Reading Difficulties* by Marie M. Clay (1979) has been used in the United States as a screening device for reading readiness (Stallman & Pearson, 1990). The checklist helps determine the knowledge a child has about how books work and how print works in books.

The Whole Language Evaluation Book by Kenneth Goodman, Yetta Goodman, and Wendy Hood (1989) has samples of kindergarten checklists, a writing checklist, and a thinking and language checklist.

An excellent 'Response to Literature Checklist' can be found in *Grand Conversations* by Ralph Peterson and Maryann Eeds (1990). They have also included checklists for recording students' participation in literature studies.

Two more global checklists are currently available. The Whole Language Behavior Inventory in *The Administrator's Guide to Whole Language* by Gail Heald-Taylor (1989) is a very complete checklist which covers speaking, listening, writing, and reading. This checklist is also designed to cover kindergarten through sixth grade. A complete evaluation package that includes observation forms developed in England is the *Primary Language Record Handbook for Teachers* (ILEA/Center for Language in Primary Education, 1989). The Primary Language Record is designed to be used for a child's entire elementary school years.

Deciding which checklist to use requires a knowledge of the behaviors that can be observed as a child's experience with language increases. It is helpful to become familiar with the literature on literacy development before using any developmental checklist.

Teachers should freely modify existing checklists or develop their own. One of the most powerful characteristics of developmental checklists in their adaptability. As a teacher gains experience using the checklists and his or her knowledge of literacy development grows he or she will want to revise the checklists he or she is using.

Interviews

The second most common observation instrument used in whole language evaluation and assessment is the interview sheet. Interview sheets are also known as conference recording forms.

Format of Interview Sheets

In general form an interview sheet has a set of questions that the teacher will ask the student and blank space to record the child's response. However, there are many variations of the interview sheet. One type used with older students suspends the interview and has students fill out the sheet independently. Another variation uses a forced choice response format where the student selects from a given set of responses the one that best matches how he or she feels or thinks. An example of an interview sheet titled 'Literature Interview Form' can be seen in Figure 5.2.

Figure 5.2 Sample of an Interview Sheet

Literature Interview Form

Reader's Name _____   Date ____/____/____

Interviewer's Name* _____

Book Title _____

Author _____

1. Whom did you like the most in the story?

2. Whom did you least like?

3. Where does the story take place?

4. When does the story take place?

5. Why did the story keep your interest?

6. Did the author do any thing which surprised you?

7. What was the saddest part of the story?

8. What was the happiest part of the story?

9. Did any part of the story make you laugh or cry?

10. What do you wish you could ask the author?

11. What do you think you will always remember about this book?

12. What type of person do you think would most enjoy reading this book?

*Interview may be done with the teacher, another student, or independently.

Purpose of Interview Sheets

The purpose of most interviews is to gain insight into how the student views his or her own literacy ability or feelings toward some literacy event.

Uses of Interview Sheets

Interview sheets can also take many forms and have many uses. The Reading Interview in the *Reading Miscue Inventory* (Goodman, Watson, & Burke, 1987) is an interview sheet in which the interviewer asks the child questions such as: "How did you learn to read?" and "What do you do when you come to a word you don't know?" The child's response is evaluated to gain insight into how the child views the act of reading and how he or she processes print.

Regie Routman, in *Transitions From Literature to Literacy* (1988), describes a simple two question interview used with her first graders. She wanted to determine the impact her classroom had on her students' views of reading and writing. On the last day of school she asks the students in her class "What is writing?" and "What is reading?" The responses were very enlightening.

Interview sheets can be used to conference with individual students about how their writing is progressing or how they respond to a piece of literature they have read. Examples of interview sheets used for writing conferences can be found in *Understanding Writing: Ways of Observing, Learning, and Teaching*, edited by Thomas Newkirk and Nancy Atwell (1988) and in *A Researcher Learns to Write*, by Donald Graves (1984).

The interview is used by the teacher to confirm other observations or to gather new information about the child. Self-evaluation occurs for the student when they answer to the interviewer's questions.

Journals and Logs

In whole language classrooms journals and logs are primarily used for instruction. But, journals and logs are excellent records of a student's language development for use in assessment and evaluation, as well.

Format of Journals and Logs

Journals and logs generally take the form of a booklet. Several blank pages are stapled together with a front and back cover. The pages can include dates for entries into the journal or log and designated spaces for the entries.

Purpose of Journals and Logs

Students may write anything they wish in their journals, while logs provide a place for learners to respond to some agreed upon topic. The evaluation uses of journals and logs change with the age of the student. Teachers however, should make clear to students at all levels exactly how their journals and logs will be used for evaluation.

Uses of Journals and Logs

The use of journals with beginning writers lends itself to both instruction and evaluation. The first journal entries of the writers in a kindergarten provide the teacher with an initial opportunity to determine the children's level of development in writing.

Students' journal entries may be pictures (picture stage), some may have scribbles like writing with their pictures (scribble stage), others may have random letters along with their pictures (alphabet stage), while still others may have written stories in invented spelling to accompany their pictures (invented spelling stage). A knowledgeable teacher can recognize that each of these groups of students is at a different level of development in writing.

By responding to each child in writing, using the child's words in the response, a teacher can provide a model for the kindergarten writer. The journal becomes a dialogue between the teacher and student and provides a constant source for evaluation of the students' writing development.

The journal becomes a record of the child's development from a picture stage, to the level of invented spelling. It also shows when the child abandons a particular invented spelling and moves to the arbitrary standard spelling.

The journal is also a method of self-evaluation for the kindergarten writer. The teacher's response gives the child feedback about the meaning he or she was able to put in his or her writing. The words and sentence structure used by the teacher provides a model for the child to compare with his or her own writing.

The more capable a writer becomes the less journal entries should be evaluated by the teacher. The self-evaluation role of journals will be viable with writers at all levels of sophistication. But, the day may come when the journal writer does not want the teacher to write in his or her journal or to even read it.

A child can use literature logs to give a response to books he or she has read. He or she can make entries while the book is being read or after it is finished. The teacher can respond in writing to the child's entries and establish a dialogue about the book. Literature logs can also be established for specific books. Each child who reads the book can write an entry and can compare his or her reaction to the book with those of his or her peers.

Children can also start logs to enter their views of their own writing. They write how they feel about how their current writing project is progressing or what they hope to express in their stories and the teacher can respond. In this way, a dialogue starts that focuses on the children's writing.

Writing Portfolios

Writing portfolios are simply collections of students' writing. These portfolios provide documentation of language development over time.

Format of Writing Portfolios

In general form, a writing portfolio is a folder that contains a selection of each individual student's writing. The sophistication of the folder varies from teacher to teacher, but it appears that the more professional looking the folder, the more pride the child takes in owning it. One adaptation used in some classrooms is to have the portfolio on a computer disk.

Purpose of Writing Portfolios

The writing portfolio is a place to save examples of a student's writing. The number of pieces in the portfolio should grow as the school year progresses. Permanent portfolios containing a sample of the student's best work can move with the student from grade to grade or school to school and become their property upon completion of high school.

Uses of Writing Portfolios

The major use of the writing portfolio is to document the child's development in writing ability. By comparing earlier pieces with his or her current work, progress becomes clear to both teacher and student.

Teachers can also use writing portfolios to examine the student's work for consistent errors for which he or she may need to have a model. The teacher can focus the student's attention on the model and then see if the child transfers that model to his or her own writing. The teacher can see what impact the activities in the classroom have had on the student's writing.

The evaluation of the writing samples can reveal changes in the child's writing style. Teachers can examine growth in the child's ability to write interesting stories and can evaluate the use of a specific story.

Developmental checklists can aid in evaluating the writing samples in the portfolio. And an interview with the child after reviewing the portfolio can provide additional evaluation information.

Sheila Valencia (1990) has described the use of portfolios for reading assessment. She prescribed two levels of evidence for portfolios to insure consistency in the contents of the portfolio from one student to another. The first level, required evidence, is the material that all students are required to have in their portfolios. This allows for evaluation across all students in the classroom. The second level, supporting evidence, may vary from student to student. Supporting evidence includes any material chosen by the student or the student and the teacher together which helps show the individual's level of literacy development.

Holistic Scoring

One of the few whole language evaluation and assessment procedures that results in a number is the holistic scoring system.

Format for Holistic Scoring

Holistic scoring is usually done with a piece of written work. The child is aware he or she will be scored and should have the opportunity to produce an example of his or her best work. The teacher or scorer reads the piece and awards a score from 1 to 5 based on an overall impression of the piece. It is assumed that this overall impression is influenced by the writer's ability to use the mechanics of language as well as the quality of the content.

Purpose of Holistic Scoring

Holistic scoring provides a system to evaluate a large number of pieces of writing. Holistic scoring results in a comparative ranking of the pieces of writing that were evaluated.

Uses of Holistic Scoring

Holistic scoring is used to evalutate the writing programs of whole schools or school districts. It is also used as a method of determining how well an individual's writing skills are developed in comparison to others at the same age or level of education. All students being evaluated need to write on the same topic and their work needs to be evaluated by "equivalent" scores.

A second use of holistic scoring is to evaluate students' responses on an essay test. After the test is returned a sample of answers that were evaluated at each level, from 1 to 5, can be put on an overhead sheet and students as a group can then determine why each response received the score that it did. In this way students can determine how to improve their own responses.

Making Your Own Instruments for Whole Language Assessment and Evaluation

While you can adopt published instruments for use in your own classroom, it will probably become necessary at some stage to make your own instruments using published ones as your models.

There are several stages in designing your own instruments. First, list those literacy traits you hope students will develop while in your classroom. (You may also need to include those traits the school district expects to see developed.)

Next, cluster those traits logically into the categories of reading, writing, speaking, and listening. Then subcategorize the traits by the context in which they can be observed. For example, group together all traits which can be seen in a child's formal writing, or all traits which can be observed during a literature study.

Finally, sort the subcategories by method of observation. The method of observation most appropriate for gathering evidence of the development of any given group of traits will provide the format of the checklist or interview sheet.

A Comprehensive Language Evaluation Strategy

The goal of the Comprehensive Language Evaluation Strategy is to develop a complete literacy picture of a child. A convenient way to organize the system is to break literacy into the four language functions of reading, writing, speaking, and listening. The strategy should include instruments to collect data in each of these language areas.

The teacher should evaluate each language area with at least two instruments. Each of those instruments should be used in a different context and should gather data in a different way. By gathering data in different ways at different times and in different contexts the validity of the child's literacy picture is much greater.

The teacher then enters a synopsis of each of the instruments onto the Comprehensive Language Evaluation Chart and a summary statement made for each category on the chart. A copy of the Comprehensive Language Evaluation Chart is shown in Figure 5.3.

The teacher can use the chart when conferencing with parents and/or the child, or when evaluating the effectiveness of the classroom environment for that child's literacy development.

Whole Language Assessment and Evaluation and Report Cards

One very pragmatic concern of classroom teachers is how to determine a grade for a student's report card. Many teachers feel that whole language evaluation and their current report cards are not compatible. We agree with their view and would hope that districts will either modify their current report cards so they can be used with whole language assessment strategies or that individual teachers be allowed to produce their own versions of report cards.

Figure 5.3   Comprehensive Language Evaluation Chart

Instruments Used/Analysis

		Instrument 1- _____
	Speaking	Instrument 2- _____
		Summary- _____
	Listening	Instrument 1- _____
		Instrument 2- _____
		Summary- _____
	Writing	Instrument 1- _____
		Instrument 2- _____
		Summary- _____
	Reading	Instrument 1- _____
		Instrument 2- _____
		Summary- _____

(Left margin label, vertical: **Language Area**)

Unfortunately school districts seem slow to change their practices and many whole language teachers may stiil be required to give letter grades on mandated report cards. We offer the following information for those teachers.

Grades on report cards are usually based on one of two criteria. The first criterion compares an individual student's performance with the other students in the class. Points are totalled in some manner and each child's total ranked in the class. Arbitrary levels are then established for each letter grade. In this system most students would receive an average or middle grade. While comparisons with other students is not part of whole language evaluation, it is still possible to use the data collected to form a rough class ranking and then award grades based on that ranking.

The second criterion in traditional grading schemes gives some predetermined numeric level for each letter grade. Every child reaching that predetermined level receives the same grade. Data gathered in whole language assessment can be used in the same way. Each child demonstrating the development of a specific set of literacy traits or a specific number of literacy traits receives the same grade.

Both these methods are completely incompatible with whole language instruction. However, the second scheme is preferable, especially when the predetermined criteria is such that all children in the class have a chance to attain it. Also, the teacher must be sufficiently knowledgeable to set appropriate criteria. In either case, the grades awarded from whole language assessment data can be as valid as those determined by a traditional point system.

References

Atwell, N. (1988). Making the grade: Evaluating writing in conference. In T. Newkirk & N. Atwell (Eds.), *Understanding writing.* (pp. 236–244). Portsmouth, NH: Heinemann.

Bean, W. & Bouffler, C. (1987). *Spell by writing.* Rozelle, NSW, Australia: Primary English Teaching Association.

Clay, M.M. (1989). *The early detection of reading difficulties* (3rd ed.). Portsmouth, NH: Heinemann.

Clay, M.M. (1982). *What did I write?* Portsmouth, NH: Heinemann.

Goodman, K. (1986). *What's whole in whole language?* Portsmouth, NH: Heinemann.

Goodman, K.S., Goodman, Y.M., & Hood, W.J. (1989). *The whole language evaluation book.* Portsmouth, NH: Heinemann.

Goodman, Y.M., Watson, D.J., & Burke, L.B. (1987). *Reading miscue inventory alternative procedures.* New York: Richard C. Owen.

Graves, D.H. (1984). *A researcher learns to write: Selected articles and monographs.* Portsmouth, NH: Heinemann.

Heald-Taylor, G. (1989). *The administrator's guide to whole language.* Katonah, NY: Richard C. Owen.

The primary language record handbook for teachers. (1989). Portsmouth, NH: Heinemann.

Lerman, E. (1984). In N.M. Gordon (Ed.), *Classroom experiences.* Exeter, NH: Heinemann.

Peterson, R. & Eeds, M. (1990). *Grand conversations.* New York: Scholastic.

Routman, R. (1988). *Transitions: From literature to literacy.* Portsmouth, NH: Heinemann.

Stallman, A.C. & Pearson, P.D. (1990). In L.M. Morrow & J.K. Smith (Eds.) *Assessment for instruction in early literacy.* Englewood Cliffs, NJ: Prentice-Hall.

Turbill, J. (1984). *Now, we want to write!* Rozelle, NSW, Australia: Primary English Teaching Association.

Valencia, S. (1990). A portfolio approach to classroom reading assessment: The whys, whats, and hows. *The Reading Teacher, 43,* 338–340.

Chapter 6

A Collage of Assessment and Evaluation from Primary Classrooms

S. Jeanne Reardon

I notice that the subjects and verbs consistently disagree in Trang's writing. She writes "the bird fly," "kids runs," and so forth. As I sit down beside Trang I ask her how she decides to put "s" on some words. She smiles and explains to me. "Easy. 's' here (kids) I put 's' here (runs). No 's' here (bird) and no 's' here (fly.)" Now that I understand Trang's reason I can help her. I explain that, "It doesn't work that way in English. In English . . ."

This chapter brings the reader into a primary grade classroom where the children and I work to understand the written and spoken language we use together to learn and live. The classroom I refer to in this chapter is a composite of many kindergarten through third grade classrooms in which I have taught. All of these classrooms are part of a large suburban public school system (100,000 students). Most of the classrooms are in schools identified as Chapter I, having a significant number of children from low income households, many of whom speak English as a second language. Readers who are part of large school systems are familiar with the nature of the school bureaucracy and the routine use of tests to measure student and teacher performance. I have not found that the data generated by national, state, and school system tests help the students or me to understand what it is that students know and do as they use written and spoken language.

I limit this discussion to examples of assessment and evaluation which prove useful to us in our classroom community.[1]

The assessment discussed in this chapter is not a response to outside forces. I am compelled to assess because that is how I teach. There is information I need and questions that the children and I must consider in order to learn.

What's going on?

When does Shirley revise her speech, reading, writing—and how?

How do we know if someone understands what we're saying. . .or writing—and what do we do when they don't understand? What makes us keep reading a book— or stop reading?

What does Jenny do in her writing to make us laugh?

What do you do when you can't read the word?

How do you know your story is finished?

I am constantly searching and re-searching to understand—to understand language, and the child as a language learner and one who uses language to learn. Put quite simply, what I assess is what I teach and value—understanding, revising, and wondering. It is also how I teach.

Before I give specific examples of how I assess children's language use and language learning, it is important that we begin together, by recognizing the assumptions upon which my teaching and assessing is based: I always assume that children's language activity is purposeful—that children have reasons for what they are doing. Assessment enables me to see language from the perspective of the child, to begin with the child's reasoning and extend the child's understandings.

I accept the complexity of the literacy behaviors of young children. I agree with Taylor (1990) that children's literacy does not develop in an orderly, sequential, predictable, manner.

Finally, I believe that evaluation demands simultaneous understanding and wondering. I don't think we can understand without wondering first, and wondering comes from noticing, and noticing comes from wondering, and our understanding may be limited to that specific situation and time. The ambiguity, complexity, and confusion of the previous statement will not surprise you if you live with children in a primary grade whole language classroom. You recognize that assessment will be ambiguous, complex, and sometimes confusing. That is what makes it so fascinating and exciting.

Imagine that you are in an art gallery studying a collage. At first you are attracted by the colors, shapes, and materials, but confused by the seemingly unrelated juxtaposition of the elements. You do not follow the interaction, or feel the relationships between the distinct forms. Then, after studying the collage, the artistic design emerges. This chapter presents an assessment collage. There are distinct elements: the teacher assessing, the child independently evaluating, the data collected by both teacher and child. There are intersections and overlappings as children and teacher collaborate and share in the evaluation process. Because assessment is a collage, the design of the chapter may at first appear confusing. However, by the end, the meaning and use of assessment and evaluation will become clear. Keep in mind, children have reasons for their literacy behaviors. Our job as assessors of language is to discover and understand their reasons so that we may teach from their perspective.

The Teacher's Data Collection

Assessment for understanding literacy requires data, and in a whole language classroom there is an abundance of data! The teacher's biggest problem is what to collect. Then come the questions of how to collect and organize all of this information so that we can use it. I find observations, conferences, collections of student writing, and reading records are my most useful sources of information.

Observations

Most of the data that I use for assessment is gathered through observation. I observe children in the process of learning and I observe their products. Often the terms "formative" and "summative" are used to describe these broad categories of observation. I prefer "process" and "product" because "summative" suggests that assessment is limited and somehow final. "Product" is a nonrestrictive term that includes observation of a range of products. Within each of these broad categories I use two types of observation to meet two different needs. The first is an open observation to collect data so that I can describe and document what is happening with individual children and in the classroom as a whole. In these observations I record as much as possible of what I see and hear. (This means that I make wide process observations, and wide product observations.) The second type is focused observations to answer specific questions. (Again, I make focused observations of process and close observations of products.) Remember the collage? All of these observations are not going to be distinct and separate; some are going to overlap.

Our classroom is active most of the day, an ideal setting to observe language learning. It is easy to say one should observe all of the time, but in practice some times work better than others. Within our day's structure there are times that especially lend themselves to both wide and focused observation. One such regular observation time is the first 45 minutes of the day.

When children come into the room each morning they sign in and return books checked out overnight from our room. They order lunch, look over the Message

Board, put up their own messages, and read. Some read alone, others read in twos or threes. Most read on the floor and out loud. (By third grade those who read alone usually read silently.) This is an informal, social reading time for the children. I tend to the beginning of the day routines and talk with the children about the books that went home overnight, then I walk around and observe and listen to children reading. Some children select books immediately, others select children and read whatever their friends are reading. There are those who come in already knowing what they are reading, those who always go to the "New Books" display, and others who read the familiar first. The children record their reading in their Reading Record and bring their books to the rug for Reading Talk.

I have an opportunity to observe natural reading, writing, and conversation during this block of time. My book check-in conversations focus on the home audience and response to reading. When Amy checks in *Strega Nona* (dePaola, 1975) I find that Grandma only knows Russian, but she

> . . . likes to listen to me read and she looks at the pictures. I can't talk to her much . . . I can tell when she figures out the story. . . She started talking a lot in Russian when the pasta was coming out of the pot and all over the floor, and she laughed when Big Anthony came slidin' out of Strega Nona's house on top of all that pasta. When Papa came home he told me about a Russian story like that. That's what Grandma was talking to me about. It's just like all the different Red Riding Hood stories.

Six-year-old Amy understands personal response to literature and uses her understanding to select the books she reads to her grandma. She knows that there are many versions of folk tales and that frequently her grandma knows these tales. Amy has begun using a storyteller's voice when she retells stories. ("Big Anthony came slidin' out of Strega Nona's house on top of all that pasta.") I make a note on my self-stick note pad. (See Figure 6-1).

Children informally talk with each other about the books they are returning. They ask questions of their fellow readers to decide if they want to read a book, and may recommend books to each other. Every day I gather important information about response to literature during the 10 to 15 minutes I spend taking lunch count and checking in books.

The book check-in is at a large rectangular table adjacent to the Message Board. Many children sit there while composing their messages. I watch and listen as children write notes. Often they begin talking with a friend about something that has happened, then decide to write a message about the event. "Tell 'em where you found it," Mike says as Carl writes about his silver rock. Mike's sense of audience is just beginning; only two weeks ago he was writing, **KM C ME** (Come see me) and pinning it unsigned on the board with little thought to the needs of the reader. I make a note of this comment before I leave the table. (See Figure 6-1.)

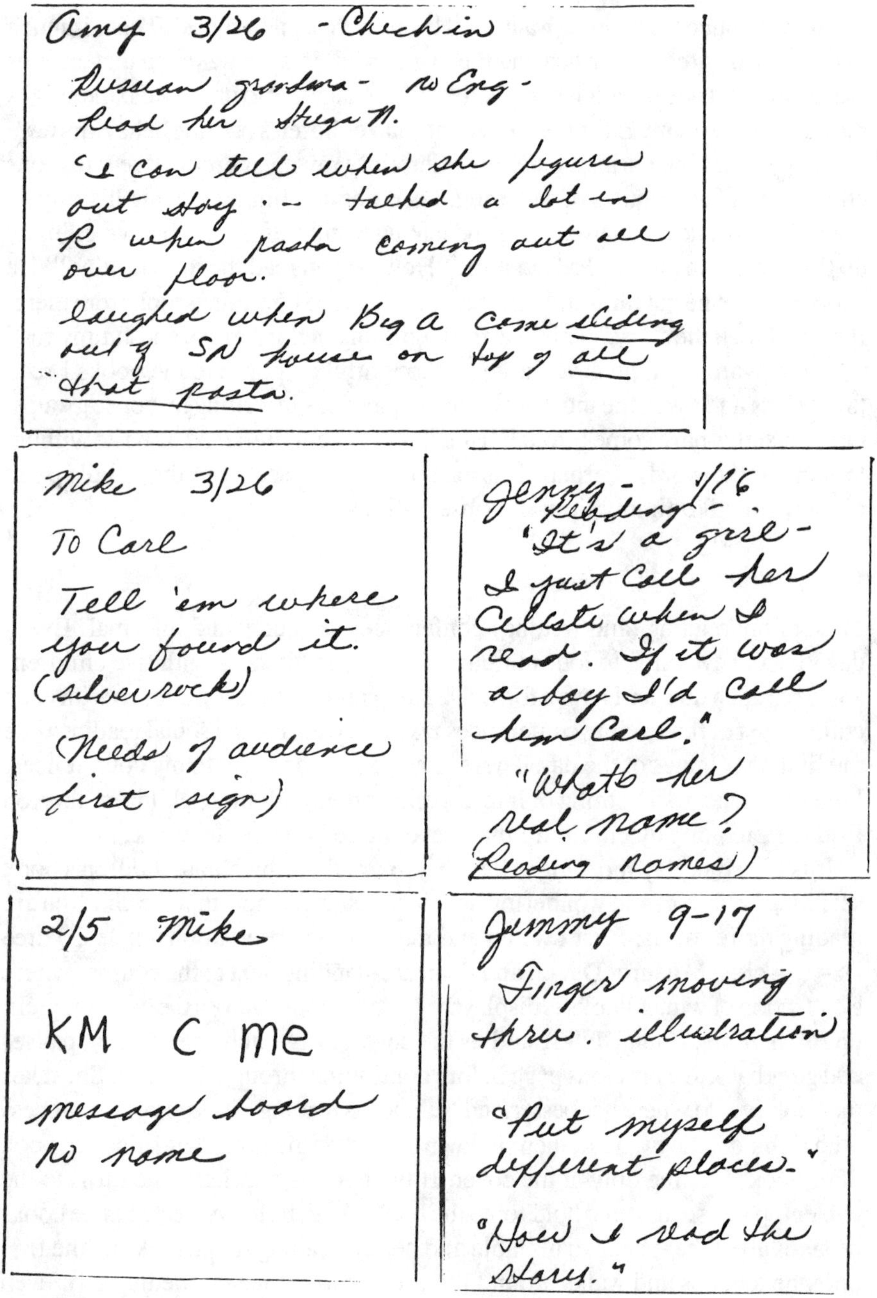

Figure 6.1 Examples of Observational Notes Taken from Student Pages in the Red Notebook

I move around the room to watch and listen as the children read. There is much to be learned without even hearing the words read. It is the watching that enables me to move outside my adult perspective of language and to understand the child's purpose. Some of my most useful insights into children's reading behaviors have begun by watching without listening. Certainly my most productive questions come after a few minutes of watching. I had noticed Jimmy moving his fingers through illustrations, often pausing and talking to himself. After observing Jimmy do this with many books I asked him, "How do you read the illustrations?" He explained that he put himself "different places to see how things look from there. It's how I read the story." This was the beginning of third grade and Jimmy read very few words, but he gave the most thoughtful response to the books I read to the class and asked the most provocative questions in writing response groups. Other insights have come through listening while children read or write without looking at the words. Perhaps it is easier for me to see from the child's point of view if I, like Jimmy limit my observations.[2]

Conversations and Conferences

Most of my reading (and writing) conferences are quick and informal. Every day I try to have three to four minute informal conferences with five children, and once each quarter I have a formal reading and writing conference with each child. Most of the reading conferences take place during the social reading time the first 45 minutes of the day. There is no particular order to my conferences. I see or overhear something of interest and confer with these children, then on Friday I pick up any children I may have missed during the week.

It is a Wednesday morning in January; I am thinking about children's book selecting behavior, and wondering how it has changed now that the children are reading more words. First I watch and make some observational notes. Three six-year-olds, Milagro, David, and Sean are standing next to the counter where a collection of winter books is displayed. Milagro looks across the counter, picks up *Brave Irene*, (Steig, 1986) studies the cover, turns each page slowly, pauses and goes back to a previous page before continuing through the book. She takes the book over to where her best friend Kehinde is reading. She repeats the process with Kehinde, the two talk, then sit down to read on the rug. David picks up book after book, looking only at the cover. If the book is nonfiction he turns to the contents page, scans it and holds onto the book. After he has collected three books he takes all of them back to his table and begins reading. Sean picks up the first book he touches and walks around the room with it, never opening it or even glancing at it. He returns it and picks up another book. After three trips to the display he leaves and goes over to sit with two boys who are reading to each other. He listens to them read for the next 15 minutes.

On that Wednesday morning I spent a few minutes observing, then I had short conferences with David, Milagro and Kehinde, Sean, and another reader, Jennifer. My notes show that David came to the winter display with several questions and was looking for books that would answer them. When I talked with him he pointed to the table of contents in one of the books. He was trying to decide which of the chapters would answer his questions about snow and ice crystals. I showed him the index in the back of the book. David located "crystals" and began telling me what he already knew about crystals. I left him looking for answers to his crystal questions. Milagro said her older sister had been reading fairy tales to her and she thought that the "pictures in *Brave Irene* look like fairy tale pictures." The two girls read a couple of pages to me. Both substituted words freely and the story came out fairly close to Steig's—not his text, but his story. Sean and I talked about the stories he had listened to his friends read. We discussed what he liked about those stories, and about listening to them. My next conference was with Jennifer who was using her modification of a reading strategy she had overheard me discussing with another child. I had been explaining that sometimes when I read I don't know how to pronounce the name in a book, but this does not keep me from understanding and enjoying the book. When that happens to me, I said, I just make up the name the best I can, or if it is a very long complicated name I use the first letter. Jennifer explained to me that she was substituting the name of someone she knew whose name began with the letter of the unknown name. (See Figure 6-1.)

All of my notes go in a looseleaf notebook. It doesn't have a name—the children call it The Red Notebook. There are pages of unlined paper for each child in the class, and I stick my notes on the child's page. I have found it much easier to keep pads of self-stick notes in my pocket, than to carry around a big notebook. The sticky notes are wonderful. I can take notes in any order, there is nothing to copy and I can rearrange my notes as I read them over and begin to see patterns. (I also write analytical notes in the notebook.) One year, at a friend's suggestion, I decided to use pads of three different colors. Blue was for reading, yellow for writing, and green for speaking. The idea was that it would help me see threads that crossed expressive and receptive modes. That's not how it worked. I would pull out the wrong color pad from my pocket and write on it. Then I'd have to copy my notes onto the correct color. I quickly abandoned the idea. Record keeping is a very individual matter; each teacher must experiment and find a system that will work for him or her.

For the formal Reading and Writing Conference I use forms to focus our discussion and provide a basis for comparing responses over the year. (See Figures 6-2 and 6-3.) Before the first quarterly conference we talk about what interests us, is important to us, and what we know about ourselves as writers and readers.

READING AND WRITING CONFERENCE- (writing)

Name: Conference on *11/16*

* Writes during journal writing time and writing workshop.

(usually)   sometimes   once in awhile

I write a lot in my Journal

* Knows and uses several ways to get started. *Draw the pictures*
* Knows what s/he likes--and when writing works.
When say the word over — like far, far away.
* Enjoys playing with words. *faster and faster + faster*

(quite a bit)   some   not really

* Has tried out different kinds of writing: (letters), stories,
lots of (about self writing) explaining, poetry, how-to writing,
informing, lists, thinking/figuring out writing, riddles,
plays, . . . *phone numbers, messages*

* Helps classmates by listening to and talking about their
writing.

(pretty often)   · sometimes   hardly ever
        my friends

* Thinks about other kids' suggestions.

usually   sometimes   (not really)

* Uses supports in the room: other children, charts, books,
adults . . .   *just want to still in books*

pretty often   (sometimes)   once in awhile

* Changes writing to make it better.
pretty often   (once in awhile)   not yet
                        when I leave out some of it

* Participates in sharing time as a listener and reader.

(almost always)   once in awhile   hardly ever

Plans: *Finish my soccer book and write another
one.*

Figure 6.2   Reading and Writing Conference (Writing)

```
              READING AND WRITING CONFERENCE--(reading)
    Name:                                Conference on  11/9

    * Reads during Everybody Reads time.

    usually          ( sometimes )            not very much
                       a little and  a lot
    * Can explain how s/he chooses books.
  favorite books - you read.      What I like    I ask somebody
                                          that can read it.
    * Talks about what s/he reads.  Know what s/he likes.
                                           yes
    a lot to say        some           not much to say



    * Likes to read to ( self--and others.
                       ( sometimes to friends if they ask me


    * Reads different kinds of materials: ( stories, information,
    how-to, ( messages ) signs, poetry,  pictures, ( books ), magazines,
    ( letters ) plays, jokes, riddles, experiments, records, cards . .
      phone numbers, menu.     Happy Birthday Moon
                               K. Egg and Ham     Didn't Frighten me
                               Oh- Bother
    * Uses illustrations to figure out words and to check meaning.

    a lot            ( sometimes )          not much


    * Use the rest of the writing to figure out words and check
    for meaning.
    ( quite often )       sometimes        hardly ever
        I read it all over from the very beginning
        and when I come to it I know the word
    * Uses letters and sounds to figure out words and check for
    meaning.

    quite often         sometimes        ( hardly ever )

    * Can read words as soon as s/he sees them.

    ( quite a few words )   some words      just a few words

    * Plans:
        just do what I'm doing . maybe read
    slower so I can talk more about it.
```

Figure 6.3 Reading and Writing Conference (Reading)

When I teach kindergarten we have only two formal conferences—one each semester. I also share what I am interested in talking about. (By November the children are quite used to me making notes and sharing "I noticed . . . I heard . . . I wonder . . ." and they just assume that it is the way we learn in this room.) I type up the form which will be used as the basis for our discussion and share it with the class so everyone will have a chance to think about his or her response. Nancie Atwell (Atwell, 1987) works differently with her middle school students. She has quarterly evaluation conferences that begin with an interview response to questions. Three of her four or five questions remain the same through the school year.

The children and I look forward to these conferences. It takes one week for us to complete the writing part of the conference and one week for the reading part (five to ten minutes per conference.) I have tried doing both parts at the same time, but have found with young children that the conference works better if we talk about writing while children are writing—and reading while they are reading. And so we do them separately. We do think of them as a Reading and Writing Conference even though it comes in two parts. When we have the second half of the conference we take some time to talk about writing and reading and how they fit together. As the year goes on we compare our current response to earlier responses and talk about how we have changed as writers and readers. Parents are always fascinated by the conference sheets, but it is the Red Notebook that interests me.

Collections of Student Writing

Writing samples are an important source of information for me. In our room each student keeps a Writing Folder, a Thinking/Learning Log, a Reading Record, and a Journal. (The Writing Folder is a comprehensive collection of the child's writing for one quarter of the school year. The Thinking/Learning Log contains quick writes and responses to prompts across the curriculum. The Reading Record is simply the student's dated list of his or her reading, and the Journal is personal writing of thoughts and rememberings.) There are many student writing samples that do not fit into any of these categories. There are signs, notes, lists, phone numbers; there are cards, letters, and gifts that go directly to the recipient. There are games, messages, how-tos, sign up sheets, casual scribblings. . . . How can a teacher, let alone a child keep track of all this writing? We don't keep track of it all, but we save enough to construct an understanding of the child as a writer.

My writing observation and conference notes, made on self-stick pads, join other notes in The Red Notebook. These notes are about all kinds of writing—single draft and multiple, finished and incomplete—across all content areas. At the end of the day I look over the room for environmental writing that I may have missed during the day.[3]

My writing observations are about the children's composing processes, the forms, functions, and purposes for their writing, themes of their writing, structure, and use of writing conventions. Each week I try to review writing folders, journals, my observational notes and so forth of three or four children and then make entries in the Red Notebook. (See Figure 6-4.) This means that I look closely at the child as a writer every two months. Usually I copy one or two selections. Figure 6-5 is a selection written by the child referred to in my notes in Figure 6-4.

Our writing curriculum requires that over the course of the year each primary grade student will write, and take through the writing process at least one piece of expressive, literary, informative, and persuasive writing. My comments in The Red Notebook include the intent or purpose of the writing, the audience, theme, or topic. Beyond that I comment on what I see as prominent features of the piece rather than covering all of the items on some checklist (See Figure 6-4.)

Children's writing has been an interest of mine for years. I have studied thousands of pieces of children's writing, and have read widely from books and articles about writing and writing research. For those who have had little practice looking at the composing processes and writings of young children I would suggest meeting with teacher consultants from state branches of the National Writing Project and reading books and articles about writing. I would particularly suggest reports from the Center for the Study of Writing and books and articles by Dyson, Hansen, Atwell, and Bissex (see bibliography).

At the end of the quarter children select one piece of writing to keep in their folder and the rest of the writing goes home. At that time I photocopy any additional pieces that I want to save. Nine weeks is a long time to wait to take home something as valuable as writing and so we have established a policy of checking out pieces of writing overnight—just as the books in our room. We try to wait until the end of the quarter to take home all of the writing, but it doesn't really belong to me and so often I let special writing go home. Of course student-written letters and notes go out daily as they are written.

As I stated in my earlier observation discussion, wide observations describe and document the process or products, and focused observations and conferences respond to specific questions about process and products. My observations of writing samples and follow up questions have confirmed my belief that there are many roads to literacy. Some are more heavily traveled, but there is not one correct, best, or normal route. I work to understand the various routes. This work is a kind of assessment.

One alternate route which I have observed is the "copy" route. For many years I would observe one or two children in my classroom who would copy from books rather than compose their own writing. I would be disturbed by this, and say something to the child, "Oh, that book has already been written. Do you want

2/1   Poetry, continuing seasonal/weather theme
new idea - put 4 short poems into long
poem with refrain. Repetition of
-ing words. Lines getting shorter,
feeling stronger, rhythm
stronger.
First evidence of large scale revision in
poetry - Change in form.
Had not worked on poems since Winter
Break - Distance?? Ask
Wants to publish or add to Poetry Collection

2/5 - 2/12   Chicken pox

2/12 - 2/20   Wandering, watching others (Between
writing behavior as earlier)

2/26   Drawing, underwater ships, sea creatures,
labels, cartoon bubbles, lots of action
in drawings. Audience eff. ~ Pete -
Gave 2 drawings away.

3/3   Working w. Yy. Pete on filmstrip adventure
Sharks, Subs, People   Conflict: Can you
add to somebody's illus? Who gets to
decide story line

3/19   Ninja Turtles. (see sample pg!) completed
6 pages. Pages end w. dramatic tension.
"Almost like how Chptrs. end." Illus.
are moving off or coming onto page - each pg.
Literary language.
Standard end punct.   "   " around
speaker rather than
Signs of revision   dialogue
adding on

Figure 6.4   Notes About Writing Samples of First Grade Boy Taken from the
Red Notebook

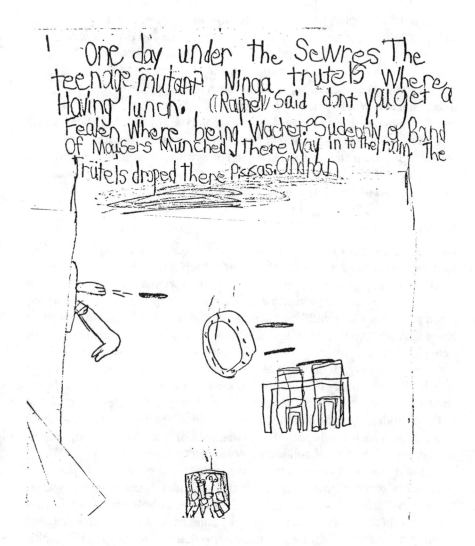

One day under the Sewres The teenage mutant Ninga trutels Where Having lunch. (Raphel) Said dont you get a Fealen Where being Wachet? Sudenhly a Band Of Mousers Munched there Way in to the room. The Trutels droped there Pssas. Oh no no

Figure 6.5 Writing Sample of Child in Figure 6.4

to take it home to read?" or, "I can make a copy of the page for you on the copy machine. Right now we are writing for ourselves." Or I might ask, "What are you doing?" And the response would come, "Writing." Then I would go on with my "You don't need to write it again. It's already been written."

Many of these copiers had begun school in other countries or inner city schools, and I attributed their behavior to previous experience and expectations. But it continued to bother me, and I worked hard to stamp it out. Eventually, (sometimes I'm a little slow in figuring things out) I decided to watch a little more closely. In the past two years I have decided that this is just another way into writing for some children. What begins as the copying of a page, gradually shrinks, until only the lead sentence is copied and the rest is composed by the child. After several months the child has mastered that genre, form, or theme and writes on his or her own. But when attempting a new kind of writing the child will again begin by copying. If I had not observed closely over a long period of time I would not have respected nor accepted this as a legitimate way of learning.

Reading Records

Records are another source of data. In our room there are three types of reading records: the reading records that the children keep of their in-class reading, my overnight book sign-out record, and their homework reading slips. I look for patterns in these records. I notice that in each class reading session Kehinde begins reading with "an old friend"—something familiar, and then moves to something new. Other patterns relate to length, difficulty of reading material or genre. For example, there are patterns of long and short, short, short; patterns of difficult and easy, easy, easy; of one kind of genre or one author for months and then a switch. (Because of my observational notes I know that some children choose children to read with, rather than books to read, and so the titles of books read by these children do not tell me about their personal reading habits.) Book sign-outs may indicate the influence of audience on book selection; only my conversations with children and conference notes can tell me.

The Red Notebook contains the literacy data for our classroom. It is a broad collection of observation notes about the children's literacy development, writing samples, and summaries of the children's Reading Records. But it is more than just a collection of data. It also contains my reflections, generalizations, and analytical comments. It functions for me in the same way that the Descriptive Biographic Literacy Profiles do for the New Hampshire teachers who work with Denny Taylor (Taylor, 1990). It enables me to know the children and talk, teach, and learn with them in a different way. Certainly my teaching is more child specific, but there is something else. The more I know and am able to see through the children's eyes the more I share their goals. Perhaps because I understand more I am better able to adjust to fit the children's goals. Such assessment keeps my teaching honest.

Student's Self-Evaluation

The Red Notebook and my increasing understanding of how children learn and use language is part of the assessment collage; another part is the children's evaluation of themselves as language learners and language users. Just as assessment is an integral part of my learning and teaching, self-evaluation is a natural part of the students' own learning. Children engage in evaluation without our help, and we need to understand their personal forms of evaluation. This section explores the self-evaluation of speaking, reading, and writing that goes on in our classroom.

When children revise as they are reading or talking they are demonstrating a form of self-evaluation. Reading teachers use the term "self-corrects" when a child goes back and gives an accurate word reading of the text. I find it more helpful to think of the behavior as evaluation and revision. It occurs quite early and naturally in speech, and continues through adulthood. (Only a few minutes of observation of yourself or other adults speaking will provide numerous examples of revised speaking. I assume that is the result of evaluation based on knowledge of audience and the intent or purpose of the talk.)

I have found that self-evaluation also occurs naturally in reading. While reading, young children frequently revise the printed text to fit or make their own meaning. If we think only of correctness and errors in the match between print and spoken text then we miss understanding how the child is reading. The realization that children purposefully revise the printed text to fit or make their own meaning came after many years of teaching and I believe it is very important. Recognizing how a child is reading is critical to a teacher's planning. When I listen to a child's thoughtful and meaningful, but inaccurate, reading I note revisions that fit logically into the whole. I an not listening at the word level, as in miscue analysis. I am speaking of meaning analysis. I listen for revisions that produce coherence in the whole piece, that fit the literary structure of the piece, that are consistent with the child's experiences and knowledge. This revision of the text to fit the child's construction of meaning is one form of self-evalaution.

Another form of reading self-evaluation is revision of one's meaning to fit the printed text. This is the type of evaluation teachers have typically valued. It is not helpful to the child to judge one type as better than the other. Both are evidence of evaluation and understanding of language—just different understandings.

Young children whose primary speech is not standard English automatically revise the text as they read, substituting their own speech for the author's. Randall was a child who would match his reading to the printed text ("accurate reading") then stop and go back to translate it into his own English. When he was in my third grade classroom he had perfected this to simultaneous translation. I may not have understood what he was doing if he had not been in my first grade classroom. In first grade I noticed that when he read a book with a predictable pattern he would begin with accurate word reading and as soon as he recognized the pattern would shift to translation, inaccurate word reading. In a few pages when the pattern changed he would catch himself—revise his language to match the new printed pattern, then once it was established begin translating into his own English again.

When we teachers make open observations and follow them with focused conversations about how children are reading or using language, then we see from the child's perspective and are open to understanding. If we observe only from our own, limited sense of correctness, we are often closed to understanding and unable to help the child learn.

When thinking about revision we more typically think of writing revision than speaking and reading revision. In whole language classrooms where writing emerges as a natural form of interaction and expression, children seem to engage in writing evaluation and revision on their own. Kindergarten children often tell stories from their written text. I do not think of this story telling as writing evaluation, but when children add thoughts and words in the oral rendition of the written text then they begin to evaluate their writing. My experience with third grade children who have not had opportunities to write for themselves, but have only experienced taught writing, is that they do very little self-evaluation and revision of their writing. On the other hand, when I have had the same children in first grade and again in third I frequently see evaluative comments written in the margins of writing in progress. My favorite example is Maggie who would write such comments to herself as, "Starts here—the good part," or "Think about this." She also would make little caricatures of faces in the margin which she explained to me were her readers. (Her audience was on her paper as well as in her head!)

I don't want to leave the impression that all I and other teachers need to do is provide the environment and evaluation will take care of itself. Our job with naturally occurring evaluation is to recognize it, make the child aware of what and how he or she is evaluating, and make the many forms of evaluation apparent and available to other members of the class and community. I point out how and what we are evaluating by having the children talk and write about their own evaluation, and I expect it. My frequent invitations to evaluate begin, "I noticed . . ." and continue, "Can you explain what you do—or how you . . .?"

And there are the "almost by yourself evaluation" times when I push or nudge. There are times when I pause to recognize or listen for effective language while reading aloud to the class, and ask the inevitable questions, "How do you think (Robert McCloskey—or an author in our room) wanted you to feel?" "Why do you think . . .?" There are times when I direct the children to evaluate their own or other printed text. Remember the collage? I am moving into the area of greatest overlap—collaborative evaluation.

Collaborative Evaluation

In collaborative evaluation I assist the children by focusing attention on a particular facet of language or language learning. The evaluation may begin with reflective questions posed to a single child during a conference, a small group of children or the whole class. Later such questions become part of the children's own inner evaluative conversations—part of the repertoire of self-evaluation.

As I sit down at a table where children are writing I am asked, "Want to hear my story?" Andrew begins to read, hesitates, and stops. "I can't read what I wrote." "You were writing about when the monsters chased you and locked you in the closet. Just make it up," helps Philip. Andrew continues reading his story. We talk about the story, and I say to the children at the table, "I've noticed that sometimes it's easy to read what you write and sometimes it's hard. What do you think makes it hard or easy?" (My question is an invitation to analyze, and a model question for the self-evaluation process.) They think about themselves as readers and writers. Andrew doesn't have any ideas yet. "I can just read it or I can't," he reports. Katie is very clear, "I know a lot of letters and I talk and write it at the same time. Only the spaces are hard. You know, the spaces aren't the same when you talk and when you write." She shows us her writing. "You have to put in lots more writing spaces than you do talking spaces, an' sometimes I can't remember where they go," she pauses. "You say it, 'Onceupona time,' (two words, one space) but you write it like this." (**1Z AP N A TM**, five words, four spaces.) "There's lots more spaces." Philip explains, "I draw lots of pictures, and write, and draw some more, so I can read the pictures and the letters at the same time."

In our room assessment requires collaborative data gathering to help us think about and understand our literacy questions. One morning I overheard six-year-old Laura ask Ferhad, "Will you help me read *The Snowy Day* (Keats, 1962)?" I bring this up during Reading Talk and Laura explains what it was that she wanted when she asked for help. Then we all think, write and discuss our response to the questions, "What helps you read?" For days we ponder these questions as we read and ask for and receive help from each other. Together we assess help and how it works for each of us as we write, talk, read, and listen. (This is an example of self-evaluation of a process.) The children share their understanding of help. During the discussion I also share what I know about myself as a writer, what I have figured out about the help I need, how I get it, and how I use it. We evaluate, we share, and we enlarge and modify our personal understanding. That is how collaboration works. If the assessing we do and the data we collect does not lead us to an understanding of what we are doing then the assessment has no value.

When having a whole class discussion we take time to write before we talk. This gives us all time to think and reflect and it commits us to our own ideas.

Every child tends to contribute to discussions if given an opportunity to write first. Examples of evaluative questions we have discussed are listed in Figure 6-6.

Figure 6.6   Examples of Evaluative Questions to Help Children Become Aware of How They Know, What They Think About Writing

---

How do you decide if writing is good writing? What makes one piece of writing better than another piece of writing? How do you decide if your writing is good writing?

If someone asked you to help them write a (story, poem, report, description . . .) what would you do for them?

Does it make a difference whom you are writing for when you write? Whom you are writing to?

Who helps you write? How do they help you? What do they do when they help you? If you could get someone to help you write a _____ what would you have them do to help you?

How do you go about writing? What do you do when you write? Do you ever get stuck? What do you do then?

What part of writing do you like the most? the least? How do you explain that?

What are some of the things that writers do?

Often the collaborative evaluation discussion springs from one of my observational notes. We are all meeting together just before we have Writing Workshop. I begin, "Yesterday I heard Jimmy asking Guillermo about the end of his story. Can you two describe the problem for us?" Jimmy explains that he can't tell when his story is finished. Guillermo's solution is to write **THE END**, that's what he does. I ask the class to think about how they know when a story is finished—to think about their own writing and about stories and books they have read. All of us write in our Thinking/Learning Log and then the discussion begins. Some may call this problem solving, others call it reflection. I call it self-assessment. In this case each one of us is assessing what he knows about story structure and how it works. (This is a self-assessment of knowledge.) During the discussion which follows our Quick Write we have a chance to rethink our understanding, maybe modify or add to it, as we listen to our friends' ideas.

Other times the evaluation topic comes directly from a class member to the group. Marla, a third grader, says, "In our response group we never raise our hands and we do just fine. How come we have to raise our hands during Reading

Talk?" We have a discussion (mostly raising our hands) about talking, listening, and how it works. "How do you get into a small conversation? "Who stops when two begin talking at once?" "Can you talk to someone if they're not looking at you?"

A large group of children decides to investigate our questions. Splinter groups form around different issues. Teams of investigators observe in our classroom, the lunchroom, on the playground, and at home. Reports come back over the next month. The class decides that six is the magic number—"Sometimes six can really talk and listen, but any more and you have to have some way to take turns." Is this research? Yes. Is it evaluation? I think so. Certainly these children now know more about how spoken language works and how they and others use it in a variety of situations, for a variety of purposes. They have assessed and evaluated the data. They have revised (modified and extended) their understanding—they have learned.

These accounts are examples of individual evaluation in a whole class setting. Evaluation does not need to be solitary and silent to be effective evaluation (Eidman-Aadahl, 1988). How one reaches an understanding (or if one understands first) is not important. What is important is that one becomes a literacy insider, a person who understands how written and spoken language works for oneself and for others. Part of my job is to provide the time, the space, the atmosphere, and questions so that this becoming a literacy insider will happen. I am not the only one who assists in self-evaluation. The children continually assist each other through their responses and questions. Evaluation and learning are social activities. Social interactions provide peer feedback which almost demands self-evaluation.

There is another, more formal way in which I assist the children with evaluation. Just as I use a formal Reading and Writing Conference sheet, (Figures 6-2 and 6-3) to assist me in assessing the current state of a child's language understanding, the children use formal evaluation sheets to assist themselves in self-evaluation. Each year the children develop new response sheets for a variety of purposes. The sample in Figure 6-7 was developed to help third grade students look at their persuasive writing. We have developed other sheets to evaluate our understanding of literary forms, reader's threatre presentations, handwriting that is to be read by the public. . . The evaluation sheets are always developed by the class after analyzing the important features of the particular genre, form, and so forth.

The Evaluation Sheet for Writing to Convince came in response to a flurry of persuasive writing. Young children engage in persuasive speech as a part of normal interactions with their peers and adults. Some children are experts at verbally convincing others of the importance of an idea or action, others have a very limited repertoire of techniques to persuade. One year in third grade there were many children with a limited understanding of how verbal persuasion

Figure 6.7   Evaluation Sheet

EVALUATION SHEET FOR WRITING TO CONVINCE   *Mom and Dad*
(person)

Chris
(author)

Meg
(partner)

	author	partner	Mrs. R.
PERSUASION			
What I want the reader to do or think is clear. *Not walk my sister to school*	✓	✓	✓
There are logical reasons given. *Yes*	✓	✓	✓
There is evidence that I know the reader and have anticipated and answered problems or arguments the reader may have.	✓	✓	✓
CONVENTIONS			
Paragraphs are used for separate ideas.	✓	✓	✓
Punctuation follows our rules sheet. (Ending punctuation, commas, apostrophes)	✓		✓
Capital letters are used where needed.	✓	✓	✓
Words are circled that may be misspelled. (draft) Words are spelled correctly. (final copy)	✓	✓	✓
Handwriting meets our standards for writing that will be read by others.	✓	✓	✓
WRITING PROCESS			
I told my partner all about the person who had to be convinced.	✓	✓	
I tried out my persuasion with my partner.	✓	✓	
I told my response group what to listen for.	✓	✓	
I considered the comments and questions of my response group.	✓		
I listened and reacted as the person to be convinced when other kids read their letters.	✓		
REVISION HELP			
The purpose sentence is underlined in red. The reason sentences are underlined in blue. The anticipation of problem sentences in green.	✓	✓	✓

worked. They tried other avenues of persuasion—increased volume, higher pitch accompanied by hitting, grabbing, and shoving were favorites. Through drama, discussion, reading, more discussion, and practice the class became more adept at verbal persuasion. Then letter writing took hold. These children were very serious about their ideas, and the importance of convincing others to change or act. This response sheet reflects the class's analysis of persuasion, understanding of audience, conventions of written language, and a writing process. The entire class helped in its development, I typed it, and it was available for those who were doing persuasive writing. Those students mailing their letters had conferences that utilized the draft letters and evaluation sheet.

It is not this particular evaluation sheet nor any of the others we develop that is important. What is important is the process used to develop the sheet, the student analysis of language, and the function it plays in revision. Self-evaluation leads to revision, and revision, the modification and extension of understanding, is learning.

Before I conclude I must acknowledge my familiarity with a more common form of evaluation which is called grading. However, I do not put grades on papers or students. (I recognize that grades and grading are a concern that must be addressed. In this chapter I have limited the discussion to assessment which is useful to the children and me. Assessment and communicating with parents, or assessment for accountability are different issues for other chapters.) I am a teacher of children, and comparative (or numerical) evaluation does not meet my needs. It does not assist me in my assessment and understanding of children as language users and language learners. Grades given by me, even if based on my assessment and understanding of a child's emerging literacy, cannot substitute for the child's self-evaluation. Grades given by me will not lead children to become literacy insiders engaging in self-evaluation, but my careful assessment and collaborative evaluation will. I leave comparative and mathematical evaluation to those who have some use for it.

Summary

Back to the collage—I had planned to summarize with a collage—a visual representation of assessment and evalution which would show all of the component parts and their relationships. There would be the teacher who must notice, wonder, question, analyze, revise, understand, question, share, collaborate. There would be children who, in the midst of written and spoken language, are also noticing, wondering, questioning, evaluating and revising. There would be observation, converstion and conferences, reading records, writing samples, and the relationships would now be clear. I tried to construct the collage, but found that I needed three dimensions, not two. Perhaps it should be a mobile.

What is clear to me is my goal: that the children become literacy insiders who routinely engage in self-evaluation. It is self-evaluation that leads children to revision. And revision, the modification and expansion of understanding, is learning—that is what teaching is about. While I believe children engage in self-evaluation on their own, I also believe they are assisted by collaborative evaluation with teachers who use assessment as the foundation for their teaching.

Endnotes

1. For a discussion of a teacher's handling of mandated reading assessment see Reardon (1990).
2. The collection of articles in *Observing the Language Learner* (Jaggar & Smith-Burke, 1985) is useful to the teacher who is interested in learning more about observation.
3. See Loughlin & Martin, (1987) especially Appendix B "Environmental Evidence for Literacy Growth."

References

Atwell, N. (1987). *In the middle. Writing, reading, and learning with adolescents*. Portsmouth, NH: Heinemann Educational Books.

Bissex, G. (1980). *GNYS AT WRK: A Child learns to write and read*. Cambridge, MA: Harvard University Press.

DePaola, T. (1975). *Strega Nona*. Englewood Cliffs, NJ: Prentice Hall, Inc.

Dyson, A. (1988). *Drawing, talking and writing: Rethinking writing development*. Occasional paper No. 3. Berkeley, CA: Center for the Study of Writing, University of California, Berkeley.

Dyson, A. (1988). *Negotiating among multiple worlds. The space/time dimensions of young childrne's composing*. Technical Report No. 15. Berkeley, CA: Center for the Study of Writing, University of California, Berkeley.

Eidman-Aadahl, E. (1988). The solitary reader: Exploring how lonely reading has to be. *The New Advocate, 1*,(3) 165–176.

Hansen, J. (1987). *When writers read*. Portsmouth, NH: Heinemann Educational Books.

Jaggar, H. & Smith-Burke, T. (Eds.). (1985). *Observing the language learner*. Urbana, IL: IRA/NCTE.

Keats, E. (1962). *The snowy day*. Bergenfield, NJ: Viking Press.

Loughlin, C. & Martin, M. (1987). *Supporting literacy: Developing effective learning environments*. New York: Teachers College Press.

Reardon, S. Putting reading tests in their place, *The New Advocate 3*, (1), 29–37.

Steig, W. (1986) *Brave Irene*. Scranton, PA: Farrar, Straus & Giroux.

Taylor, D. (1990) Teaching without testing: Assessing the complexity of children's literacy learning. *English Education. 22*, 4–74.

Chapter 7

Holistic Assessment in Intermediate Classes: Techniques for Informing Our Teaching

Yvonne Siu-Runyan

Good teaching . . . is created and crafted through a continual process or revision. (Bird, 1989, p. 15)

Assessment and instruction go hand in hand. Assessment enhances teachers' powers of observation and understanding of learning. (Teale, Hiebert, & Chittenden, 1987, p. 773)

To use assessment information for revising one's teaching, as these experts suggest, requires a different kind of data collection. It requires going beyond relying on numerical results from the commonly used standardized and criterion-referenced tests packaged by publishers or developed by school districts.

While numerical scores from standardized and criterion-referenced tests can yield useful information about how well students, schools, and districts do in comparison to others, they do not provide information useful for daily instruction. A numerical test score cannot tell us:

- What our students think about reading and writing.
- What strategies they use when reading and writing various texts.
- How they use reading and writing to make meaning, to evaluate the relevance of knowledge, to verify and revise their own thinking, and ultimately to direct their own learning.

Further, scores from tests are not helpful for teachers who want to involve their students and themselves in the process of continual self-evaluation for reflective teaching and learning. They cannot help both teachers and students seriously examine questions such as: "How am I doing? Are things going as I planned? What can I do to see that things go better next time?" (Goodman, 1989, p. 13).

Because of the limited information test scores can offer teachers, and because teachers want assessment data that can empower them to revise their teaching, many teachers are asking, "What else can I use that's more helpful than test scores to inform myself about what my students know, what they are struggling with, and what do I need to help them become more strategic readers and writers?"

Assessment Techniques for Intermediate Classrooms

When discussing assessment, several experts point out the need for overcoming our habit of using once yearly, product oriented assessment techniques. They suggest putting more emphasis on using:

- Assessment data which reflect ongoing student learning over long periods of time (Jaggar, 1985).
- Assessment data that reflects the active nature of learning and can be used as feedback for reflective practice and as the basis for cooperative decisions about curriculum and instruction (Brown, 1989; Costa, 1989).
- A broader range and variety of assessment techniques (Valencia & Pearson, 1987; Pikulski, 1989), which include teachers' assessments (Hiebert & Calfee, 1989).
- Authentic assessments such as direct observation of behavior, portfolios of student work, long-term projects, logs and journals, student interviews, video- and audio-tapes of student performance, and writing samples (Costa, 1989; Shepard, 1989).

From my past experiences as a classroom teacher when working with children in grades 3–6 in a mountain schoolhouse that has approximately 40 children (K–6), I have learned that there are several sources of information that yield information valuable for assessing student understanding and ability, and directing instruction. These techniques involve talking with students, using anecdotal records, involving students in long-term projects, learning from student portfolios, and observing how students use reading and writing in their everyday lives and how they talk about their own literacy and the literacy of others. In addition, teachers may want to use other assessment techniques such as audiotapes and videotapes, and logs and journals, neither of which are addressed in this chapter.

Regardless of what assessment procedures teachers decide to use, we need to keep in mind that these procedures need to reflect the dynamic, constructionist nature of language learning and not the mastery of discrete skills. Further, I encourage teachers eager to move toward holistic assessment techniques to jump right in and do it. Don't feel as though you need to know everything there is about these techniques before you try them. There is no rigid formula for their use. As you use the various assessment procedures, you will learn what works best for you and your students. You will learn from your mistakes and refine your own techniques.

Talking with Students

Some of the most useful sources of information we teachers can use for assessment are the conversations we have with students about their reading and writing. These conversations can inform us about:

- Student understanding of reading and writing.
- How reading and writing affect students' thinking and learning.
- The things teachers do that are helpful and not helpful to students.
- Student interests—the things about which students like to read and write.
- The areas where students want help.

To learn about one's teaching and how students view reading and writing.

Two questions that lead to interesting conversations with students and that I have found to be extremely useful for assessment and teaching are:

1. What kinds of things do I do that help you as a writer?
2. What kinds of things do I do that help you as a reader?

When I first asked my students these questions, I received either no response, very little response, or general statements that had little value for instruction. Besides having limited or no experience responding to questions like these, I think the students were unsure of my sincerity. They didn't want to be penalized for being honest with me. Initially, students typically offered comments like these:

You help us. (Zephyr, 3rd grade)
You like us. (Travis, 4th grade)
You help me with spelling. (Geoff, 5th grade)
I don't know. (Ashleigh, 4th grade)
You don't yell at us. (John, 6th grade)

However, because I was interested in finding out what my students thought about my teaching, I kept asking them these two questions. After awhile, the students finally realized I was sincerely interested in finding out what they thought. They learned they could trust me, and began giving honest feedback that I could use to improve my teaching.

What did I learn from asking these two questions?

From Zephyr (3rd grade), I learned how important the language I use with children is. He said, "I like when you (long pause), I mean some teachers I've met are really serious and if I get something wrong they'll yell at me. I like that you don't do that. You offer suggestions, but not meanly. And then I choose if I want to follow your suggestions. I don't feel stupid."

Zephyr was the first to point out that how I spoke with the students was important. As a result of Zephyr's response, I became much more aware of how I spoke with the students. I noticed that when I was dictatorial and directive, the students tuned me out. And that when I offered suggestions and spoke with them as reader to reader and writer to writer, they were much more invested in their own learning.

With practice and close attention to the kind of teacher talk I used, I became more of a facilitator of children's learning, rather than the director of their learning. Zephyr taught me that helping children learn is more a matter of what **we** do than of what we ask our students to do.

As I became more skillful at using language that empowers them as learners, appreciation for the way I talked with them was later expressed by other students.

> I like the way you talk to me about the stories I read. You're really interested in what I like. . .and by getting to know us and the kind of stories we like to write. (Stephanie, 5th grade)
>
> I like the way you talk to me about the stories I write, and how you help me put conversation in my stories. (Cara, 4th grade)
>
> I like the way you talk to me to help me when I get stuck (Travis, 4th grade)
>
> I feel good after I talk to you about my story. You tell me what you like and you help me think about what I want to say. (Geoff, 5th grade)
>
> I like when you share your writing with us. (Lucas, 4th grade)
>
> I like it when you read stories to us and we discuss them. It gives me ideas for my own stories. Learning how to write from a web was also helpful. (D.J., 6th grade)
>
> I like it when you read to us. It makes me want to read the book too. (Ben, 5th grade)
>
> When you show us what you do when you read and write. (Mike, 6th grade)

From the comments like the ones above, I learned several things:

- To stop and think before I speak.
- The students understood that writing is using written language to communicate. They are first concerned about their message instead of the mechanics. This indicated to me that they have a good grasp of the writing process.

■ The books we read and discussed helped my students generate ideas for their own pieces.
■ It was important for the students to share their pieces with others.
■ Teaching them how to brainstorm and web ideas were helpful strategies to them as writers.
■ That students liked it when I read, wrote, and shared with them.

Two other questions that were much more difficult for students to answer are:

1. What kinds of things do I do that are *not* helpful to you as a writer?
2. What kinds of things do I do that are *not* helpful to you as a reader?

I found that when I asked students these two questions, they had a much more difficult time formulating their response. Nevertheless, I had some brave souls who broke new ground for my thinking. From Silas (4th grade), I learned that just telling kids to get busy and write isn't always helpful. In response to these two questions, Silas said, "I like that we can read what we want. But, I don't like it when you tell me to just get busy and write. I have a hard time getting busy when I don't know what to write about."

Stephanie (5th grade) taught me that when a student is sitting and daydreaming, it doesn't mean he or she isn't writing. Stephanie related, "I don't like it when you tell me to get busy. Lots of time I'm thinking about my story. And when you tell me to get busy, it makes me nervous."

And John (6th grade) taught me that reading magazines is as engaging, useful and important as reading books. He said, "I don't like it when you tell me to read a book during silent reading time, when I'd rather read a magazine. I like magazines. I learn interesting things in them."

Missy (5th grade) taught me that it was important for them to share their reading and writing with one another. She offered, "I don't like it when we are right in the middle of a discussion about a book or a story we are writing, and you tell us to stop."

As a result of the information gleaned from asking students to tell me the ways in which I was helpful and not helpful to them as readers and writers, I became a much more reflective and responsive teacher, and in the process I improved my teaching. For the first time in my life, I was not afraid to ask these hard questions. In fact, I learned that in order to be an effective teacher, I had to seek answers to these difficult questions.

To find out what students want to learn next

The way curriculum guides and published materials are developed and packaged leads many teachers to rely on them to direct their teaching. We rarely, if at all, ask students what they want to learn next in order to become a better reader and writer. And yet, this may be one of the most important questions we can ask our students. Jane Hansen (1989, p. 21) offers, "Asking kids these kinds of questions is really important to teaching. I'm wondering how in the world I ever taught before because I didn't ask students what they wanted to learn, nor did I ask how I could help them. So I was putting things together in my head very differently from the way children saw things. No wonder school didn't seem to be all that meaningful."

What did I learn from my students when I asked this question? I learned that students can articulate what they want to learn. From this information, I could better assess their understanding of reading and writing, and this influenced how and what I taught next. I learned that teaching became a lot easier, more dynamic, and fun for all of us. I learned that I was a more effective teacher when I took my lead from the students. I learned that the students were more invested in learning when they focused on things important to them.

When I first asked the question: "What would you like to learn next in order to become a better reader or writer?" I received very little response from the students. When they did offer comments, they were vague ones like:

Learn how to read better. (Ben, 5th grade)
Write better. (Geoff, 5th grade)
Who knows? You're the teacher. (Travis, 4th grade)

After about a month of asking this question over and over again, students slowly began telling me what they wanted to learn next. Here is a sample of some of the things they wanted to learn:

I want to learn how to read inside my head, instead of out loud. (Ben, 5th grade)
I want to learn how to put conversation in my stories. (Ashleigh, 4th grade)
I want to learn about other words to use in place of said. (Mike, 5th grade)
I want to learn how to punctuate the convertations in my stories. (Lucas, 4th grade)
I want to learn how to find topics to write about. (Silas, 4th grade)
I want to learn how to type on the computer. Finding the keys is hard. (Cara, 4th grade)
I want to learn how to develop my characters. (D.J., 6th grade)
I want to learn how to spell the word "probably." (Thomas, 5th grade)

From the children's comments, I learned that they knew a lot about reading and writing. They knew that reading is not sounding out words, and that writing is not primarily spelling words and forming the letters of the alphabet correctly. They knew that one reads for understanding, and one writes to communicate. And, most importantly, their suggestions showed me that students can tell us what they want to learn if we just ask them.

Using Anecdotal Records

Anecdotal records include teachers' observations about any of the following:

- What students are reading and writing.
- Student comments about reading and writing.
- How students approach reading and writing.
- How students respond to instruction.
- How students use reading and writing to learn.
- Teacher questions and comments.

While it is helpful for teachers to record their observations daily, it isn't always feasible. Nevertheless, if teachers can write a minimum of only one sentence every day about their observations, they will learn a lot. This information is vital if teachers are to move from being managers of materials to being reflective, decision makers in charge of their own teaching. Sometimes teachers feel as though they must make insightful comments or evaluative comments about their observations. But I have learned that just recording one's observations is often enough. Insightful or evaluative comments are drawn from the many observations recorded over time.

To illustrate what I mean let's examine some excerpts from my anecdotal records.

8/31/87—Most of the children are struggling with their pieces. They want to write grand stories, but don't know enough about their topics to write well. They want to write fiction, and not personal narratives which is what I think would make a difference for them.

9/2/87—The students are abandoning pieces like mad. Even though I did a lesson on brainstorming ideas for writing topics, most are still struggling with topic choice.

9/8/87—Thomas is writing a piece about war. It's really a replay of the war stories on television.

9/14/87—I wish the kids were more invested in writing. They are wasting a lot of time, because many don't know what to write about. I am getting worried.

10/7/90—Kids of concern: Zephyr, Tom, Travis, Geoff, Cara, Ashleigh, Lucas, John, Ben, Missy, Mel, Rojana, and Mike. These kids are still not invested in their writing. I'm beginning to feel like a failure.

When I reviewed the observations recorded on the dates listed above, I knew I had to do something to help these children and soon. I then realized that I hadn't written with them, nor had I modeled how literature inspired me to write. "Perhaps, if I model this technique, the students will take their lead from me," I thought. "It's worth a try."

So, the next day (10/8/87), I read *The Important Book* (1949) written by Margaret Wise Brown. After reading the book, I said, "You know reading this book has given me an idea for writing." Then during writing time, I wrote my own important story, which included every student in my class. I shared my emerging drafts and read the final story to the students.

Entries in my anecdotal record notebook dated after the 10th of October reveal what happened when I used this approach.

10/14/87—Lucas and Melissa are writing their own important stories. I am so pleased that they are trying their hand at this. Perhaps now others will use literature to help them learn about writing. Now to keep the momentum going. I must be careful about what books I choose to share. I must remember to select personal narratives with an obvious design. I think this will help the kids a lot.

10/20/87—Read *My Mom Travels A Lot* (1981) by Caroline Feller Bauer. Discussed the design of the book. Created several stories verbally following the opposite design pattern of this book. Today Cara developed her own story from the model presented. Great!

10/26/87—Read *Fortunately* (1964) by Remy Charlip. The design of this book is very similar to *My Mom Travels A Lot*, except that the events are connected. Guess who decided to write a similar story? Cara. She's really taken off on using the opposite design pattern for her stories.

11/2/87—Read *If You Give A Mouse A Cookie* (1985) by Laura Joffe Numeroff. Discussed circle plot structure with the class. Made up two stories verbally. Thomas is starting his own story modeled after this book. Wonderful. Thomas has a hard time organizing his thoughts. I wonder how he'll do.

12/7/87—Since the beginning of November, Thomas has written several stories modeled after *If You Give A Mouse A Cookie*. He's written "If You Give A Chipmunk A Peanut Butter Bread," "If You Give a Bear Some Crumbs," and "If You Give A Goat Some Grass." Tom is obssessing on this pattern. I'm wondering if I should be concerned. But he is writing. And his stories are more organized than they have ever been before. He had definitely learned how to spell the word, "probably." Rhoda, the special education teacher told me that he has never written anything before as organized as these three stories. We think the structure of the design helped him to organize his thoughts. Rhoda also said that Tom loves the word, "probably." He refused to take it out of his story. Now that's investment.

From my anecdotal records, I discovered the importance of discussing the design of stories with my students. I also found out that if I wanted to encourage my students to take risks in writing, that I must write with them, model how I use the writing process and literature to help me write, and become one of the participants in our reading/writing workshop.

Further, to help my students understand that effective authors write from a position of knowledge and experience, I started asking, "What do you think the author had to know or experience in order to write this piece?" Once we started discussing their responses to this question along with the design of various pieces, I noticed the empty war stories and TV violence replayed on paper slowly vanished.

In addition, anecdotal records have also been useful in helping me determine the areas in which my students need help in order to improve their writing style, and how they use reading to help their writing.

11/23/87—Students are writing, writing, writing. They love writing and share it easily with others. I have noticed however that there are a lot of wents, gots, and saids in their stories. Perhaps now would be a good time to discuss strong verbs.

11/30/87—D.J. Is noticing character development in the story he's reading. In fact, it is not uncommon for him to follow me around the class reading excerpts from his book to me.

12/2/87—Steph's piece has the words *tree GAP* in it. She said she learned that from the book, *Tuck Everlasting* (1975) by Natalie Babbitt.

12/7/87—Kids still think that revision is editing. They do not really understand **RE-VISITING** a piece.

12/11/87—I need to get the kids to become more independent. They need to learn how to rely on each other more, instead of always coming to me. Help!!
    They need to learn how to ask each other questions so that revision can occur.

12/14/87—D.J. said that he wants to write descriptive leads instead of leads which put the reader right into the action.
    The kids are moving along very well. They are learning about writing from the stories they read. Pointing out things that authors do when they write in the books we are reading and discussing is proving to be useful for me personally and for the students, too.

When reviewing the previous anecdotal records, I learned that I needed to now focus attention on:

- Making public how and what the students were learning about writing from their reading.
- Helping the students learn how to ask questions that help the writer with revision.
- Helping students understand how important it is for them to write about something they know.
- Using strong verbs.

It is interesting to note that these four very important aspects of reading and writing are not part of the district's language arts/reading curriculum guide. Had

I taken my direction for developing lessons from the curriculum guide only, I would not have seen the opportunity to teach my students how to learn about writing from the literature they read, how to ask each other questions which help with revision, and how to use strong verbs rather than weak ones.

Involving Students in Long-Term Projects

Assessment should determine whether students are able to monitor their own understanding, use strategies to make questions comprehensible, evaluate the relevance of accessible knowledge and verify their own solution. The best way to check for these indicators is to make assessment measure resemble learning tasks (Shepard, 1989, p. 7).

In the school district where I last taught, a task force was organized to develop a plan for assessing students' writing ability. The plan that the committee finally approved was suggested by Miles Olson from the University of Colorado. Because we wanted this activity to be an authentic task for students, Dr. Olson suggested having the school librarians write a letter to the students in their respective buildings asking for input about the authors, topics, and books they would like in their school libraries. A sample letter was developed for teachers to follow. In this letter, the students were asked to help select books by telling who their favorite authors were and the topics about which they were interested. The students were also told that it would be helpful if they included in their letters titles of books by their favorite authors and titles of books on their favorite topics. And finally, students were informed that decisions about which books to purchase would be based on how well the students were able to convince the school librarian that their choices were the best ones, and on how well their letters were presented. The students were given two weeks to finish this project, and all writing had to be done in school.

In order to complete this assignment, the students decided they needed to have a discussion about how to proceed. (I merely acted as facilitator. I did not direct them nor give suggestions about what to do.) Their discussion surprised me. I discovered that the students knew a lot more about the writing process and books than I had originally thought, and that they had definite opinions about the authors, titles, and topics they wanted to read. These were the activities in which the students engaged to complete this project:

Rehearsal:
1. They brainstormed favorite authors and topics.
2. They talked with one another about favorite authors and topics.
3. They did research to find titles of books written by favorite authors.
4. They did research to find out titles of books on favorite topics.

5. They went to the card catalogue to find out what books and how many copies of certain titles were already in the school library.
6. They developed and conducted surveys to find out if other students wanted the same authors, titles, or topics they had chosen.

Drafting:
1. They wrote and shared their emerging persuasive letters with one another to check for clarity.
2. They used each other as well as the resources in the classroom to find spelling and punctuation errors and correct them.
3. They used the language arts textbooks to clarify the correct form for writing letters.

Final Copy:
1. They wrote final copies in long hand or on the computer using correct letter format.
2. They had concrete reasons for their choices
3. They had suggestions for titles, authors, and topics.
4. Their letters were organized.
5. The understood a lot about punctuation. A few of the 3rd graders, most of the 4th graders and all of the 5th and 6th graders underlined the titles of books and used the colon appropriately. Most of the 3rd and 4th graders and all of the 5th and 6th graders used ending punctuation and commas in a series correctly.
6. They all demonstrated their knowledge of writing and literature, their love of books, and their ability to research, collect, and analyze data.

Here is Silas's (4th grade) letter at rehearsal and in final copy. Notice that his preparation for writing his draft is thorough. He first brainstormed all his favorite authors and topics. Then he selected his most favorite topics and authors and did research to determine how many books, if any, were included in the collection. After that Silas interviewed the other children to find out if they were interested in reading books on topics and by authors he had selected.

Once he collected all the data needed for writing his letter, he proceeded to write his draft. After the draft was written, Silas shared his emerging letter with other students, received feedback from them, and wrote the final copy.

Notice how much Silas understands about the writing process and the skills he knows. Silas knows how to brainstorm ideas, gather data using the card catalogue and *Children's Books in Print*, conduct a survey, organize the information, and write a persuasive letter from draft to final copy. Silas also knows how to use ending punctuation, the colon, commas in a series, parentheses, and capitalization. In addition, he also knows correct letter format and that book titles need to be underlined.

Figure 7-1

Silas 2-22-89

FEB 24

Brainstorming Sheet

Author	TOPICS
1. Franklin W. Dixon *	1. Mystery *
2. Wilson Rawls	2. Adventures *
3. Richard Adams *	3. Survival *
4. Winthrop	4. Fiction *
5. Jack Pearl *	5. Wild Life X
6. Beverly Cleary	6. Mamels
7. Chris VanAllsburg X	7. Drama X
8. E.B. White	8. Dogs
9. Shel Silverstein *	9. Cats
10. Gary Paulsen X	10. Rodents X
11. Sheila Burnford *	11. Secpenc
12. James Howe	12. Reptiles X
13. Audrey + Don Wood	13. Poems X
14. Jack London *	14. Forest X
15. Brock Cole X	15. Lizard
16. Robert N. Peck X	16. fishing X

Figure 7-2

Library Research

Silas 2-27-89

Authors	Topics
Franklin Dixon	Mysterys
	We have: 63
We have: 7	
	Adventures
Richard Adams-	We have: 1
We have: 0	
	Survival
James Howe	We have: 10
We have: 5	
	Sports
Jack Pearl	We have: 0
We have: 0	
Jack London	
We have: 2	
Shel Silverstein	
We have: 1	

Figure 7-3

Silas MAR 06 1989   1989   X

RESONS

1. I like Franklin W. Dixon. Other kids like him to. These are some people: Lucas, Ben. B, Adam, and Sean and other people do to.

2. I like Franklin W. Dixon because he writes exsideny Mystery/Adventures. He writes Hardy Boys. Here are a few of his case file book: "Border line," "Perfect Get Away," "Cult of Crime," "Edge of Destruction," and "Lazus Plot." Another Author that I like is Richard Adams. He writes books about Ficional anamals. They would bring enjoment to the class (Espexaly D.J.). These are a few books I would like you to order: "Shardik," "Watership down," and "Pleage Dog."

Figure 7-4

March 8, 1989

Dear Gail,

    I like Franklin W. Dixon. Other kids in our class like him, too. These are a few people that like Dixon: Lucas Ben.B, Adam, Sean, and other people in our class.

    I like Franklin W. Dixon because he writes exciting mystery/adventure stories. He writes the Hardy Boys Here are a few of his casefile books: Bordrer Line, Perfect Get Away, Cult of Crime, Edge of Destruction, and See No Evil.

    Another author is Richard Adams. He writes Fictional novels. They would bring enjoiment to the class (Espcially D.J.) These are a few books I would like you to order: Shardik, Watership Down, and Pleage Dog.

Sincely,

Silas

The results of this project showed me my students' knowledge of writing and literature. It also provided me with insights about instruction. When reviewing the rehearsal activities, drafts, and final copies of the letters, a glaring hole in my instruction surfaced. I noticed that not one student developed a graphic organizer of the information they wanted to include in their letters. Consequently, that was one of the strategies I immediately taught my students how to use when writing. We had used graphic organizers (webs) when studying content areas and for reading comprehension, but I had neglected to teach them how to use graphic organizers for writing.

This long-term, persuasive letter project gave the students the opportunity to write a real piece for a real reason. It was developed so that the writing situation was a natural one, and revealed not only what the children knew about writing, but also about books and authors. The students were given sufficient time and a supportive environment where they could actually demonstrate their ability to use the writing process and the resources needed to complete this project. In long term projects like these, students are better able to demonstrate their knowledge in an authentic, meaningful ways.

Learning from Student Portfolios

> Portfolios allow teachers to get to know their students-as readers, writers, thinkers, and as human beings (Reif, 1990, p. 24).

Using portfolios for assessment is valuable for teachers, students, and parents. Since ". . . portfolios should be viewed as a growing, evolving description of students' reading and writing experiences" (Farr, 1989, p. 264), it shows growth over time and provides useful information about the unique literacy development of each student in the class in the following ways:

1. Portfolios can help parents understand the ongoing development of their children as readers and writers. With this kind of frame, parents are less likely to put undue value on the results of test scores. They come to realize that numerical scores provide only limited information about their children's abilities.
2. By putting together a portfolio students can examine concretely for them-selves how they have grown as readers and writers.
3. Portfolios can help teachers discover the strengths and weaknesses of their students and thus better develop lessons and literacy experiences for them.

When putting together literacy portfolios, I ask students to do the following:

1. Select samples of your best writing and arrange them in some way.

2. In preparation for our conference about your portfolio, think about why you selected the pieces you did, and what you want to say about them. Think about:
    a. What parts of your piece do you really like and why?
    b. What you were trying to accomplish in this piece and if you think you were successful?
3. Look at all the pieces you selected for your portfolio and think about what you learned about yourself as a reader and writer by putting together your portfolio.
4. Now that you've thought about your development as a reader and writer, what goals do you have for yourself as a reader and a writer?

To illustrate the value of portfolios and its ". . . potential for placing teachers and students—not tests and test scores—at the very center of the assessment process (Pikulski, 1989, p. 81), I have chosen to share D.J.'s portfolio. I chose D.J. because of his ability to reflect on and talk about his reading and writing, and use this information to self-evaluate his reading and writing development and to set goal for himself in these areas.

According to his 5th and 6th grade results on the California Achievement Tests (Forms E&F), D.J. scored:

	5th Grade Results	**6th Grade Results**
Vocabulary	NP=75%; Range=67–82	NP=89%; Range=84–93
Comprehension:	NP=62%; Range=56–69	NP=79%; Range=70–85
Total Reading:	NP=70%; Range=63–75	NP=87%; Range=82–89
Language Mechanics:	NP=39%; Range=28–54	NP=62%; Range=49–74
Language Expression:	NP=30%; Range=23–38	NP=65%; Range=54–75
Language Total:	NP=33%; Range=27–40	NP=63%; Range=54–71

While D.J.'s scores on the CAT tests indicate that he scored above the national average (50th percentile) for reading while in 5th and 6th grades, below the national average for language while in 5th grade, and above the national average for language while in 6th grade, these scores do not provide me with information useful to guide my instruction. In fact, these scores did little in terms of informing me about D.J. as a reader and a writer. The scores also didn't tell me anything about how D.J. uses reading to inform his writing, or what he thinks about himself as a reader and a writer. Compare the usefulness of the scores from the CAT tests with the information gathered from D.J.'s portfolio.

D.J. selected nine pieces (3 realistic fiction, a biography, an essay, 2 adventure stories, a science fiction, and a folktale that used a story within a story plot structure with a surprise ending) to include in his portfolio. When I asked him why he selected these pieces, he responded with, "I picked these because they show more of my strong points."

D.J. ranked his piece entitled, "The Season," (realistic fiction written in grade 6), as his best. Here is a portion of the conversation I had with D.J. about it.

Yvonne: Why did you choose this piece as your best?
  D.J.: This is the fourth piece I was really pleased with and I took it around and showed it to people. I am really proud of this piece.
Yvonne: What was good about it?
  D.J.: I like the descriptive words I used to show what my character is like. I also like how my story flowed.
Yvonne: Was this hard for you to write? Did it take a lot of effort?
  D.J.: The part that took a lot of effort was trying to describe the character's feelings and show what this character is like.
Yvonne: Look through this piece and pick out some of the parts where you feel you did a good job of accomplishing your objective of showing what the character is like.
  D.J.: In this part, Jim had just gotten through with practice in the story.

> At the end of practice I was exhausted. I slid into my 1970 V-8 orange jeep and sped out of the parking lot.
> "I don't know how I could hit so many red lights."
> The light turned green.
> VROOM! SCREECH.
> "I hate coaches!" I sighed. "Why do I have to play their way?"
> I looked back only to see lights flashing. I slowed down and turned to the side of the road.
> A wirey haired man came up beside me and looked at me. His square jaw moved mechanically as he said, "Do you know how fast you were going?"
> "Ya! Thirty-five like the sign said!"
> "Try sixty-five," the officer said curtly. "Will you step out of your jeep please? Now, can you walk a straight line?"
> Jim walked a straight line.
> "Can I smell your breath, please?"
> "Sure."
> "Just in a hurry, huh?" the officer sighed.
> "Yeah."

Yvonne: Why did you like this part?
  D.J.: It showed how he was aggravated because he had not done well at practice and he was angry at the coach, and it showed how he took out his frustrations. It shows what kind of person he was.
Yvonne: What were you trying to do in this particular piece?
  D.J.: In the whole piece I was trying to bring his attitude from a pretty bad attitude to a good attitude where he would be always trying and listening.

I wanted to show that he was basically a good player with a good attitude, but at first he was too cocky to play with the majors.

Yvonne: And do you think you successfully did that?

D.J.: Yes, I think successfully brought the story around to where Jim learned he had to change attitude if he wanted to play in the majors.

Yvonne: Was this hard for you write?

D.J.: It was kind of hard. It was a fun piece, but it was hard to get everything just the way I wanted it.

Yvonne: Did you learn anything about writing from writing this piece?

D.J.: I learned how to use experiences from my life and put it into a story. I learned I could describe things better if I knew something about it.

When discussing the other eight pieces D.J. chose to include in his portfolio, it was interesting for me to learn that he selected them because in each one there were three common threads. In each, D.J.:

- had tried something that was new for him.
- had learned something about writing.
- felt he had accomplished what he had set out to do in the piece.

What follows is a listing of the other eight pieces D.J. chose to include in his portfolio, and unfortunately, because of limited space, only a sample of what he said about each one can be shown here.

2nd Best—'Alexi Grewal,'' biography written in grade 6.

This was the first time I had actually done a web to help me with my writing. I made up questions to ask him. Then I interviewed Alexi on the tape recorder. I thought this was very good, because as I listened to the interview on tape, I webbed the information. As my questioning went to different things I just brought out different circles, and as I went to write the piece I looked at my whole web and decided what I wanted to say first, second, third and on down. This was a lot easier than working from notecards.

I learned how to take notes and ask questions and how to use the answers to write a biography. I also learned how to web the information and write from a web. I thought it was a good piece for a short biography. If I had to do this again, I would ask more questions, and I would look to see what areas I didn't have as much information on and I would ask him about those things so that there is more complete information about him in the piece. But this was only my first biography.

3rd Best—''The Wrong Game,'' realistic fiction written at the end of grade 5.

I chose this piece, because in this piece, it was the first time I thought about developing my characters. I got the idea of developing characters from a book

I read by Clive Cussler. Cussler really does a good job of developing his characters and I like that in his books. I wanted to show how sometimes good kids get caught doing bad things because of peer pressure. And I wanted to show that because he was basically good, he had trouble with his conscience. Here is one part I like:

> Tony thought to himself that it sure was lucky they were all spending the night together, but something kept bugging him. Who else were they going to meet at midnight? Tony had a hard time sleeping that night. But finally he dozed off. Suddenly Tony felt a nudge on his ribs.
> "Come on, come on," whispered B.J.
> Tony had butterflies in his stomach as they jumped out of his bedroom window. He sure hoped his parents slept real sound tonight.

I like it here, because I think I did a pretty good job of showing what kind of person Tony really was. Tony just got in with the wrong gang, but basically he was a good kid. He knew the difference between doing good and bad.

4th Best—''Mesa Verde,'' folktale with a story within a story design and a surprise ending written in grade 5 (This piece won third place in a young writers' competition sponsored by the Colorado Council of the International Reading Association).

I got the idea for Mesa Verde after you read us a book about an Indian grandmother. We talked about the plot structure of the book and how the author used the story within a story design for the story. After we talked about this, I was getting ready to write a piece and I thought why not try it out. And I had just gotten back from taking a trip to Mesa Verde this summer so I thought why not put the setting there. I liked writing this piece. I had a good time writing it.

5th Best—''Why I Love Reading and Books,'' essay written in grade 6.

This was just a little thing I had written telling what I thought about reading and books for an essay. I thought I had written it well. I liked it when I wrote this part: "Books are like friends. You start to read one and you want to read more, just like you want to see your friends more." I like it because it tells what I think about books. When I find a book I really like I want to find out how the story ends, but when it ends, I wish it was still going on. And it's kind of like losing a friend.

The piece tells you that I categorize books as friends and that I like to read. And when I start liking something, I just don't want to stop reading. Like the essay says, I also read books to learn how to write. And I read to learn about cultures and things like that too. When I read a book I can go into another world and just have fun reading. From reading books, I learn more about words and ideas and things like that.

As a writer, I use books to help me learn different words and get ideas for my stories. And if you have ever seen me reading a book, then you probably have seen me using ideas I learned from the books in my writing.

6th Best—*Adventure story with no title written in grade 6*

Even though I really like this piece, I put it towards the back because I didn't really write this piece. Gary Paulsen really did. I liked the book *Hatchet* (1987) so much that I wanted to rewrite the story. And I liked the way Paulsen repeated his words in the story. So, I though of writing an adventure story following Paulsen's style. I think I did a pretty good job of following his style, but I also rewrote his story. So that's why I put this towards the back. I like this part:

> I realized the worst thing that could've happened had happened. The pilot was dead. I screamed three times and thought, "Get a hold of yourself. You are Corry Williams. You are in a plane, and the pilot I think had a heart attack. What should I do? I might be able to fly the plane, but after the pilot had jerked the plane, I don't know which way to go. I am like a bat without sonar, helpless."
>
> I realized I would have to go down, but trees meant certain death. I had no parachute. I would wait till the plane ran out of gas. I began to cry.
>
> "Death, death, I was going to die."
>
> Suddenly, the plane roar stopped. I had to glide to a lake and skid along the edges. "Lake, lake," I thought. Then I saw the lake.

This part shows how I used Paulsen's style of repeating certain words to make it sound almost like a poem.

7th Best—*'Futuristic Fiddle Faddle,'' science fiction written in grade 5.*

This was just a fun piece to write. I like it because it was a different kind of writing I don't usually do. I just wanted to have some fun. I really got into conversation in this story, and used different words for said. Like here when I wrote.

> "That's it!" Frank and Joe yelled spontaneously.
>
> "Give us a hundred"
>
> Joe and the guy got in a big fight. While they were fighting, Frank picked up fifty Pepsi's and started shoving them down his pants and anywhere else he could find. He did the same with Joe. Then he saw an EXIT sign. They ran out clanging all the way. Finally they reached the ship. They jumped in.
>
> "I am driving," yelled Frank. He took off full bore. Joe fell to the floor. "You!"
>
> "I'm just going to your motto!" Frank laughed.
>
> "Let's start hyper-warp drive," Joe said.

"Warp 1, 2, 3. . .9.9, BOOM!

They went full bore so they could coast in with no power. They lined up with the runway and flew in. Boom! The light were out.

"EMERGENCY POWER!" Frank bellowed. Then the lights were on.

8th Best—"Pool," realistic fiction written at the beginning of grade 5.

Even though this piece is short, I think it shows what I was trying to do. In this piece, I was trying to write about something that I wish would happen to me. I was playing a lot of pool with my friends and I always wanted to get all the balls in at once. And so that's what I decided to write about. I like my beginning when I introduce Don. It sort of sets up the situation. "Don Majestic woke up in a cold sweat after dreaming Allan Wiggins, the worst pool player in the world, beat him in a game of pool. Don was the fifth best player in America." I think it shows the tense situation he was in.

9th Best—"World War VIII," adventure story written at the beginning of grade 5.

I din't use any conversation in this piece. I just told what happened. When I wrote this piece, I never used to think much about conversation. In this one, I like all the action. I like some of the words I use like "counter-attacked," "kicked-rear," and "got nailed in the knuckle." I like how I used these words to show action. I can't believe I used to write stories like this.

I learned a lot about D.J. as a reader, writer, and learner from having him put together a portfolio and talking with him about the pieces he chose to include in it. I learned that D.J.:

1. Loves to read, and that he uses reading not only for personal enjoyment and pleasure, but he uses reading to learn about life and other cultures, and to inform his writing. D.J. reads deeply, critically, and in a most sophisticated way. He reads with the eye of a writer.
2. Enjoys writing. He likes to try out different things that he has learned about writing in the pieces he crafts. He is able to use techniques which show rather than tell his readers some aspect of the character or the situation, use conversations in the stories he tells, and use graphic organizers (webs) to help him organize ideas for writing.
3. Needs additional help with noticing how and where authors use figurative language in their pieces. Focusing on this aspect of writing will help D.J. write even better pieces.
4. Needs to widen his spectrum of writing. He especially needs opportunities to experiment with writing essays and poetry.

In addition, when I asked D.J. what he learned about himself as a reader and writer from putting his portfolio together, he said:

> I learned from putting together this portfolio that I like to read and write about things I can relate to, things I know about. It is from these things that I can write about and describe best. I like strong words like verbs that build up what you are describing.

D.J.'s comments about what he learned about himself tells me that he understands that writers use their knowledge and experiences to write; that unless he knows his subject, he probably will not be able to weave as good a tale as he may like.

When discussing goals for himself, D.J. said that he would like to read more books, learn how to read quicker, but still be able to understand the meaning expressed by the author. Another goal is to spend more time writing in his journal, to put more effort into making his pieces the best they can be, and to keep trying to excel in writing.

When I think about how much I learned about D.J. as a reader and writer from having him put together a portfolio, it makes me realize how little I knew about my students before I used this technique. I also learned how portfolios can not only help the teacher develop instructional plans, but how portfolios can help students reflect on their own literacy development and set goals for themselves. Probably, the most important reason for having students put together portfolios is to help them evaluate themselves and in the process discover what it is they do well and areas where they need help, and then to set goals for themselves. In this way, evaluation is put where it belongs, in the hands of our students, and it is we, their teachers, who benefit.

The one area that I didn't have the foresight to have students include in their portfolios concerned data about their reading. I should have had my students:

1. Keep track of the many books, magazines, new articles, and so forth they read. This activity would have given us (students and me) interesting insights into their reading diet.
2. Copy quotes, sayings, phrases, and so forth from books that caught their fancy. This activity would have given us information about the things my students pay attention to when reading.
3. Write their thoughts about those books which really made an impression on them and why. This activity would have given us wonderful data about the ways in which books influence them.

Observing Students

The best alternative to testing comes from direct and, in most cases, informal observation of the child in various situations by the classroom teacher. (Y. Goodman, 1989, p. 119).

Once I learned how to be a kid-watcher, my teaching became more relevant. But what kinds of things are most useful for teachers to notice? Every day provides many opportunities to collect data about our students' literacy development. I have developed two simple guidelines which have helped me become a better observer of students.

1. Notice what students say about their own and each other's reading and writing.
2. Notice how students use reading and writing in their everyday lives.

Noticing what students say.

When I started paying more attention to the literacy events in which students engage and what they said about one another's reading and writing, I learned a lot about them. For example, here is part of a conversation that occured when several students had a conversation with undergraduate students about their reading.

Adult: Have any of you read *The Chronicles of Narnia* (1982)?

Silas: Yes, but I don't like reading science fiction. But, Sean Griffith, a third grader in our class, really likes them.

Lucas: What about Sean Kaley?

Silas: Oh yeah, Sean Kaley really likes them too; he read all of them last year.

Adult: How do you get ideas for your stories?

Emily: For my story, "The Electric Dream," I got the idea from a book I read about sound waves. In the book, it said that sound waves have arches. So I used this information in my story.

Silas: I like to read before I write. It helps me when I can't get into my writing.

D.J.: I got the idea for how I was going to organize a story from a book that Yvonne read. The book had a story-within-a-story plot. After we discussed it, I decided to try it out.

Adult: Do you guys read at home?

Emily: That's the first thing I do when I come home from school everyday. I love to read.

Lucas: I always read before I go to bed.

Silas: Me too. I read before I go to bed and also when I get home from school.

D.J: I read everyday. I always read before I go to bed.

Adult: How do you choose books to read.

D.J.: I like to read books by favorite authors. And my mom reads a lot, and she gives me books to read that she thinks I might enjoy.

Silas: I read the blurb on the book jacket. Sometimes I asked other people if the book they're reading is interesting. There's not too much I don't like. I just like reading.

Emily: If I couldn't read, I'd be bored.

Lucas: I like to read any books about animals and nature. I love animals. Sometimes my friends will tell me to read a book because they know I might like it.

D.J.: When I read *Hatchet* I wanted to rewrite the book. It was so good. Practically every fifth and sixth grade boy read that book, because it was so good. We kept passing it from person to person. Everyone wanted to read it. Remember, Yvonne, you couldn't read it, because everyone else wanted to read it.

This conversation astonished me. I knew my students enjoyed reading. But, I was surprised at their knowledge of each other's tastes in reading and the influence reading had on their writing. I also was pleased to know that my students enjoyed reading so much that they choose to read outside of school.

Noticing how students spontaneously use reading and writing for personal reasons.

There are many occasions for engaging in reading and writing that occur throughout the day. The ways in which our students spontaneously take advantage of these opportunities tell us whether or not they view reading and writing as useful and powerful tools. Here are three examples of the ways my students on their own used writing to try to influence others.

Halloween was on a Monday. Several children in my class were upset because they had to go to school the next day. So these children took it upon themselves to write individual letters to the President of the School Board expressing their dissatisfaction with this policy. To the delight of the children, the Board President even wrote back.

Another occasion presented itself when a guest speaker came into the class to talk about the depletion of the rain forests and the possible consequences of this current situation. After the guest speaker left, Lucas was so bothered by the apparent lack of concern to this serious condition, that he wrote the following letter to Colombia.

At the mountain schoolhouse where I previously taught, the enrollment has slowly increased over the years. Because of the greater numbers of children, there was less room on the school playground to play active running and catching games safely. Even though the land adjacent to the school sits vacant, the children are not allowed to play on it—it is private property and not landscaped properly for play. Frustrated with not having enough playground space, several students decided to write a letter to the owners of the land requesting that they sell it to the School District.

These kinds of literacy events showed me that my students are empowered writers. They understand the power of the written word and use their knowledge

Figure 7-5

May 10, 1989

Dear Columbia,
    I was wondering if you could stop cutting down your
rainforests, because if you don't we will have the green house affect.
    Our ozone is almost gone. Do you want to dye? If you cut down the
rainforest, you will be killing yourself and everyone else too, plus
animals and some of the most endangered animals. I would not mind
living in a rainforest. You are very lucky to have so many different trees
from America, and if you cut down the trees we will have less oxygen.
Because trees give us air. Trees are living things.
    And when you use your chainsaw it pollutes the air. It is all up to
you to save everyones lives not just yours. Do you know you don't have
to have live stock to get money or wood? You could sell fruit from the
trees.
    And I bet you would get a lot of money fromfrom fruit. I really hope
you don't cut down all the trees.
    Well, I hope you will write to me.

                                    From,
                                        Lucas albrighton
                                    4th grader at Jamestown
                                    School in Colorado.

of writing to inform, persuade, and communicate their ideas and feelings to others. For them writing and reading are not filling in blanks, drawing lines to, or circling. My emphasis on creating authentic reasons for using reading and writing has empowered my students to read and write for their own reasons, not mine. Consequently, they read and write more, and in the process they learn about the strategies and skills literate people use to help them learn.

Becoming Literate

Being literate means more than being able to read, write, and pass standardized tests. Unfortunately, I have encountered too many individuals who know how to read and write, and who passed standardized tests, but who choose not to read and write. These individuals are friends and students in my university classes who have told me that they haven't selected a book to read for personal reasons in years, and that they feel insecure about writing and dislike it immensely. When I pressed them to discuss the reasons for this negative attitude toward reading and writing, many related that they did not have experiences which engaged them in authentic literacy events where reading and writing were used for personal reasons, nor were they involved in examining and evaluating their own progress in reading and writing.

Despite current and past criticisms about our youngsters' ability to read and write, the problem is not that test scores are dropping, but concerns its overemphasis. Holistic techniques for collecting data about how students do in reading and writing can help not only teachers plan meaningful instruction, but provide a powerful tool for helping students honestly evaluate themselves as readers, writers, learners, and thinkers.

As Dr. W. Edwards Deming (1986, p. 93), the genius who revitalized Japanese industry, said about running a company on visible figures alone (for which he credits Lloyd S. Nelson of Nahua Corporation), ". . .the figures that are 'unknown and unknowable' are even more important."

References

Bird, L.B. (1989). The art of teaching evaluation and revision. In K.S. Goodman, Y.M. Goodman, & W.J. Hood (Eds.), *The whole language evaluation book* pp. 15–24. Portsmouth, NH: Heinemann.

Brown, R. (1989). Testing and thoughtfulness. *Educational Leadership, 46,* 31–33.

Costa, A. (1989). Re-assessing assessment. *Educational Leadership, 46,* 2.

Farr, R. (1989). A response from Roger Farr, director, Center for Reading and Language Studies, Smith Research Center, Indiana University, Bloomington, Indiana. In Questions & answers: Portfolio assessment, edited by K.S. Jongsma. *The Reading Teacher*, *43*, 264.

Goodman, Y.M. (1989). Evaluation of students: Evaluation of teachers. In K.S. Goodman, Y.M. Goodman, & W.J. Hood (Eds.), *The whole language evaluation book*, pp. 3–14.

Interview with Jane Hansen. (1989). *The Colorado Communicator*, *12*, 1, 21.

Hiebert, E.H., & Calfee, R.C. (1989). Advancing academic literacy through teachers' assessments. *Educational Leadership*, *46*, 50–54.

Jaggar, A. (1985). On observing the language learner: Introduction and overview. In A. Jaggar & M.T. Smith-Burke (Eds.), *Observing the language learner* (pp. 1–7). Newark, DE: International Reading Association.

Pikulski, J.J. (1989). The assessment of reading: A time for change? *The Reading Teacher*, *43*, 80–81.

Reif, L. (1990). Finding the value in evaluation: Self-assessment in a middle school classroom. *Educational Leadership*, *47*, 24–29.

Shepard, L.A. (1989). Why we need better assessments. *Educational Leadership*, *46*, 4–9.

Teale, W.H., Heibert, E.H., & Chittenden. E.A. (1987). Assessing young children's literacy development. *The Reading Teacher*, *40*, 772–777.

Valencia, S., & Pearson, P.D. (1987). Reading assessment: Time for change. *The Reading Teacher*, *40*, 726–732.

Walton, M. (1986). *The Deming Management Method*. New York: Dodd, Mead & Company.

Children's Books Cited

Babbitt, N. (1975). *Tuck everlasting*. New York: Bantam Skylark.

Bauer, C.F. (1981). *My mom travels a lot*. New York: F. Warne.

Brown, M.W. (1949). *The important book*. New York: Harper & Brothers.

Charlip, R. (1964). *Fortunately*. New York: Parents' Magazine Press.

Lewis, C.S. (1982). *The chronicles of Narnia*. New York: Caedmon.

Numeroff, L.J. (1985). *If you give a mouse a cookie*. New York: Harper & Row.

Paulsen, G. (1987). *Hatchet*. New York: Bradbury Press.

Chapter 8

Whole Language Assessment and Evaluation: A Special Education Perspective

Hilary M. Sumner

Introduction: The Gnawing Dilemma

Assessment and evaluation for the special educator is a fact of life. For the holistic teacher it is the gnawing dilemma of coping with local, state, and federal regulations while orchestrating an authentic, purposeful, child-centered program. Ken Goodman (1989) writes that whole language has been a grassroots movement motivated by teachers who are knowledgeable about the learning process and language development. Whole language teachers believe that evaluation must occur in authentic, meaningful ways within the natural context of a students' learning environment. Most traditional evaluation is inappropriate and often underestimates a child's growth in the functional use of language. Goodman explains that whole language teachers represent a courageous group rejecting imposed teaching methods and narrow curriculum. They rebel against behavioral objectives and traditional evaluation, especially standardized tests, because they are contrived, synthetic, confining, and dated. Whole language teachers instead, engage in ongoing, interactive assessment as part of their whole program.

So how does the special educator, whose belief system embraces holistic learning theory, deal with the shackles of differing definitions, varied eligibility criteria for identification, questionable assessment practices, Individual Educational Plans (IEPs), and federal, state, and local regulations? It's not easy!

The purpose of this chapter is to explore this dilemma through both past and current practices, and to discuss some possible avenues to remain in legal compliance while still promoting a special education program that evaluates student development in a holistic and relevant way. In order to assess something appropriately, we need a definition of just what we are assessing, trustworthy methods of data collection that lead to an improvement of some kind, and above all, a purpose for the evaluation.

Learning Disabilities: The Definition Dispute

The field of Special Education encompasses a broad range of mildly to severely handicapping conditions. For the discussion in this chapter, I will be focusing on the group of individuals identified as having learning disabilities. The predecessor of the condition now known as a learning disability was termed dyslexia. Bartoli and Botel (1988) explain that historically, dyslexia was believed to have been organic in nature: the result of a supposed neurological defect, either genetic or induced by minimal, nonobservable brain trauma.

As a result of much litigation, the United States Congress passed the compulsory education law called the Education For All Handicapped Children Act of 1975 (U.S.O.E., 1977). A legal definition of learning disabilities was included in this act and it reads as follows:

> learning disabled pupils are those who demonstrate a disorder in one or more of the basic psychological processes involved in understanding or in using language, spoken or written, which may manifest itself in the imperfect ability to listen, think, read, write, spell, or do mathematical calculations. The term includes such conditions as perceptual handicaps, brain injury, minimal brain dysfunction, dyslexia, and developmental aphasia. The term does not include children who have learning problems which are primarily the result of visual, hearing, or motor handicaps, of mental retardation, emotional disturbance or environmental, cultural, or economic disadvantage. (p. 65083)

Salvia and Ysseldyke (1985) explain that eligibility criteria, for learning disabilities services, vary considerably from state to state. Furthermore, additional testing for causes of the disorder may or may not have to be administered, depending on a particular state's educational code. Dr. Lynn Rhodes (1988) noted that in the past speculation about the causes of learning disabilities has focused on conditions intrinsic to the child. This is a convenient explanation for most of our more severe reading failures. Rhodes points out the child, not the curriculum or the standards for achievement, is seen as the problem.

Since the mid-1950s dyslexia has never been pinned down, nor has any etiology, or cause, ever been shown to be conclusively valid. Moreover, the instruction that was based on the motor and perceptual deficit theories of dyslexia has not proved effective in the teaching of reading. Bartoli and Botel (1988) concluded from their research that since it is not possible to distinguish organic causes from other causes for the basis of a reading handicap, the academic term learning disability is more appropriate than the medical term dyslexia. In fact, they even preferred the terms "less developed" or "low progress reader." These terms seemed more consistent with their developmental outlook of learning and their belief in the potential of the student to become a more efficient reader.

Poplin (1988) reports that the field of learning disabilities has struggled to move beyond the early medical definitions. She reviewed the popular models of learning disability theory that have developed over the past 40 years. Although each model defines learning disabilities differently, they all are similar in their reductionistic learning theory. Poplin explains that reductionism is the process by which we break ideas, concepts, and skills into parts in an attempt to understand and better deal with the whole. She suggests that the teaching methods many are currently using with learning disabled children are all examples of the erroneous belief that a complex whole such as human learning can be broken into its component parts. This task analysis is done in a genuine attempt to design more effective means of instruction and assessment, but in fact it has fragmented and disrupted the natural learning process.

In contrast to what is now known about natural language acquisition and holistic learning, the earlier models of learning disability theory have several things in common. They segmented learning into parts. They believed that instruction was most effective when it was tightly controlled, leaving the learner basically passive. The diagnosis for each model also became the intervention, and instruction was usually focused on student deficits rather than strengths. Each model held that there was a right way to learn something, which revealed a basic distrust of student minds and the belief that appropriate learning would not develop without direct instruction. Teaching and learning were considered unidirectional, in other words the teacher alone knew what was to be learned and the student was expected to learn it (Poplin, 1988). As long as instruction and assessment in Special Education continue to adhere to this dated theory, the natural language and learning processes will continue to be disrupted, perpetuating the gnawing dilemma.

Obstacles to the Identification of the Learning Disabled Child

Cecil D. Mercer (Vaughn/Bos, 1987) emphasizes that the need for more accurate definition and useful assessment of learning disabilities has never been more pressing. He points out that not only professionals in Special Education, but also parent and political groups continue to seek better methods of identifying and teaching the learning disabled student. Mercer describes the following obstacles in our search for better identification practices:

1. A lack of consensus regarding the definition of learning disabilities makes it difficult to agree on the criteria to be used in the identification process.
2. The heterogeneity of the learning disabled population makes it difficult to establish a set of identification criteria suitable for the wide range of students. One learning disabled student may have very different characteristics from another.
3. Many currently recognized definitions of learning disabilities include a discrepancey factor (the significant difference between a student's ability and achievement). The tests and formulas used to determine the significant differences have been severely criticized in the professional literature. There is little agreement as to just how much of a difference is significant (Berk, 1984; Cone & Wilson, 1981; Forness, Sinclair & Guthrie, 1983; Reynolds, 1985).
4. Many assessment instruments used to identify learning disabled students are inadequate, lacking a sound empirical base (Coles, 1978), and lacking sufficient reliability and validity (Shepard & Smith, 1983; and Salvia & Ysseldyke, 1985).
5. Many school districts are not able to provide adequate services to low achievers and the teachers do not receive the training or support system they need to help these youngsters. Consequently, in an attempt to get help for both classroom teachers and low-achieving students, there is an increase in the number of students who are inappropriately referred for evaluation and placed in learning disabled programs.

Special Education Legislation: Public Law 94-142

Most of the current assessment practices are a direct result of legislation. The Education For All Handicapped Children Act, otherwise known as Public Law 94-142, (U.S.O.E., 1977) was to guarantee services to all children who needed them. It was intended to guarantee that all decisions regarding special education were made in a fair and appropriate manner. The act was to set requirements for management and auditing of special education services at all levels of government, and it was to provide federal dollars to the states for handicapped children (Salvia & Ysseldyke, 1985).

P.L. 94-142 specifies that all handicapped children between the ages of three and 21 have the right to a free, appropriate, public education (FAPE) and that each handicapped student has an individualized educational plan (IEP), designed by the school including long-term goals and short-term objectives. The IEPs must be based on a comprehensive individual assessment by a multidisciplinary team (MDT). The team must specify not only the goals and objectives, but the how, when, and where of the services and the means by which a student's progress would be evaluated. The IEPs are written with the student's parents and the parents have a right to a due process hearing to resolve conflicting opinions if they disagree with the school. To ensure that handicapped students are educated in settings that maximize their opportunities to interact with their non-handicapped peers, P.L. 94-142 mandates that they are placed in the least restrictive environment (LRE) possible to meet their special needs. (Salvia & Ysseldyke, 1985)

Congress included specific provisions in the law regarding assessment for these handicapped children. In order to ensure that testing was fair, equitable, and nondiscriminatory, eight requirements were listed:

1. Tests are to be selected and administered in such a way as to be racially and culturally nondiscriminatory.
2. Students are to be assessed in their native languages or primary mode of communication.
3. Tests must have been validated for the specific purpose for which they are used.
4. Tests must be administered by trained personnel in conformance with the instructions provided by the test producer.
5. Tests used with students must include those designed to provide information about specific educational needs, and not just a general intelligent quotient.
6. Decisions about students are to be based on more than performance on a single test.
7. Evaluations are to be made by a multidisciplinary team that includes at least one teacher or other specialist with knowledge in the area of the suspected disability.
8. Children must be assessed in all areas related to a specific disability, including—where appropriate—health, vision, hearing, social and emotional status, general intelligence, academic performance, communicative skills, and motor skills. (Salvia and Ysseldyke, 1985)

These eight provisions do not mandate the specific assessment tools, nor do they require the reductionist view of evaluation that has become so prevalent in special education today. They do require equity, validity, and nondiscrimination. They stipulate a team assessment approach, multimeasure decisions, and an evaluation based on specific educational needs. Furthermore, the eighth provision actually mandates a look at the whole child. There is nothing in the eight requirements that is inherently in opposition to the values and beliefs of the holistic educator.

The Latitude of Eligibility Assessment

Assessment in the field of learning disabilities is a continuous process, with many different purposes. Special education teachers must collect specific district, state, and federally mandated assessment data throughout the school year. The assess-ments usually include the prereferral process, referral, eligibility, IEPs, goals and objectives, instruction, and end-of-year assessments.

Typically these evaluations involve standardized tests in which a child is removed from his regular classroom to a special testing room. Sometimes the evaluator is a stranger and the child is caught basically unprepared for the experi-ence. Or perhaps the child knows that he or she is being tested because he or she has failed in some way. Even the most talented of specialists has a big job getting reliable data from such a scenario. All too often, decisions about whether a child is handicapped are made on very few tests, in a single testing situation. The special education assessment process can indeed become a maze of standardized tests, diagnoses, eligibility formulas, and labels. However, special education programs and assessment can also be an interactive, responsive evaluation process that genuinely looks at the talents rather than deficits of a whole child in the context of that child's natural environment.

Learning disabilities specialists, who are responsible for eligibility assessment, are commonly expected to identify children in terms of the ability/achievement discrepancy. This is usually done by comparing an intelligence test (or comparable cognitive assessment) and measures of academic achievement. Many school districts dictate which cognitive tests psychologists and learning specialists are expected to administer. The collection of achievement data allows the holistic teacher more latitude. The comparison of responsibly collected, trustworthy academic data will do much to improve the eligibility process.

Valencia and Pearson (1987) lament the extensive reliance our schools have placed on standardized test scores. Teachers are led to believe that the data from either standardized or basal tests are somehow more trustworthy than the data they collect each day as part of their teaching. Valencia and Pearson suggest the best assessment of reading would seem to occur when teachers observe and inter-act as their students read authentic texts, for genuine purposes, in the process of constructing meaning. Campione and Brown (1985) referred to this model as dynamic assessment. This model was designed as a result of Vygotsky's theory. Vygotsky wrote about a learner's "zone of proximal development." This refers to the zone or distance between what a learner can do in isolation and what he can do in the presence of others. For instruction (or assessment) to be effective, it must be aimed at the student's proximal level. If aimed beneath what a child can do, it is a waste of time. If aimed above the proximal level, it is also inap-propriate and can be damaging to the child. Instruction and assessment is best at the level in which a student stretches just beyond his or her current level of competence, into his or her next level of learning. With this theory, assessment means the measure of a student's ability is not a score, but an index of the type and amount of support required to advance learning.

Eligibility decisions are probably the most difficult decisions special educators must make. Once a child is determined to qualify for special services, the goal of assessment changes. Ysseldyke and Algozzine (1984) believe that

> the ultimate goal of assessment is improvement of instruction for the learner. The only valid special education process is one in which assessment leads to treatments that have known outcomes. . .To the extent that collection of assessment data leads to improvements in instruction, collection of those data is a reasonable activity.

If it is a fundamental belief that educational assessment should lead to better instruction, then why are we accepting so much assessment data from questionable tests and ignoring the wealth of data available from teacher observation and student self-assessment?

Let's Bring Learning, Teaching, and Assessment Back Together

Dr. Brian Cambourne (IRA, 1990) explained that when we engage in evaluation of any kind, it is based on our prevailing set of beliefs. As a result of the reductionistic view, most instruction and assessment used today reduces the learning process to discrete measurable parts in an attempt to be scientifically objective, reliable, valid, and controlled. He quoted Frank Smith lamenting that we "backed the wrong horse when we backed psychology" and we now are saddled with behavioral objectives and a lack of trust in our own observations. It is time for us to rethink our assessment model and the set of beliefs upon which it is based.

Many special educators erroneously interpret the public law. They believe that all assessment must be standardized, and based on behavioral objectives of minute subskills. As early as 1982, Dr. Peter Hasselriis (1982) examined the law in relation to whole language. He reported that the law does specify that we must prepare an IEP containing a statement of present levels of educational performance, and it must be presented in terms of objective measurable observations "to the extent possible." The law *does not* exclude subjective measures and it leaves the choice of assessment tools and criteria up to the educator. The law further states that annual goals should stem from the present levels of student performance and that short term instructional objectives must be measurable steps between this present level and the stated annual goals (U.S. Department of Education, 1980, p. 20). Measurable steps have, unfortunately, been interpreted very narrowly by many educators. The public law does not require that the learning process be fragmented into subskills, or remediated by drills and less than meaningful, repetitive tasks. The goals and objectives ought to be consistent with the educator's belief system of the learning process. Dr. Hasselriis (1982) specifically states that holistic measures such as interviews, anecdotal observations, writing samples, and reading miscue inventories (Goodman & Burke, 1972) are perfectly legal and show measurable, developmental growth that provide much information into the student's strategies as a learner.

Dr. Jan Turbill (IRA, 1990) discussed the implications of a shift in belief about assessment. She suggests that we bring learning, teaching, and assessment back together. We need to focus on the process of learning rather than the product and we must include the learner as part of the process. She and Dr. Cambourne acknowledge the enormous superiority of the knowledgeable human over the formal test instrument. In other words, teachers' observations can be rigorous, credible, and trustworthy without the need to be purely objective and standardized. Dr. Turbill compared this to what parents do naturally when they evaluate their own children. Parents use a variety of ways to assess their children's development, in many different contexts, constantly interacting with them. They use lots of observation and interaction based on a coherent theory about growth and development.

With this shift in belief to a more holistic program, the special educator can make significant changes within his or her classroom to more approximate what parents do at home. The special education program can become a place where authentic learning happens and is responsibly assessed by the teacher and student alike. This shift is happening and the legal obligations are being satisfied, perhaps more ethically than ever before. The remainder of this chapter will suggest possible ways a resource room program can function within the constraints of federal mandate and still remain authentic, and meaningful within the natural context of a student's learning.

The Shift in Belief: A Holistic Resource Room

So what does authentic learning look like in a resource room? A holistic program is based on the belief that all children can learn and the process of learning is a process of constructing meaning. We do this through the interaction of what we already know, the context of the situation, and the new experience (Poplin, 1985). Learning is an active process which is controlled by the student, not the teacher. Learning disabled students often have a mismatch with the new experiences, the context of the new learning, and their background knowledge. This can occur because the child is not developmentally ready for the new learning. It can occur because the child's background knowledge is not sufficient for the experience to be meaningful. Learning might not occur because the child is expected to remain passive and the necessary interaction cannot take place. Unfortunately, too often the learning is incomplete because of the teaching process and/or the learning environment rather than a deficit within the child.

Curriculum is a critical factor in the resource program. A holistic resource room is developmentally appropriate, interesting, relevant, and congruent with the students' background experiences. It invites participation and inquiry, and it encourages the program to be child-driven. Since learning disabled youngsters have a greater difficulty with the curriculum match, the program in a resource room must be adapted to each individual. It should encourage literacy through the constant interaction of the student's listening, speaking, reading, and writing experiences. Thematic units are particularly successful ways to create this interaction. They not only accommodate a learning disabled child's background knowledge, learning style, and developmental stage, but they invite discovery, experimentation and cooperative learning. A literacy approach is profoundly more appropriate for learning disabled students than the typically controlled, remedial approaches used in the past.

The role of the teacher is that of a facilitator who supports the individual's learning process. The program should be cooperative rather than competitive. The holistic resource teacher orchestrates a program that is relevant to the child's classroom learning and outside life. In the daily activities the teacher models efficient strategies by doing the projects right with the kids. She or he writes when they write, reads when they read. And the teacher includes the students in the assessment process.

Finally, a holistic resource program needs to consider the purposes and audiences of the assessments. The special educator's gnawing dilemma has a great deal to do with the type of assessment data needed.

Dr. Jan Turbill (1990) asked "Who are the stakeholders?" Are teachers testing for the children? The other teachers? The principal and administration? The parents and community? The policy makers? Each audience has different needs and purposes for the evaluation data and each may have a different understanding of the learning and evaluation process. The policy makers might want the evaluations to tell them very different information based on current special education local, state, and federal regulations. Are the literacy standards across the nation increasing? Is the money justified? Who qualifies as handicapped? Is overplacement in special education happening? Are special education programs helping? For whom and as a result of what?

The teachers might assess to answer the questions: Are the children becoming more efficient language users? Are the strategies I'm teaching relevant? Are my materials inviting discovery? Are my students becoming more efficient readers? Parents might want the assessment to tell them how their child is doing in relation to other kids.

According to Valencia and Pearson (1987), the underlying assumption about assessment is that different decisions must be made at each level, and each type will require different assessment. But across all assessment, certain features should remain constant. The assessment must reflect a sound model of the learning process. The attributes being assessed are interdependent and cannot be measured discretely (that is, there is no scope and sequence). And whatever is worthy of assessment should be assessed in a variety of contexts.

This chapter has examined the holistic special educator's dilemma of dealing with legal mandates while remaining authentic. We have explored the differing definitions of learning disabilities and the constraints of eligibility criteria. We have reviewed the federal law and its latitude, which is often misinterpreted. And we have described a holistic resource program by theory. In order to demonstrate the unique assessment issues of special education and some ways to accommodate them responsibly, the remainder of this chapter describes a scenario. A regular, second grade classroom teacher needs help with a low-achieving, frustrated student, who may be eligible for special services in the learning disabilities resource program.

Scenario: Classroom Teacher Refers Child for Assessment Referral

Mrs. Ferraro refers Kyle to the learning disabilities specialist. She wants to come to the MDT meeting to discuss Kyle's special needs and his frustrations in the classroom. She has tried everything she can think of and nothing seems to work. He is making very little progress in reading and writing and has become rather disruptive in class. What can she do? How can she help him? Does he have a handicap, is she overlooking something, or is he just being lazy?

Mrs. Hayman, the learning disabilities specialist, spends some time talking about Kyle with Mrs. Ferraro. When did she first notice this? Is there a specific time of day, activity, situation when his behavior is more pronounced? What do his parents say? Has she discussed this with them? What does Kyle's last year's teacher report say? Is this frustration new? Mrs. Hayman takes preliminary notes about the problem. Mrs. Hayman asks Mrs. Ferraro to complete a prereferral form. She asks for a history of the problem. She asks for Kyle's present level of functioning in all subjects and the ways Mrs. Ferraro assesses Kyle to determine this. She asks what information the teacher is seeking from the MDT and what contact the teacher has had with the family concerning this problem. Mrs. Hayman includes questions about Kyle's general health and history of absences. What were the interventions the teacher has tried to improve the situation and the results? How well does Kyle function in different learning situations (individual, pairs, small group, cooperative groups, whole group) and which curriculum did she use with Kyle? Finally, Mrs. Hayman asks Mrs. Ferraro what she hopes to achieve with this referral. With this information Mrs. Hayman hopes to develop a picture of Kyle's learning needs and his environment. She also is validating Mrs. Ferraro's ability to kid watch (Goodman, 1978) and is helping her to become aware of the importance of looking at the whole picture of Kyle's learning.

Mrs. Hayman and Mrs. Ferraro present their concerns at the next multidisciplinary team meeting and the team decides that a full evaluation should be completed to determine how Kyle's learning environment can be improved to meet his special needs, and whether he qualifies for special education services. Mrs. Hayman and any other specialists the team determines appropriate (for example, the speech and language specialist, the school nurse, the school psychologist, the motor development team, and so on), are then responsible to assess Kyle's learning. Mrs. Hayman requests that the classroom teacher make the intitial parent contact to discuss her concerns about Kyle. Mrs. Ferraro should have been in touch with the parents for some time before the referral was inititated. In fact, many interventions with the parents and the child should have been attempted long before special education was considered. If teachers were willing to take a look at curricular changes and individual learning styles more often, fewer students would be referred for such evaluations.

The parents then conference with Mrs. Hayman about Kyle's needs and the process of the evaluation is explained. The parents are required to give written permission for any special assessment. Mrs. Hayman interviews the parents to learn as much as possible about their expectations and Kyle's history. Once she has permission, and a little background knowledge about Kyle, Mrs. Hayman visits Kyle's classroom to observe him within the context of the whole class. As she watches and notes his involvement, she records the activity of the whole class and that of one other random child. Without this comparative information, Mrs. Hayman might record an unfair picture of Kyle. If the whole class is active and up and about, using the classroom, then Kyle is not off task or inappropriate if he is also up and about. Mrs. Hayman's observation also includes information about the lesson she is watching, the size of the learning group, and the types of interactions Kyle has with the teacher and other classmates. In other words, an appropriate observation needs to consider the entire academic and social interactions in which the student is engaged.

After Mrs. Hayman visits in the classroom, she then meets with Kyle in person. All too often, we specialists get tunnel vision and think only of our assessment tools and formulas. We forget the child. Think of the irony of our testing behavior. Isn't it curious that we would bring a child into a testing situation and just start testing. When has someone ever gone to a doctor and not told him where it hurts. Can you imagine the task a doctor would undertake to diagnose if the patient didn't first explain his symptoms? Yet we rarely ask the student where his reading or writing hurts. Mrs. Hayman takes the time, as she visits with Kyle, to listen as he tells her about his schoolwork and his special needs. Then, with all the information from the parents, the classroom teacher, and from Kyle himself, Mrs. Hayman can responsibly begin to assess Kyle's needs.

Eligibilty

Mrs. Hayman's school district (like many districts today) uses a discrepancy formula to help determine learning disabilities eligibility. This formula is supposed to indicate whether a student demonstrates a significant discrepancy between cognitive ability and academic achievement. Mrs. Hayman assesses Kyle's potential as she must by law. Intellectual ability is frequently determined by such tests as the WISC-R (Wechsler, 1974) or the Stanford-Binet Intelligence Scale (Terman & Merrill, 1973), and in Mrs. Hayman's district, those tests are administered by the school psychologist. She might give the Woodcock Johnson Psycho-Educational Battery (1978) which is designed to assess cognitive ability, scholastic aptitude, and academic achievement. By using these or other like measures she determines relative potential and rules out mental retardation. She reviews the interview data and student records to learn what she can about Kyle's health, his attendance, and the effects of his cultural environment on his present learning situation. Then Mrs. Hayman takes a look at Kyle's literacy level.

In the past, parents and other teachers were interested in grade level equivalencies. They wanted to know just how many months behind the child was. Now we know that there are better ways to look at Kyle's literacy. The key to holistic assessment is to look at what Kyle CAN do. This is different from his grade level and rate of fluency. Grade levels, of tests and curriculum, are an odd and arbitrary system of supposed difficulty. They are based on the assumption that normal kids follow specific, predetermined scope and sequence of development. They suggest that the levels are a set of sequenced, discrete skills a child should master in order to become literate. We know that learning is not static mastery. It is dynamic interaction. In order to genuinely assess Kyle, and to communicate that information to his parents and teachers, Mrs. Hayman might need to enlighten them (if you will) with some background about natural learning and authentic assessment.

At this point, Mrs. Hayman is collecting assessment data for the purpose of eligibility for special education. Most information at this level is not specifically designed to provide instructional direction. Mrs. Hayman continues her collection of data about Kyle's learning by asking the teacher to gather work samples over time and in different contexts. As part of the prereferral form, Mrs. Hayman gets information from other staff members that come in contact with Kyle regularly (i.e. the physical education and music teachers, the playground staff, the principal, the secretary, the media specialist, instructional aides, and so on). They will have valuable information about how Kyle functions in other subjects, in social situations, with peers. Perhaps they have known Kyle for some time. Are Kyle's learning problems generalized (are they noticable in most contexts), or are they specific to Mrs. Ferraro's class?

Mrs. Hayman also assesses Kyle's literacy. She would have Kyle read a selection into a tape recorder and then retell it to her so that she could analyze the quality of his miscues and the efficiency of his reading strategies (Reading Miscue Inventory, Goodman, Watson, Burke, 1987). If her student was developmentally young, she might use Marie Clay's Concepts About Print Test (1972) to assess his understanding of text and print conventions.

She might have Kyle write an independent piece on a topic of his choice. She would ask him to take some time to think about his writing first, then write it the best he could, completely unaided. He may use any resource he chooses, except to have editing assistance from an adult. It is critical here for Mrs. Hayman to kid watch to make note of the resources he uses as he writes and self edits.

Depending on her school district and special education department, Mrs. Hayman may be expected to administer some standardized reading, language arts, and math tests. Although she is aware of the dangers of such measures, her administrators still are uncomfortable with her using no standardized tests. Districts vary widely as to the tests considered worthwhile. In her district, standardized reading tests such as the Gates-MacGinitie Reading Tests (MacGinitie, 1978), and the Woodcock Reading Mastery Tests (Woodcock, 1973), and the Test of Early Reading (TERA, 1981) are often used by reading specialists. Mrs. Hayman prefers to have Kyle complete a writing sample rather than a formal test in order to study his language arts development. Some specialists might administer the Test of Written Spelling (TWS-2, Larsen & Hammill, 1976), or the Test of Written Language (TOWL, Hammill & Larsen, 1983). These tests are easier to diagnose, but you would miss the unique and natural language manipulation a child uses in his independent writings, and his or her self-editing strategies. In the area of math she might have her students complete the Test of Math Abilities (TOMA, Brown and McEntire, 1984) which investigates not only math calculation skills, but attitude, vocabulary, general math information, and story problems. She might administer the Keymath (1971), or the Test of Early Math (TEMA, 1985) for much younger students. Mrs. Hayman also gathers as much observable data in a variety of contexts, (student work samples, reading lists, progress reports, etc.), as possible to balance the assessment.

By the time the MDT meets again, Mrs. Hayman is well prepared to discuss Kyle's cognitive assessment, his literacy and his present achievement. She has a profile of the student from many sources, and the team is then much better equipped to decide Kyle's eligibility for learning disability services. One of this most difficult things to decipher, when making eligibility decisions, is the affect of his classroom and his home environment on a child's school achievement. We know how powerful the learning climate is. We also know how delicate the subject of change is. It is unfortunate, but not surprising that special education has focused on inter-child deficits and eligibility rather that change in the learning environment.

Individualized Educational Plan and Resource Room Services

Assuming the team does determine that Kyle has a learning disability, he would then need an individualized educational plan (IEP) designed by the teachers and parents, so that he may receive service through the resource program. Each school serves special needs students differently. Some resource models pull children from the regular classrooms and instruct them in a small group or on an individual basis. In some programs, the specialist goes into the classroom and assists the child in his or her regular environment. Some learning disability specialists serve as consultants to the regular classroom teachers and do not instruct the children directly but spend a majority of their time inservicing staff. Most programs involve a combination of all of these.

In this case, Kyle is determined to qualify for services from the learning disabilities program in language arts (reading and writing). Mrs. Hayman contacts Kyle's parents, and teacher as she sets up an IEP conference. At this meeting they design Kyles's program for the year. They write annual goals and short term objectives to meet his special needs. As discussed earlier, the objectives do not have to be written in task analyzed steps, nor do they have to be measured in percentages. An example of holistic language arts goals for Kyle's IEP are presented in Table 8.1.

Mrs. Hayman includes Kyle in a language arts lab in the resource room. Kyle is immersed in lots of good literature, and thematic units which cross most curricular areas. Mrs. Hayman coordinates the units with his classroom studies and his personal interests, as much as possible. Kyle reads, writes, researches,

Table 8.1   Suggested Holistic IEP Goals

Kyle P. Reader	Grade 02	Language Arts

ANNUAL GOAL
Kyle will use BEGINNING LITERACY strategies.

Short Term Objectives:
Kyle will read predictable stories matching his spoken words with the words of the text.

Kyle will read and print-match his dictated stories.

ANNUAL GOAL
Kyle will use efficient reading strategies to correct his miscues.

Short Term Objectives:
Kyle will use all cueing systems (Graphophonic, syntactic, and semantic) to predict, confirm, and correct his miscues or to make substitutions in close activities.

When Kyle comes to a word he doesn't know, he will either substitute a word that makes sense, or skip the word and continue to read for meaning.

When Kyle's reading doesn't make sense, Kyle will stop, go back to the beginning of the sentence, substitute new words based on the context and letter sounds, and continue to read for meaning.

ANNUAL GOAL
Kyle will improve his reading strategies in different materials.

Short Term Objectives:
Kyle will learn to use the following strategies to improve his comprehension:
a. activating prior knowledge
b. predicting
c. substituting and/or saying skip and reading on
d. going back and rereading
e. retelling and summarizing

ANNUAL GOAL
Kyle will show efficiency with emerging writing literacy.

Short Term Objective:
Kyle will use invented spelling in his writing, as he improves his use of standard English conventions.

ANNUAL GOAL
Kyle will demonstrate the writing process, including brainstorming, drafting, editing, and publishing.

Short Term Objective:
Kyle will write in his journal daily.

Short Term Objective:
Given his rough draft, Kyle will edit in the following ways:
• proofing for voice and content
• proofing for sentence structure
• restructuring paragraphs
• proofing for conventions
• proofing for spelling

Short Term Objective:
Kyle will write, edit, and sometimes publish his writing.

Evaluation
These goals will be evidenced by the contents of his portfolio such as: work samples, self-evaluations, literacy checklists, attitude surveys, interviews, teacher observation notations, reading miscue inventories, tests, and quarterly reviews. (Sumner, 1990; Reser, 1990)

interviews, gathers information from many different sources, and writes for more information if necessary. He keeps journals, notes, recordings, pictures, and artwork. He learns to organize his information with maps, clusters, webbings, and traditional outlines if he desires. In short, Kyle generates a wealth of assessment data in his own, daily discovery. At the same time, Mrs. Hayman is gathering information about Kyle and his development. She is recording his reading development, several times weekly, as they engage in whisper conferences. She is looking for the strategies Kyle uses when he comes to words he doesn't know, and she watches his use of all the cueing systems. She is noting the resources he uses (dictionaries, encyclopedias, fellow students, and so forth) and how well he can locate the information he seeks. She is not only recording his progress, but she is interacting with him in the process.

Mrs. Hayman is assessing her learning disabled students all the time. She isn't necessarily recording every observation but her continous assessment of the children drives her instruction. She uses checklists and a teacher's journal of anecdotal records to keep track of all her students' growth. But by far the most used assessment tool in her room is the brag box. This is the classroom portfolio box. The portfolio holds examples of real learnings that happen to include the use of skills. Each student has a file in which the teacher or student can add any piece of student work, any test, or whatever. This brag box holds a history of the child's development. It is a living example of the students' development over time. The student is welcome to bring work samples from home or from his regular classroom to add to the file. It is a collection of their favorite works. And it is an enormous source of pride in the room.

Portfolio Assessment: The Brag Box

Just as the artist collects the treasures that exemplify his or her depth and artistic development in a portfolio, so can the student collect his or her work, projects, creations. Portfolio assessment is the opportunity for authentic, collaborative, and contextually varied assessment over time. Valencia (1990) suggests that "no single test, single observation, or single piece of student work could possibly capture the authentic, continuous, multi-dimensional, interactive requirement of sound (portfolio) assessment." The portfolio is more than the traditional student file. It is a collection of student work selected by the student and/or teacher. It is a place to collect student self-assessments. It is a place to save letters, journals, reading logs, literature study projects, tests, checklists, surveys, and progress reports. It is a rich communicator to parents and regular classroom teachers at conference time. Portfolio assessment is collaborative, continuous, and accessible.

Mrs. Hayman uses the portfolio, or brag box, to keep not only student samples, but she keeps routine testing, standardized measures, and report cards in it too. She does not believe that grades and test scores should be kept a secret from the students. In fact, she has found that the more the students know about her grading system the more they'll know about the strategies she values, the ones she believes promote literacy. She might have her students write a guide to their portfolios describing what they choose to include and why they thought that was important.

Each district needs to decide how they choose to use portfolio assessment. As mentioned earlier, assessment has many different purposes. Valencia (1990) reminds us that while the flexibility of the portfolio is its greatest asset, it may also be one of its problems. There is concern that portfolios could easily become a source of inconsistency, unreliability, and inequity. To protect against that, Valencia recommends two levels of assessment data, the required evidence and the supporting evidence. Districts need to communicate what expectations and criteria they wish their teachers to use as they develop portfolios. Teachers need to participate with the administrators who make the required assessment decisions and share with them their knowledge of the learning process and authentic assessment.

Donald Graves (1990) cautions that we all must have an experimental stance with portfolios rather than the "here it is" attitude. He said to be careful what you expect or require in a portfolio. It could easily become a curriculum evaluation. Jongsma (1989) warns that portfolios should not become collections of the week's graded papers. They should be viewed as a growing, evolving description of the students' reading and writing experiences.

Mrs. Hayman saves a rich, representative sampling of Kyle's work, testing, and self-selected pieces. At the end of each quarter, she might go through the portfolio with his parents to share Kyle's growth, and to discuss the focus they should have to help with Kyle's literacy the following quarter. Her special education department requires her to evaluate Kyle on his goals and objectives each quarter. The contents of his portfolio make these judgments easier for Mrs. Hayman and Kyle. She asks Kyle how he evaluates himself on each goal and writes whatever he says on the report card (under student self-evaluation) in addition to her assessment. It sends a very powerful message to Kyle as she records his self-evaluated grade next to hers.

At the end of the school year, Mrs. Hayman must write new IEPs, goals, and objectives for her students. The collection of masterpieces, and assessments in the student portfolios are an extraordinary communication tool. Parents and classroom teachers are often amazed at the growth in the student. We forget just where the child's literacy really was way back in September. As they analyze the development and adjust the focus for instruction in the fall, Mrs. Hayman, the teacher, and the parents can see the rate of growth, the projects that were interesting and exciting to the student, the projects that weren't so thrilling, the needs, and the celebrations. The new IEP is easily prepared and the objectives refined, using the portfolios as a starting point.

Educators often ask what is to become of the contents of the portfolios the next year, and so on. Won't they just become a management nightmare? Mrs. Hayman believes that representative samples of growth are important data to use in instructional planning. She picks three or so samples of Kyle's work over the year to keep. These will be useful to compare with Kyle's work after the summer break and the same points next year. She saves standardized tests that she was required to administer, or the major assessment tools used in Kyle's eligibility. She keeps all special education forms for the referral and IEP process. She keeps the four progress reports, an end of the year literacy checklist, and a spring attitude survey. Ideally she would complete a summary sheet for the year end describing the projects, materials, and strategies worked on. The remainder of the contents should go to the student and parents to take home.

If the child moved to another district, Mrs. Hayman would organize the special education working file to include the formal IEP forms, eligibilities, parent contacts, and required standardized tests, arranged together with the summary cover sheet. She would insert the portfolio in the working file including the annual assessment pieces described above. She hopes that the organization, the choices of assessment tools, and the summary sheet tell enough about her beliefs to the new district, that they will look at the child in a new way.

Portfolio assessment is ongoing, interactive, and trustworthy. It is assessment that demonstrates a philosophy that honors both the process and the products of learning as well as the active participation of the teacher and the students in their own evaluation and growth (Valencia, 1990). There is no compelling reason why special education programs cannot embrace holistic learning theory and a compatible philosophy of authentic assessment. It may be the most ethical move in special education since the enactment of P.L. 94-142.

Summary

Educational assessment today no longer fits the literacy in our classrooms. Most traditional forms of assessment are designed to show comparisons, percentiles, mastery scores, and other quantitative statistical information (Winograd & Paris, 1988). They do not provide teachers with instructional guidance. They rarely are consistent with teachers' goals and most traditional assessment tools are incompatible with what we know about learning.

Johnston (1987) argues "the functional goals for all educational evaluation is optimal instruction for ALL children." He suggests that we look toward assessment in terms of responsibility, rather than accountability (Johnston, 1990). We have the responsibility to provide our students with learning that is relevant, useful, and engaging. We have the responsibility to evaluate our students in such a way as to honor their process and celebrate their products. We have the responsibility to take great care in making eligibility decisions which affect these youngsters for the rest of their lives. We have the responsibility to follow legal mandate to educate all children, but also to educate the community and the policy makers. They need to know what we now know about the natural learning process.

Public Law 94-142 was the result of a lengthy, concerted effort from parents advocating for the rights of their handicapped children. It is in all respects a human rights document. Education and assessment have indeed changed as a result of community pressure and court litigation. If we are really looking for a universal shift in belief about the learning process and a change in special education assessment based on these beliefs, then I suggest we collaborate with our parents again.

References

Bartoli, J. & Botel, M. (1988). Reading/learning disability: An ecological approach. New York: Teachers College Press, Columbia University.

Berk, R.A. (1984). An evaluation of procedures for computing an ability-achievement discrepancy score. *Journal of Learning Disabilities, 17*, 262–266.

Brown, V. & McEntire, E. (1984). *Test of math abilities.* Austin, Texas: Pro-Ed.

Cambourne, B. (1990). Paper presented at IRA annual conference. International Reading Association Convention, Atlanta, Georgia.

Cambourne, B. (1990, May). Beaverton School District Inservice, Beaverton, Oregon.

Clay, M. (1972). Concepts About Print Test. Hong Kong: Heinemann.

Campione, J.C. & Brown, A.L. (1985). *Dynamic assessment: One approach and some initial data.* Technical Report No. 361. Urban, IL. Center for the Study of Reading.

Coles, G.S. (1978). The learning-disabilities test battery: Empirical and social issues. *Harvard Educational Review, 48*, 313–340.

Cone, T.E. & Wilson, L.R. (1981). Quantifying a severe discrepancy: A critical analysis. *Learning Disability Quarterly, 4*, 359–371.

Conolly, A., Nachtman, W. & Pritchett, E. (1971). Manual for the Keymath diagnostic arithmetic test. Circle Pines, MN: American Guidance Service.

Forness, S.R., Sinclair, E. & Guthrie, D. (1983). Learning disability discrepancy formulas: Their use in actual practice. *Learning Disability Quarterly, 6*, 107–114.

Goodman, K.S., Goodman, Y.M., & Hood, W.J. (1989). *The whole language evaluation book.* Portsmouth, N.H.: Heinemann.

Goodman, Y.M., Watson, D.J., & Burke, C.L. (1972). *Reading miscue inventory.* New York: Macmillan Publishers.

Goodman, Y.M., Watson, D.J., & Burke, C.L. (1987). *Reading miscue inventory: Alternative procedures.* Katonah, N.Y.: Richard C. Owen Publishers, Inc.

Goodman, Y.M. (1978). Kid-watching: An alternative to testing. *National Elementary School Principal, 57*(4): 41–45.

Graves, D. (1990). Paper presented at IRA annual conference. International Reading Association Convention, Atlanta, Georgia.

Hammill, D. & Larsen, S. (1983). Test of written language. Austin, TX: Pro-Ed.

Hasselriis, P. (1982 January). IEPs and a whole language model of language arts. *Topics in Learning and Learning Disabilities.* 17–21.

Johnston, P. (1990). Paper presented at Annual Conference. International Reading Association Convention, Atlanta, Georgia.

Johnston, P. (1987). Teachers as evaluation experts, *The Reading Teacher, 40,* 744–748.

Jongsma, K.S. (1989). Portfolio assessment. *The Reading Teacher, 43*(3), 264–265

Larsen, S. & Hammill, D. (1976). *Test of written spelling.* Austin, TX: Pro-Ed.

MacGinitie, W. (1978) *Gates-MacGinitie reading tests.* Chicago, IL: The Riverside Publishing Co.

Poplin, M. (1988). The reductionist fallacy in learning disabilities; Replicating the past by reducing the present. *Journal of Learning Disabilities, 21*(7): 389–400.

Poplin, M. (1988) Reductionism from the medical model to the classroom: The past, present and future of learning disabilities. *Research Communications in Psychology, Psychiatry, and Behavior, 10*(1, 2) 37–70.

Reynolds, C.R. (1985). Measuring the aptitude-achievement discrepancy in learning disability diagnosis. *Remedial and Special Education, 5*(3), 19–23.

Rhodes, L. & Dudley-Marling, C. (1988). *A holistic approach to teaching learning disabled and remedial students.* Portsmouth, N.H. Heinemann.

Salvia, J. & Ysseldyke, J.E. (1985). *Assessment in special and remedial education,* (3rd. ed.). Boston, Mass: Houghton Mifflin Co.

Shepard, L.A. & Smith, M.L. (1983). An evaluation of the identification of learning disabled students in Colorado. *Learning Disability Quarterly, 6,* 115–127.

Sumner, H.M. & Reser, P. (1990) Unpublished drafts of holistic IEP goals. Revised from Special Education Goals and Objectives, Beaverton School District, Beaverton, OR.

Terman, L. & Merriel, M. (1973). *Stanford-Binet Intelligence Scale.* Chicago: The Riverside Publishing Company.

Turbill, J. (1990) Paper presented at annual conference, International Reading Association Convention, Atlanta, Georgia.

U.S. Department of Education, Office of Special Education. (1980, May 23). *Individualized education programs (IEPs).* OSE Policy Paper.

U.S.O.E. (1977, December, 29). *Assistance to states for education of handicapped children: Procedures for evaluating specific learning disabilities.* Federal Register, 42.

Valencia, S. (1990). A portfolio approach to classroom reading assessment: The whys, whats and hows. *The Reading Teacher, 43*(4), 338–340.

Valencia, S. & Pearson, D.P. (1987). Reading assessment: Time for a change. *The Reading Teacher, 40*(8), 726–732.

Vaughn, S. & Bos, C.S. (1987). *Research in learning disabilities: Issues and future direction.* Boston, Mass: College Hill Publications, Little, Brown and Company.

Wechsler, D. (1974). *Manual for the Wechsler intelligence scale for children–revised.* Cleveland: The Psychological Corporation.

Winograd, P. & Paris, S.G. (1988). *Improving reading assessment.* Lexington, MA. The Heath Transcripts.

Woodcock, R. (1978). *Woodcock-Johnson psychoeducational battery.* Hingham, MA: Teaching Resources Corp.

Woodcock, R. (1973). *Woodcock reading mastery tests.* Circle Pines, MN: American Guidance Service

Ysseldyke, J.E. & Algozzine, B. (1984). *Introduction to special education.* Boston, MA: Houghton Mifflin Company

Chapter 9

Assessment and Evaluation in Bilingual and Multicultural Classrooms

Dorothy King

Introduction

Whole language multicultural and bilingual classrooms are rich environments in which students and teachers learn from one another. The attitudes of whole language teachers, including sensitivity to individual differences and acceptance of diversity, are critical to effective multicultural and bilingual programs. The principles and forms of evaluation and assessment that one finds in whole language classrooms apply to multicultural and bilingual classrooms. Evaluation is intentional and expansive to help teachers, students, and the community facilitate learning as curriculum is created to take into account variations in interactional, communication, and behavioral standards.

Tomacita is five years old and attends a bilingual/biliteracy school in the Navajo Nation. One morning her mother called the teacher aside and told this story:

> As Tomacita ate with her family, she spied a jar of dill pickles on the table and asked what they were. Her uncle told her that the jar contained prairie dog. Tomacita had seen many prairie dogs and protested that the jar did not contain prairie dogs. Her uncle told her that when prairie dog is cut up, salted and preserved, it looks like that. Tomacita tentatively conceded. When the label was turned toward her she said, "Oh, dłǫ́ǫ́," and pointed to the word "dill" with satisfaction. (Dłǫ́ǫ́ is the Navajo word for prairie dog.)

When Tomacita's teacher heard this story, he was thrilled. He had been working very closely with the parents of the children in his class so that they would be able to recognize the evidences of their children's literacy learning. He was happy to add this incident to Tomacita's evaluation folder as an example of Tomacita's growing awareness of print. Tomacita's response was a perfect example of a reader getting meaning and then looking to the print to confirm that meaning. She demonstrated that she expects print to make sense in its context (Harste, Woodward and Burke, 1984).

> During recess, the student teacher talked to Devon about ways to make the playground safer. When the kindergartners gathered for a class meeting after recess, she called on Devon. "What would you do to make the playground safer, Devon?" Devon sat and looked at the floor. She asked again and he remained silent. The teacher smiled and said, "Let's get into groups and talk about what we can do to make the playground safer." The children got into their current teams and started talking. Devon talked quietly with the others. Later the groups presented their ideas and Devon was the reporter for his group.

The teacher explained to the student teacher that Devon's family held traditional ideas about behavior and that Devon would do nothing intentionally to call attention to himself as an individual; he would be quiet, reserved, and anonymous. At five and a half, Devon is already concerned that he be part of his larger society. Among his Navajo classmates, Devon's behavior is appropriate. The teacher and student teacher began to evaluate the classroom environment and their plans for the year to specifically include experiences that would help the kindergartners realize that the larger culture values behaviors that may differ from their own.

Like all whole language teachers, Tomacita and Devon's teacher is a dedicated and proficient kidwatcher (Goodman, 1978), fascinated by his students' language and social learning and eager to learn from his students. Most of his students begin schooling with Navajo as their first language or with Navajo English as their predominant dialect and they come from families that have traditional Navajo values and standards of conduct. As they learn to speak and read and write in English and Navajo, and as they learn about other ways of social interaction, he finds many things to be excited about.

Collecting language stories and behavior anecdotes is a vital and integral part of the ongoing evaluation that whole language multicultural and multilingual teachers use to inform the curriculum they and their students create. Whole language accepts learners and builds on their strength.

Ken Goodman (1986) summarizes these teachers' beliefs and goals for their classrooms:

Schools should build on the language development children have attained before they start school, and on the experiences they have outside school. Whole language programs respect the learners: who they are, where they come from, how they talk, what they read, and what experiences they already had before coming to school. That way there are no disadvantaged children as far as the school is concerned. There are only children who have unique backgrounds of language and experience, who have learned to learn from their own experiences, and who will continue to do so if schools recognize who and where they are. (p. 10)

Bilingual and Multicultural Classrooms

The United States has a long history of trying to assimilate and homogenize its peoples; the "melting pot" metaphor is a familiar one. Recently a general, though not unopposed, attitudinal change toward recognizing the fundamental values of cultural and linguistic diversity has occurred. This change is responsible, in part, for legislative and funding support for bilingual and multicultural programs.

The term bilingual simply means being able to speak two languages. Programs labeled bilingual in schools show a great variety. Bilingual may mean that the language of instruction or the language favored for instruction is different than the students' first language. Some classes begin instruction in the first language while teaching another language and by the middle grades phase the first language out of instruction. Other classes and schools may support the first language by conducting part of daily instruction in the first language or by supplementing the language of instruction with explanations of concepts in the first language. Some schools have the goal of having all students proficient in two languages (Zintz and Maggart, 1984; Tenorio, 1990). Because of the relationship of language and culture, bilingual classes should be multicultural, though in practice some are not.

Multicultural classrooms are those in which a conscious effort is made to make the cultures of the students an integral part of instruction, and to promote understanding, appreciation and acceptance of cultural differences. Multicultural education is based on the unwavering belief that all people's social, ethnic, cultural, and religious backgrounds are valid and of value. Multicultural education is predicated on the concept that all learners can be enriched by perceiving different ways of viewing the world. There is no inferiority or superiority of language or people; there is appreciation of diversity.

Multicultural classrooms show infinite variety. A multicultural class may consist of a teacher and students from mainstream culture and one student from Viet Nam; it may consist of a majority of students from diverse cultures from many parts of the world; or the teacher may be the class member who is from the divergent culture.

Monocultural classes—those in which students are seemingly homogeneous in terms of culture—may also be multicultural if instruction has a pluralistic focus. If all the subcultures of any country are taken into account, then all classes could be considered multicultural.

Language and Culture

The system of a language reflects the entire culture of the people who create and use it. Language reflects the interpretation and perceived relationships of phenomena and experience for members of that culture. Culture defines ways of feeling, thinking, and behaving. It provides the concepts for determining and shaping the view of the world that the people in that culture hold. Cultural differences in language practices represent very different ways of understanding the world and human beings' place in it. Culture defines what is logical, what is reasonable, what is appropriate, what is true. Language reflects all these (King and Goodman, 1990).

Children learn the rules of the language(s) around them without explicit instruction. They learn the language and the cultural rules for use of that language because they have a need to communicate in various settings and for various purposes. Immersion in language settings that provide for real and authentic transactions among language users fosters the intense and personal involvement in language use necessary for language learning.

This authentic language use is a strength of whole language bilingual and multicultural classrooms. The ways people use oral and written language are inextricably bound up with patterns of cultural belief and conceptual principles characteristic of their culture (Heath, 1983). Multicultural classrooms display a variety of learning activities meant to build on diverse learning styles and patterns of social interaction. The classrooms capitalize on research findings that academic and linguistic gains are made when curriculum integrates and expands the languages and experiences of learners (Tikunoff, 1984).

Evaluation and Whole Language Bilingual and Multicultural Classrooms

Evaluation and assessment in whole language multicultural and bi- or multilingual classrooms serve the same purpose they do in whole language classrooms that do not have the designation. Evaluation and assessment serve to help students and teachers plan how to learn and to find out if they are accomplishing what they want. Evaluation is an integral part of the curricular and decision making process.

As in other whole language classrooms, evaluation in multicultural and bilingual classrooms is intentional. Teachers, students, and the community are consciously aware of what they are doing and why they are doing it. They observe, analyze, and make decisions based on knowledge of themselves in particular and of learners in general. Learners are evaluated in real situations during authentic acts.

The Importance of Whole Language Evaluation to Linguistically and Culturally Diverse Learners

Misleading and inaccurate ideas about linguistically and culturally diverse learners have dominated educational thinking because these learners have not been dealt with fairly. They've been asked to play in games they don't know. They've been judged by standards that make no sense to them. As a result they've been labeled "disadvantaged" or "deficient" or a number of other labels that say "You don't fit; you can't make it." A situation in which one is considered inferior, where self-confidence is threatened, where one is expected to perform correctly without the requisite linguistic and cultural knowledge, can hardly be supportive of learning.

Phenomena and practices that occur in non-whole-language classrooms and lead to false pictures of students' abilities and performance are precluded by the very nature of a whole language classroom. These phenomena have to do with teacher attitude, school and classroom climate, instructional practices, and the kind and purpose of evaluation used.

Teacher Attitude

Whole language teachers believe in learners and in every learner's ability to learn language and behavior in accordance with what he or she needs and wants to learn. They understand that the intent to learn is always determined by the learner (Smith, Goodman and Meredith, 1976). They view their task as helping the learner decide to learn by providing contexts in which learning is useful and meaningful. They also respect the learner's decision of whether something is useful to learn at any particular time. For learners of diverse language and culture, the faith in their ability to learn and succeed and the respect for the time it may take to understand the usefulness of learning something are important considerations.

Whole language teachers understand the relationship of language, culture, and development. They are committed to appreciating cultures and understanding them at more than a surface level. They know that culture is far more than how groups dress, the words they use, their recipes, or their ways of acting. They actively seek to ready themselves for how students think and perceive the world. Teachers will be avid consumers of research about specific cultures; they will read autobiographies and biographies of those from cultures with which they interact; they will be careful observers and questioners of learners' reactions and interactional patterns, questioning from the belief that behavior is purposeful and reasonable; they will study perspective-perceptual sources such as music, poetry, religion, folklore, and other cultural expressions (Gold, Gant and Rivlin, 1977). Because whole language classrooms operate as part of the larger community outside the school, teachers will learn from their natural participation with community people in their cultural value systems and socializations. Teachers will observe colleagues who are successful in multicultural settings and note body language, attitudes, and rapport-building procedures used (Zukowski/Faust, 1988).

Whole language teachers have made a conscious commitment not to diminish existing ways of knowing or explaining. They know that the farther a teacher is from the culture of the students, the more alert and sensitive he or she must be.

Whole language teachers interpret the agenda of the wider culture to students and, at the same time, support the ways of knowing and the knowledge that are already valuable to the learners. They are constantly sensitive to the need of all people to maintain an identity with their community, its history, and aspirations. Teachers are committed to finding out about their students' ways of viewing so that they can better understand them and so that they can help their students expand their perceptions and views of the world to include those of other cultures, including that of the larger general society.

Because of whole language teachers' sensitivity to culture and individual beliefs, the phenomenon called "cultural discontinuity" (Garcia, 1988) is less likely to occur. Discontinuity occurs when experiences in schooling and classrooms do not accommodate or are not compatible with cultural backgrounds of students. For example, children from communal cultures of the South Pacific are likely to find that the idea of earning money for individual material gain is incongruous with what they know about social relationships and their idea of goodness in people (LeSourd, 1990). Children from Puerto Rican backgrounds may have difficulty accepting mainstream American society's preoccupation with systems and organization when their culture places paramount value on human relationships (Gold, Grant and Rivlin, 1977).

Zukowski/Faust (1988), Hall (1989) and others discuss several areas in which diverse perceptions and interactions may manifest. These include:

- time; pacing; and emphasis on past, present, future
- self-reliance, independence and competitiveness
- voice level and nonverbal communication
- directness of communication
- standards of conduct
- personal space
- authority, control, and power

Consideration of each of these phenomena and patterns will help make evaluation more accurate.

School and Classroom Climate

In whole language bilingual and multicultural classrooms differences among learners are valued; diversity of background is viewed as an asset and as a powerfully enriching resource for all class members. Language and experience are accepted and used as the bases for learning. Accommodation and understanding of all learning and social interaction styles is a goal.

Because classrooms may consist of learners from several different backgrounds who vary widely in terms of perceptions, whole language teachers and students may start out by mutually developing rules that will allow them to work together and learn about each other. These rules are developed initially with the understanding that as class participants learn more about each other, the rules will change or be interpreted to be as compatible as possible with all the cultures represented in the class. An attitude that "we are all different, but the differences among us are what make us interesting" is established (Zukowski/Faust, 1988). The intellectual and social advantages of multilingualism (Diaz, 1990) are continuously presented, discussed, and demonstrated.

The classroom community is tied to the larger communities from which students come. In this way, the artificial differences in learning in school and out of school are reduced. Community resources and people are an integral part in instruction and evaluation. For example, Lucia's grandparents returned from a month's visit to relatives in Palermo, and were invited by the seventh grade to talk of their visit and the similarities and differences they perceived in the old country Italian community and their own Italian-American community. Several students decided to do sociological studies and the grandparents were involved in the projects.

Part of the integration of culture into evaluation involves the recognition of various standards of child development for the cultures from which students come.

Different cultures focus differently on developmental characteristics according to what the culture values. Children from cultures that emphasize cooperation, communalism, and mutual aid, e.g., those from African-descent cultures, conform to different expectations than children from cultures that stress individualism (Gold, Grant and Rivlin, 1977). Whole language evaluation takes into account the different views of normal for different cultures.

Instructional Practices

Evaluation and instruction are inextricable. For too long, linguistically and culturally diverse students have been subjected to instruction in which they have little chance of success. Knapp and Shields (1990) raise questions about the value and appropriateness of the instruction which many linguistically and culturally diverse children receive, for example, skills-based, sequentially ordered, teacher controlled. MacDonald, Adelman, Kushner, and Walker (1982) point to "a largely behaviorist pedagogy (in which) language is divorced from its cultural contexts of meaning and use, componentized and taught as abstraction. This is arguably the most difficult way yet devised to promote literacy and the least responsive to the student's cultural resources."

Destroying language makes it harder to learn for anybody, but especially for learners from cultures and languages that are different from the majority because these children don't have the background to guess at what the pieces could mean. Fragmented language is without meaning. Unable to deal with the meaninglessness of their instruction, many children are considered to be deficient. In a whole language bilingual or multicultural classroom, the competence of learners is already accepted and the environment supports, respects, and builds on the language and experience learners have.

When learners are evaluated in environments in which there are multiple opportunities to express ideas in a variety of ways and time is provided to work on a variety of topics for many purposes, to reflect on ideas, express feelings, present information, entertain with a story or dance or drawing, narrate events, and express opinions to a variety of audiences, their learning is obvious (Rigg and Enright, 1986; Franklin, et. al., 1989).

Purpose and Kinds of Evaluation

Whole language strives to make evaluation fit the learner, not to make the learner fit a preconceived evaluation model. For this reason, evaluation is purposeful in facilitating learning and it exists to help learners as they engage in authentic situations and acts. It does not disrupt what is going on, but is an integral part of the ongoing activity.

Evaluation is expansive, not reductionist. Teachers and students seek to expand and get meaning from their actions, not narrow the focus to one particular item. And when different languages and cultures are involved, the rich information used and gained in making evaluations is a learning asset.

A part of this expansiveness includes evaluating the context. Whole language teachers always consider the context of the classroom and look for conditions that may serve to constrain what students and teachers can accomplish. Cultural knowledge of the students is integrated into the evaluation.

Slaughter (1988) suggests that four kinds of context are important to assessment: the physical situation (is it familiar or unfamiliar?; is it a group discussion or a one to one conference? and so forth); the linguistic and paralinguistic context (how what is expressed relates to what was communicated before and what is yet to be communicated); the social context (the social meaning of the communication; the status and relationship of the speakers; the cultural expectations held for the encounter); and the invisible context (the assumptions of each participant about background information and what is known and shared about the topic).

Because the whole language bilingual and multicultural classrooms are part of communities and consider contexts, evaluation takes many forms. Whole language classrooms allow for all kinds of evaluation. For example, some cultures may not emphasize auditory and visual expression; students from these cultures may prefer tactile and kinesthetic presentations of their learning and express themselves better through art than through reading and writing. These expressions of learning are unquestionably valid.

Learners in whole language bilingual and multicultural classrooms have a stake in their own learning. A large part of evaluation is self-evaluation, that is, learners decide if they are doing what they want and if and how to do better. After listening to fellow students discuss a draft of his report on Samoan legends, Aisa decided that he had not communicated what he wanted and revised the organization and language usage so that his points were clear.

Burke's (1990) vision of evaluation as a combination of perspective on learning (who is doing the evaluating—self, collaborative others, or larger society) with what aspect in the process will be evaluated (learner intent, engagement, or artifact) is especially important in multicultural classrooms. Such a schema for evaluation reminds the participants that multiple perspective and assessments are necessary to learners' success. Evaluation from everyone making up the classroom community or having a stake in it is valued.

A Cautionary Word

Whole language teachers may find that some of their own most cherished stances and approaches are challenged in a bilingual or multicultural classroom. Some behaviors in whole language classrooms may initially upset students from other cultures. For example, whole language teachers see themselves as fellow learners and this stance does not lead to being an authority figure. Some students expect teachers to be authorities and evince obvious leadership in terms of telling others what to do. In another example, students from Japanese backgrounds may have a strong cultural taboo against directly opposing someone else's view (Livingston, 1985). The whole language teacher may genuinely crave thoughtful discussion and questioning, the evidences of the inquiry that is learning (Watson, Burke and Harste, 1989). Whole language teachers will accept these differences and willingly work with students so that both teacher and student needs are met.

Some Examples of Evaluation in Bilingual and Multicultural Classes

Evaluation in whole language bilingual and multicultural classrooms will take the same form as it does in other whole language classrooms. Teachers will use miscue analysis and writing portfolios, holistic writing assessments and interviews. Evaluation and assessment instruments and procedures mentioned elsewhere in this volume will be used. Always the evaluators (teachers, peers, self or others) must keep in mind the perceptions and development of the students as they interact and create in the classroom.

The following are examples of evaluation in multicultural and bilingual classrooms. These examples are the authentic evidence that learning is occurring.

Observational Records

Students and teachers may keep track of their language and interactions in a number of ways. One of the basic ways is through anecdotal records.

> 11/2/88 Robin said, "Teacher, I thank you very much from me." I think this is the first time he has used the generic English "you." In his language in Ceylon he would never use a familiar form to a teacher, but would use a formal form of "you" which English doesn't have. He seems to be showing willingness to accept that English doesn't need to express such differences.
>
> 11/7/89 Carletta and Mary were writing a play. Dorothy (the student intern) was taking dictation. Carletta said, "He be working" and Dorothy wrote "He's working." Carletta said, "Shanelle say he coming" and Dorothy wrote "Shanelle say he coming." Carletta said, "That not right. Spell it right." Dorothy wrote, "Shanelle said he's coming." Both Carletta and Mary said, "Alright!! Don't do that no more," and laughed. They demonstrated that they do know Standard English, but in the informal situation prefer their Black dialect. They are proud of their play and want it written in Standard English so that others can read and appreciate it.

It is usually helpful to organize observations. This serves the purpose of helping the evaluator look at the many facets of a particular sample or evidence of learning. One way is to use lists of potential indicators of learning. The following example has proven useful in multicultural and bilingual classrooms.

The Evaluation of Basic Reading and Writing Processes was developed by Stephen Kucer (1988) for use in a bilingual (Spanish/English) classroom. Originally intended as a way to help teachers make change, for example, if the evaluation instrument is changed, the curriculum changes to match it, the grid presents a way to organize anecdotal observations as well as keep track of the reading and writing processes which students are using. Below is an excerpt from one such record (see Figure 9.1).

Writing Samples

Keeping track of samples of writing over time can reveal what students are working on and the progress toward standardization and convention that they have made. Writing samples may be evaluated for sense of story or genre convention, for example, parts of a letter; sense of audience; growth in syntax; and orthographic conventions, such as spelling, punctuation, spacing, legibility (TAWL, 1984). Writers decide if they want to focus on a particular aspect of writing.

In the excerpt sample below (see Figure 9.2) Cassandra, age 5, writes "My Tsini (sister's nickname) went to the airplane and she's going to get basic training." Her use of orthographic conventions shows that she understands spacing between words; uses invented spelling, pictures and letter strings; and uses periods. Though the piece is about a personal experience that she has told, she uses complete sentences as one does in writing and the piece engages her reader.

In the written retelling of a familiar story done a year later (see Figure 9.3) Cassandra uses less invented spelling and what she does use is more accessible to the reader.

Audiotapes, Profiles, and Other Records of Students Reading

In addition to helping the teacher keep track of changes in reading behavior over time, tapes and descriptions of reading can also be used for self-evaluation and to share with parents and others who are interested. Records kept include miscue analysis profiles, strategy lessons introduced, and reader selected miscues (Watson, 1978). In the following excerpt, Esteban, who has been in an intensive remedial phonics program for two years, focuses on the graphophonic system almost exclusively. The teacher and his peers demonstrated the strategy of asking "What should go here? What makes sense?" and used cloze procedures (Hittleman, 1978) and other strategy lessons to help Esteban focus on meaning.

Figure 9.1   Evaluation of Basic Reading and Writing Processes

Evaluation of Basic Reading and Writing Processes

Student's Name: __Marquis__   Grade: __6th__

Age: __12__   Evaluator: __M.S.__

Writing Processes	Yes	Somewhat	No
1b. Generates and organizes major ideas or concepts.	1/6		
2b. Expands, extends, or elaborates on major ideas or concepts.	1/6 "Home is good example		
3b. Integrates meaning into a logical and coherent whole.		1/6 starting to take peer advice	
4b. Uses a variety of linguistic cues -- textual, semantic, syntactic, graphophonic.		1/6 see above	
5b. Uses a variety of text aids -- pictures, charts, graphs, sub-headings, etc.			
6b. Uses relevant background knowledge.	1/6		
7b. Predicts/plans upcoming meanings based on what has been previously written.		1/6 see above	

Figure 9.2

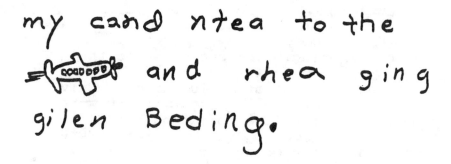

my cand ntea to the [airplane] and rhea ging gilen Beding.

Figure 9.3

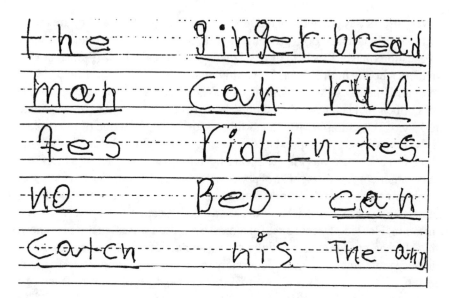

the gingerbread
man can run
fes riolln fes
no Bed can
Cotch his The ann

```
          her  gaddyk    teent              safe② ?
The huge geodesic "tent" was dark save for
   seekle  sp-       ler- who          darker
a single spot of light which (cut the) darkness
   church ringing      crowed
at center ring.  The crowd (issued the)
res-tell-lease
   restless (silence of anticipation.   Only )
mon-ments
mom                          hu
moments before, the holographic "monster"
          dawn  scales       delly ②fra-
show had drawn squeals of delightful/fright
```

from the children. (King, 1980.)

During second semester a look at Esteban's reader selected miscues shows how his reading behavior has changed.

The arena is fully lit now. Volcrnka is motioning to the generators adjusting

the angles of the riders till they are precisely where he wants them. They have

practiced the trick before; they have performed it before. It must be exactly right.

A very useful way to check on readers' understandings of what they are reading (and to evaluate classroom procedures) is to allow students to retell or respond to questions and probes in their first languages. Moll and Diaz (1987) report that readers who are multilingual frequently understand more that is read or heard in English than they can retell in English. When readers are permitted to do retellings in their first language, their comprehension of a story may be more accurately reflected. For example, after a reading lesson in English, one of the students, Sylvia, was asked to respond to the question of why the children in the story thought a classmate was lost. Responding in English, Sylvia gave a brief, hesitant, rather confused response of about twenty words. From observing this, one might conclude that she did not understand what she had read in English. Right after her response in English, Sylvia was asked in Spanish to respond to the same question. Her lengthy response (of almost a hundred words) in Spanish showed that she had easily understood the events and actions in the story. Using first language retellings may more accurately reflect students' understandings. The results of these retellings also signal the teacher to find ways to extend first language abilities into the second or other language.

Self-Evaluation Forms

Students are responsible for their own learning and decide what they want to know and how well they want to know it and of planning what to do next. Below is an example of a form on which students may plan what to do next (Crenshaw, 1990).

Figure 9.4

Today I learned:

_____

_____

I have a question:

_____

_____

_____

I worked on:	Mon	Tue	Wed	Thu	Fri
Math	___	___	___	___	___
Science	___	___	___	___	___
Social Studies	___	___	___	___	___
Reading	___	___	___	___	___
Writing	___	___	___	___	___
Computers	___	___	___	___	___
_____	___	___	___	___	___
_____	___	___	___	___	___

Summary

Teaching in a whole language bilingual or multicultural classroom is one of the best experiences on earth. It is challenging and the rewards are great. One is constantly alive and alert because there is so much to learn and feel about language, culture, and individual perception. There are always questions to be asked and answered about relationships, teaching, learning and evaluation, and making the world a better place.

References

Burke, C. (1990). Curriculum evaluation. Personal correspondence.

Crenshaw, S. (1990). Encouraging students to self-evaluate. Presentation at NCTE Spring Conference, Colorado Springs, CO.

Diaz, R. (1990). The intellectual power of bilingualism. *SWCOLT Newsletter, 6*(1), 2–6.

Franklin, L., Franklin, K., Tullie, V., King, D., & O'Brien, K. (1989). Second language learning through writing process. *Journal of Navajo Education, 6*(2), 21–28.

Garcia, R. (1988). The need for bilingual/multicultural Indian education. J. Reyhner, (Ed.), *Teaching the Indian child*. Billings, MT: Eastern Montana College.

Gold, M., Grant, C., & Rivlin, H. (Eds.). (1977). In *Praise of diversity: A resource book for multicultural education*, Washington, DC: Teacher Corps and Association of Teacher Educators.

Goodman, K. (1986). *What's whole in whole language?* Portsmouth, NH: Heinemann.

Goodman, Y. (1978). Kidwatching: Observing children in the classroom. *Journal of National Elementary Principals, 57*(4), 41–45.

Hall, E.T. (1989). Unstated features of the cultural context of learning. *The Educational Forum, 54*(1), 21–34.

Harste, J., Woodward, V., & Burke, C. (1984). *Language stories and literacy lessons*. Portsmouth, NH: Heinemann.

Heath, S. (1983). *Ways with words: Language, life, and work in communities and classrooms*. Cambridge, England, Cambridge University Press.

Hittleman, D. (1978). *Developmental reading: A psycholinguistic perspective*. Chicago, IL: Rand McNally.

King, D., & Goodman, K. (1990). Whole language: Cherishing learners and their language. *Language, Speech, and Hearing Services in Schools, 21*(4), 221–227.

King, M. (1980). *Always the edge: For Karl Wallenda*. Unpublished.

Knapp, M., & Shields, P. (1990). Reconceiving academic instruction for the children of poverty. *Kappan, 71*(10), 752–758.

Kucer, S. (1988). Evaluation of basic reading and writing processes. Inservice for Nazlini Boarding School, Ganado, AZ.

LeSourd, S.J. (1990). Curriculum development and cultural context. *The Educational Forum, 54*(2), 205–216.

Livingston, M., & Abe, H. (1985). Japanese students and the learning of English: Cultural and other sources of frustration. In S. Johnston and D. Johnson, (Eds.), *Rocky Mountain Regional TESOL '85: A collection of papers*. Phoenix, AZ: AZ-TESOL.

MacDonald, D., Adelman, C., Kushner, S., & Walker, R. (1982). *Bread and dreams: A case study of bilingual schooling in the USA*. CARE Occasional Publication #12. Norwich, England: University of East Anglia, Center for Applied Research in Education.

Moll, L.C., & Diaz, S. (1987). Change as the goal of educational research. *Anthropology and Education Quarterly, 18*, 300–311.

Rigg, P., & Enright, S., (Eds.). (1986). *Children and ESL: Integrating perspectives*. Washington, DC: TESOL.

Slaughter, H. (1988). A sociolinguistic paradigm for bilingual language proficiency assessment. In J. Fine, (Ed.), *Second language discourse: A textbook of current research*, Norwood, NJ: Ablex.

Smith, E., Goodman, K., & Meredit, R. (1976). *Language and thinking in school*, 2nd ed., New York, NY: Holt, Rinehart and Winston.

TAWL (Tucsonans Applying Whole Language). (1984). *A kid-watching guide: Evaluation for whole language classrooms*. Tucson, AZ: University of Arizona.

Tenorio, R. (1990). A vision in two languages: Reflections on a two-way bilingual program. *Rethinking Schools, 4*(4), 11–12.

Tikunoff, W. (1984). An emerging description of successful bilingual instruction. In Executive Summary of Part I of the *Significant bilingual instructional features studies*. San Francisco, CA: Far West Laboratory.

Watson, D.J. (1978). Reader selected miscues: Getting more from sustained silent reading. *English Education, 10,* 75–85.

Watson, D., Burke, C., & Harste, J. (1984). *Whole language: Inquiring voices*. New York: Scholastic.

Zintz, M., & Maggart, Z. (1984). The reading process: The teacher and the learner, 4th ed. DuBuque, IA: W.C. Brown.

Zukowski/Faust, J. (1988). The multicultural classroom. *Arizona English Bulletin, 30*(3), 18–22.

Chapter 10

Record Keeping in Whole Language Classrooms

C. Jean Church

In a land not far away and in a time not long ago, the pursuit of documenting student educational progress led teachers through reams of ditto sheets, stacks of workbooks, decks of vocabulary flash cards, and a maze of bubble answer documents, scored outside the district. Our story began sometime ago when a group of teachers met together to study this thing called whole language. As they started thinking analytically and critically about their teaching, their attitudes and beliefs about what constitutes learning began to change. They, like other teachers trying to implement whole language, discovered that the traditional methods of record keeping and evaluation no longer seemed to fit with what they were trying to do. Because story is the way in which we learn and narrative is the way in which we organize our minds, this chapter will tell our stories, those of our students, and the lessons we gleaned from the stories of others as we seek to document student progress in credible, transferable, and dependable ways.

Gone from their rooms were workbooks, gone were the packets of ditto sheets, gone were the vocabulary lists, gone were the basal reader lessons, gone were the red pens that marked all over student work, gone were the stickers and smiley faces doled out by the teacher, gone were the checklists of 4656 isolated skills once believed to add up to reading proficiency, gone, gone, gone.

Yet, all around us the accountability issue looms still. There are state requirements, there are parent expectations, there are colleagues' questions, there are administrators who put much stock in the neat numbers generated on standardized test printouts. David Dillon (1990) sadly acknowledges that there still seems to be a tremendous preoccupation with evaluation as an end in itself rather than as an ongoing, integral part of teaching and learning. All too often the learner is left out of the process.

One day as we were discussing how to document progress, one of the first grade teachers threw up her hands and, tongue in cheek said,

> How do you know when they are through? It used to be so easy, along about April or May, as my top and middle reading groups finished the first grade reader, I could wipe my hands and smile to myself, satisfied that I had duly administered first grade and we were done. Sort of like giving all the baby shots, whether they took or not. But now, the kids in my class just keep on reading and writing! I can't fill out the reading cards that tell next year's teacher what book they are ready for and furthermore, they don't fit neatly on the scope and sequence skills charts anymore. Some of them can't pass the lower level checkpoints and yet they easily pass skills at much higher levels. Their charts have gaps in them. How will I ever convince the second grade teacher that we really did have first grade?

Even though her remark brought laughter from the group, several of them were feeling the disequilibrium associated with trying to fit newly acquired knowledge of teaching and learning with past expectations of how it's supposed to be. But, if we hope to propel ourselves into a new realm of understanding of language learning and survive the outside pressures for accountability, viable evidence must be presented to students, parents, other teachers, administrators, local tax payers, and state policy makers that learning is proceeding.

In considering the issue of accountability, the teachers explored three basic areas of record keeping which they thought would help them and needed to be addressed:

1. purposes of record keeping,
2. what kinds of records would provide needed information, and finally,
3. what needs to be recorded.

Purposes of Record Keeping

To present evidence of learning, teachers must keep careful documentation of systematic observations of and interactions with children as they learn language, learn about language, and learn through language. Records provide the data from which they derive interpretations, value judgments, and evaluations. Record keeping, assessment, and evaluation can no longer be the sole responsibility of the teacher, but must be a shared responsibility among teachers, students, parents, and administrators. Although the data may be presented in a variety of different ways for a variety of different audiences, it will still be the same data. Therefore, it is important that teachers understand for whom the data is intended and for what purpose it will be used. Record keeping should:

1. help students make self-evaluations,
2. construct a history of the learner's development,
3. guide interactions and instruction, and
4. should serve to communicate with parents and other stakeholders.

Helps Students Make Self-Evaluation

One April morning I was visiting Chad's first grade classroom. Chad, instead of writing, started flipping through his Beautiful Word book. The page fell open to an entry he had made about Thanksgiving. He pored over the page and then began to carefully inspect each subsequent page, then he went back and did it again. Still no writing—I though he was just wasting time when all of a sudden he leaped out of his seat and rushed over to his teacher. "Look," he cried excitedly, "I learned to start each new sentence with a capital letter back on November 29!" Chad had revealed to us that day the importance of the learner taking responsibility for his learning and that some of the records kept must serve to help students make self-evaluations. Often in the past learners have been left out of the process of record keeping and evaluation. Because of this, many students are simply unaware that they are learning anything. Just as we found it essential as teachers to keep asking ourselves, "What are we learning?" it is also essential for the students to continually be challenged to think about and express what they are learning. This helps them begin to build internal standards for judging what constitutes good work.

Constructs a History of the Learner's Literacy Development

The work of Denny Taylor (1990) in the *Biographic Literacy Profiles Project* focuses upon teaching, learning, and schooling from the perspective of the learner. Through constructing profiles of children's observable literacy behaviors, growth can be shown. Like the Project teachers, we too began to try to describe children's personal understandings of the forms and functions of written language as they go about using language in the classroom. This history documents growth over time which is a shift in emphasis from comparing children to a predetermined standard to that of basing evaluation upon the accomplishments of the learner. No longer is it appropriate to rate kids on a scale from "stupid" to smart, rather the learner's progress must be charted as he moves along the literacy continuum.

Guides Interactions and Instruction

Think back for a minute to our colleague who worried a little that the next year's teacher would not know where to start with the children because the basal reading cards were not filled out. As we reflected upon this, we realized that the information recorded on these cards was decontextualized fragments of language. It told us nothing about the child's reading strategies; it told us nothing about the processes the child used; it told us nothing about the child's attitude toward reading and writing. In actuality it could do little to guide interactions and instruction. For records to be valuable, data must be collected in the context of children's language.

Communicates to Parents and Other Stakeholders

Another purpose for careful record keeping is to inform parents and others who have a share in the education of our nation's children. If careful thought is given to the kinds of data collected, the various audiences entitled to information can interpret it according to their needs.

Kinds of Records

Brian Cambourne (1988, p. 122) states that

> one continually builds up a store of knowledge about each child's literacy development. In this sense, the teacher becomes like a classical anthropologist. Like an anthropologist, she alternates between participant observer, detached observer, and collector of artifacts. At times she observes the "members of the tribe" from a distance, recording her observations for later analysis. At other times she asks questions of various informants about what they know and think and about the ways they produce their artifacts, all the time recording their responses. Her records become her store of knowledge. From this store of knowledge she tries to construct what reality is for the tribe or culture she's observing. In the case of the teacher building a store of knowledge about literacy development, the reality she is trying to construct is how each one of her pupils' knowledge and skill in literacy and all that it entails is changing and developing over time.

As Cambourne suggests, an anthropologist doesn't just record some events, but records a range and depth of experiences of the culture. Likewise, the teacher must record across all classroom events not just during language class. The teachers, as well as the students, in our group kept a variety of records. One important point made by all the teachers was that record keeping should not interfere with student contact. Teachers should not walk around with post it notes stuck all over them or become humpbacked from carrying around video cameras to record every little thing. Common sense and intelligence go a long way in selecting appropriate yet manageable record keeping strategies. The records kept in our group fall into three categories: those kept by the teacher, those kept by the student, and those supplied by the parent.

Teacher Records	Student Records	Parent Input
Anecdotal Records	Reading/Writing Folders	Parent Profile
Interviews	Daily Logs	Evaluation Comments
Observations	Reading Response Letters	
Conference Notes	Individual Plans and Goals	
Status of the Class		
Teacher Journals		

We have not included video and audio tapes at this point. The overriding concern of the teachers was that record keeping not dominate the teacher's time as it once did with all the tiny isolated skills she was required to test. Not all teachers used all these as separate records, for example, some teachers combined conference notes in the anecdotal record, others combined observations in the conference notes. In short, the way in which the teacher organized the classroom heavily influenced the way in which the data was collected and organized.

Anecdotal Records

Most of the teachers in the group use a loose leaf, tabbed notebook with a few pages designated for each student. Teachers usually carry these around to jot down literacy vignettes, as they work in and among the students. Other teachers prefer to jot on a packet of post it notes or address labels and transfer later to the notebook. Still others use a clipboard. (A fifth grade teacher confided that she used the clipboard because it made the kids think she was doing something important whether she was or not.) One of the kindergarten teachers keeps index cards in her pocket as she works with the children. She then has a card file box with sections for each child. Because these teachers no longer have the traditional high, middle, and low reading groups, there is time to observe and interact with students.

The purpose of the anecdotal record is to try to capture the child's literacy development. It is generally descriptive in nature and by asking the following questions, teachers seek to look at learning from the child's perspective (Taylor, 1990).

■ What does this child know?

- What can this child do?
- How does this child use language to gain membership in the classroom?
- What control does this child have over oral language? Over printed language?
- How does this child go about problem solving?
- How does this child plan, organize, and go about completing tasks?
- What kinds of questions does this child ask? Are they relevant?
- How does the child use language (listening, speaking, reading, and writing)?
- What kinds of comments or remarks does he make while working?

Questions such as those listed above, prompted the teachers to begin to look and listen differently in the classroom.

Interviews

Drawing upon the example of the anthropologist again, the teachers have learned to inquire of the children about their work. They listen for the child's process, his or her line of reasoning. One of the teachers remarked in her own journal that the more she listened, the more she learned about her students. She wrote that her teacher talk had always dominated the classroom, but now she hears the voices of the children. Yetta Goodman (1989) taught us that as we reflect on the learning of the student we can reflect on our own professional development as teachers.

Jane Hansen (1987) and Nancie Atwell (1987) believe that young students as well as those in the middle grades are quite capable of talking about their work and helping to plan their next steps in their language learning. Both researchers used interviews to gain information from children. Questions that Hansen asked the children were:

1. What's something new you've learned to do in writing?
2. What's something you would like to learn so you can be a better writer?
3. What's something new you've learned to do in reading?
4. What's something you would like to learn so you can be a better reader?

Likewise, Atwell conferenced students about their reading and writing by using the following three discussion topics:

1. The main thing they hoped to learn during the grading period
2. The main thing they did learn
3. One thing they intend to do because of what they learned.

Observation Forms

Learning to recognize literacy events takes time for teachers, but even longer time for parents. During a theme study of famous Americans, the students in

Mrs. Dooley's second grade class decided to communicate their learnings through a dramatic portrayal of each figure. They researched and gathered their information, organized the format of the presentation, wrote the scripts, sewed costumes and built sets, wrote invitations to parents, arranged for the media specialist to provide a microphone and video tape equipment. On the day of the Famous American performance, the students presented flawlessly. Mrs. Dooley was so proud until one mother said, "The kids' show was really cute, but is that all you do in here, just play?" Mrs. Dooley calmly picked up the log written by this parent's child. The children had recorded a description of the processes they had followed to put on this presentation. The parent, after reading the passages, immediately apologized and said she wasn't used to looking at learning in that way.

Most of the teachers in our group have come up with some observational forms with widely recognized literacy indicators. Yet, at the same time, they had to design those forms that were most workable for them. Included near the end of this chapter are some examples of observation forms.

Conference Notes

With the abandonment of the three reading group model, reading and writing conferences take place on a regular basis. As the student conferences with the teacher about his or her reading, writing, or content area project, the teachers make notes. Most of the teachers add these conference pages to the student's section in the anecdotal record notebook.

Included here is an example (Figure 10.1) of one of the reading conference forms used. Depending upon the level of the students and the objectives of the teacher, the specific indicators varied.

Besides individual conferences, teachers often keep notes on literature discussion sessions. Small groups of children read the same book or piece and then discuss it. Figure 10.2 shows the form on which some of the teachers keep notations about the growth of the students in understanding and comprehension.

Status of the Class Check

Even our primary teachers have found Nancie Atwell's (1987) status of the class check helps students focus on the work period with a plan. Pat Bringman's second graders utilize the media center as a natural extension of the classroom. No longer are her students scheduled in the media center for a once a week session on library skills in isolation, but they are continually in and out searching for information for their work. One requirement however, is that during the status of the class check, they need to state what they are working on and how the media center would be the most appropriate place to accomplish their goals. Pat reports that occasionally students go just to browse. Since she often browses in libraries and bookstores, she counts this as valued behavior.

Figure 10.1

Conference Notes

Name ————————————————— Date ————————————————

Title of Piece——————————————— Type of Piece——————————

Attitudes/Interests/Background

Comprehension

Fictional Text
  • main idea
  • details
  • setting
  • characters
  • inferences

Informational Text
  • facts
  • concepts
  • vocabulary

Strategies used

Further reading or extension project

Figure 10.2

BOOK DISCUSSION NOTES

Title of Book _____ Date_____

Student Names:	Comments: (Record student responses which indicate ability to elaborate, justify, explain, communicate or express feelings.)

Tim Moss, another teacher in the group, regularly uses this technique (Figure 10.3) to keep track of his multi-aged group and to help them focus their work period.

Figure 10.3

STATUS OF THE CLASS CHECK

Date _____

Student Names:	Plans for the Day	Materials or Resource Persons Needed	Comments
Sarah	*Continue work on River City Gazette (Newspaper project)*	• *Working with Mardee and Michele* • *Will interview local Historian*	*Girls are well planned and focused.* *Check on Interview Questions.*
Jason	*Starting research on fishing industry*	*Will need to go to Media Center*	
Michele	*See notes on Sarah*		*Make sure Michele gets oportunity to call Mrs. Clark to set up interview.*

Tim says the comment column helps him focus himself during the work period as well as sometimes serving as an anecdotal record. Tim has been experimenting with making weekly status of the class checks.

Teacher Journals

Recently when Don Graves spent some time with us, he inspired us to write daily for ourselves, to develop our own literacy. Daily reading and writing needs to be a life-style for us. Then when we show this to children, it becomes an authentic literacy lesson. The teachers and principal at one school involved in a special grant project to study our Wabash River, have begun to keep personal day books. On a daily basis, the teachers and principal try to capture thoughts, perceptions, images, insights into the teaching/learning situation, things they would like to learn, and so forth.

Goals for this project were:

1. teachers and principals would learn more about collaboration among teachers, administrators, students, parents and community members;
2. they would learn more about how a guided research or theme project could form the basis of student/teacher work rather than work organized by traditional subject areas or disciplines; and
3. they would learn more about working with children in multi-aged, multi-ability grouped settings. In addition to these project goals, each staff member was to generate some personal goals. At the end of the project, the staff selected pieces from their journals which demonstrated their learnings about each of the goals.

At first, it almost seemed an additional chore that had to be done. However, within a few weeks, the teachers were amazed at how much broader they seemed to view the classroom, their own lives, and the world. One teacher commented that "it feels good to look at that log book. It represents my work and my learning. It's great to hold learning in your hands."

Writing and Reading Folders

Collections of student writing are kept by the children. Patterned after the work of Graves (1982) and Harste (1988), they contain all the pieces the children are working on. In the case of our emerging authors, much of their work is completed in one or two times. However, these young learners are quite capable of stamping the date on the piece with their teacher's date stamp and filing them under their own names arranged alphabetically. By stamping the date on the work, a pattern of growth emerges over the course of the year. Older students might have several pieces in progress, but they too need to be able to see their own growing control over the form and function of written language.

Students keep track of the reading they are doing. Sometimes this is merely recorded on a reading log (see Figure 10.4), at other times written responses might be collected in a folder. Many of the intermediate teachers write letters back and forth with the students about their reading (Atwell, 1987). The letter has proven to be a natural way in which the teachers and students can carry on book conversations. In the early primary grades, the students generally just keep track of the books they are reading and make simple comments or recommendations.

Figure 10.4

READING LOG

Name _____

Name of Book/Article/Poem	Date Started	Comments or Recommendations	Date Completed

Portfolios

From the reading and writing folders, students are asked to build a portfolio that represents their learnings. Much of what we know about portfolios as documentation of the learner's knowledge can be attributed to Dr. Don Graves during his time with us. He helped us to view the portfolio as an ongoing, ever changing artifact as the students pass from one layer of learning into the next. The basic assumption is that students select those examples that best demonstrate their learning, knowledge, and growing control over language. Because portfolio as a database is still in its infancy stage, much experimentation needs to take place always keeping in perspective the question, how can we show ourselves as learners?

In selecting material for their portfolios in the river grant project, the teachers and students decided that their selected pieces should be related to their personal goals, as well as those of the project. In some cases, the students wanted to present their learnings in the form of a media presentation, others wanted to include their art work, still others had constructed some models of bridges, barges, and paddleboats and wanted to include those. It was finally agreed that "artifacts" as well as written documentation would be appropriate.

Some of the goals for the project included:

- students would become familiar with real, fictional, or legendary river characters
- students would gain familiarity with historical figures of our Wabash Valley
- students would build an understanding of the importance of the river in the settlement of the valley
- students would become familiar with art and music that pertains to rivers
- students would gain an understanding of environmental concerns.

Examples of what students and teachers might select for the portfolio based upon these goals could include:

- Samples of questions prepared to interview the city's mayor pertaining to the future plans for the river and the final text of the interview along with the student's comments
- A script written for an historical drama about the establishment of Fort Harrison along with bibliographies of resources used
- Drawings and paintings done at the river
- A musical presentation using dulcimers and other early instruments
- Original folktales written by the students, including draft copies
- A full dress portrayal of Mark Twain along with written material compiled by the student

- A video tape documentary pertaining to environmental concerns with the pesticides being used in the watershed
- Constructions of model bridges, boats, or barges along with the plans for the constructions and the procedures
- Maps and charts made of the Native Americans of the area.

As we presented, displayed, explained and shared our learnings with the parents and interested persons in the community, we felt that they did indeed receive us as learners. The teachers expressed the need to continue to work with this kind of data as an alternative to the traditional methods of testing at the end of a unit.

Parent Profiles

As David Dillon (1990) states, "It's also sad seeing educators taking on all the burden of evaluation themselves . . . when they could be sharing that responsibility with learners and their parents." In our district when children enter kindergarten, we have parents complete background cards. We had always checked addresses, phone numbers, guardianship, health information, siblings, and so on, but had not until recently, asked anything that pertained to early literacy development. Figure 10.5 shows our start at seeking parent input and partnership from the beginning of the child's school career.

In addition to this, as we experiment with developing portfolios, we developed a response sheet for the parent (Figure 10.6).

As Dillon points out, he believes that if parents were involved in understanding that viable evidences of literacy learning can be documented, they would perhaps serve as allies with us to influence policy makers as we search for better assessment and evaluation procedures.

What to Record

In our medicalized education system (Taylor, 1990), the typical procedure is to test or check for specific isolated skills and then prescribe the cure. We traditionally examine the learners for what they can't do rather than what they can do. The basic assumption underlying this model is that language learning consists of a series of skills acquired in a linear fashion; therefore, teachers should look for missing parts, supply those, and it will result in reading. But with our shift in philosophy from a fragmented view of language learning to an integrated whole, what to record from our observations of learners becomes a central issue. Like Cambourne and Turbill (1990), we found that what to record became a "value-laden enterprise." What the teachers recorded in their anecdotal records

Figure 10.5

Parent Profile For _____
                              Student Name

Date_____

Welcome to our school. Since parents are the first and best teachers the child has, we can learn much from you. Please help us help your child.

Does your child seem interested in school?   ☐ Yes ☐ No

Does your child retell stories you have read to him/her?   ☐ Yes ☐ No

Does your child show a desire to use written language?   ☐ Yes ☐ No

Does your child pretend to write or copy or trace print?   ☐ Yes ☐ No

Does your child enjoy music and art?   ☐ Yes ☐ No

Would you say your child is willing to try new things?   ☐ Yes ☐ No

Does your child respond to environmental print such as signs, labels, etc?   ☐ Yes ☐ No

Do you have a set time for reading to your child?   ☐ Yes ☐ No
If so, when and about how much time? _____

Comments:

Figure 10.6

Parent Response to_____ Portfolio
                              Student Name
Date_____

List of goals set by student for this period	Parent Comment
1. Correct spelling of high frequency words on a consistent basis.	*What do you notice about your child's developing control over spelling of high frequency writing vocabulary?*
2. Use more action packed verbs in written pieces.	*Please comment on Joey's use of verbs.*
3. Math......	
4. Social Studies	

and conference logs was influenced by what they knew and understood about language learning and it changed from one marking period to the next as the teachers built different understandings of learning. This continual change, at first, was uncomfortable. Pat Bringman wrote in her journal that, "just when I think I have a system for marking the students or a routine established, one of the students will do or say something that causes me to change all over again. But when I think about this, language learning is not systematic or routine and neither should teaching be systematic or routine."

Taylor (1990) states that observational teaching and instructional assessment cannot be packaged, for this is problem-solving teaching. Sometimes when observation forms and checklists are devised an overly simplistic view of the complexities of language arises. Each teacher must find his or her own ways to portray his or her students' evidences of developing literacy. Checklists do not yield helpful information unless designed to meet the needs of specific students.

However, Cambourne and Turbill (1990) suggest that there are certain "markers" of natural growth and development that parents use intuitively to determine the progress of their children. Likewise, teachers, through years of experience working with young children, develop signposts of literacy development. Thinking back once again to the first grade teacher's questions, "How will I ever show that my kids have learned?" we asked the whole group to go through their notes and records on the children and find out what they had intuitively recorded as being important indicators of literacy development. Although specific examples and emphasis changed over the grade levels, the following broad categories seemed to be recognized as important:

1. Developing control over the conventions, skills and mechanics of language
2. Comprehension and understanding of both printed and oral language
3. Using language for a variety of purposes and audiences
4. Social behaviors and thinking skills
5. Attitudes and interests
6. Amount of time engaged in reading, writing, speaking, and listening.

Next we turned that question back to the students, "How do I as a teacher know that you are learning? How can I be sure you've learned? What things would show others that you are getting better at using language?" The first idea students presented to us was "teachers could look at the things we do or make." Kindergarten and first grade students often suggested their drawings, their paintings, and their constructions, whereas older students referred to their writings, their theme study projects, their readings. We found that all students expressed the need to be actively involved in learning.

Secondly, the students suggested that we listen to what they say or talk about. "You can tell how much we know about reading when we talk about our books."

A sixth grader stared incredulously at his teacher when she posed the question, "How can I know that you have learned something?" Finally he replied, "I didn't know teachers really cared about what we knew. I just thought we were supposed to do the assignments, memorize some stuff, and pass the test! If you really want to know what we've learned and what we know, then you have to let us talk some of the time."

The third suggestion of the students was to pay attention to how their thinking changed, before and after. For example, fifth grader Aaron said, "I used to think all Indian artifacts, tools, utensils, clothing, weapons, and so on were pretty much the same until I started to work with my friend Jeff. He's an Indian expert, you know. Jeff told me some things and got me interested in some books, then we went to the library and got some more. Now I know that each Indian tribe was alike in some ways and different in other ways." Once again the idea that we must trust the children to learn was pointed out to us.

As we discussed the categories we had generated and what the students had said, it became clear that students must set many of their own purposes for reading, writing, and learning. One of the teachers recently had enrolled in a computer class at the local vocational technical school. Her purpose was to learn to operate the new equipment at her school and to be able to apply these skills in her classroom. However, the instructor's course agenda intended for the students to become experts in computer terminology, understand some programming, etc. She remarked to the group after her first test, "He tested me on the things I didn't know and never let me show him all the things I did know. I guess that must be the way our students feel when we don't include them in planning how they can demonstrate their learning."

What we record then must be based on the aims and objectives of the teacher and of the students. Although, according to Cambourne (1988), "there is no definitive, conclusive set of standards or levels which can be applied universally to each grade level or age group," data that permits one to draw conclusions about the learner's attitude and the learner's developing control of language must be recorded.

What follows here are some examples of what the teachers utilized. These lists and examples (Figures 10.7 and 10.8) were intended to sharpen the teachers' observational and listening skills rather than serve as the kind of checklist tool we used to use to determine whether the child measured up or not.

The information on our observation forms is in no way to be considered universal or the most important behaviors to be noted. It is merely representative of the complexities of language learning. The forms and lists will change as we become more informed about how children acquire and use language. Teachers should look for global behaviors and overall pattern in the move toward literacy.

Figure 10.7

Early to Beginning Stages

	1st	2nd	3rd	4th
Name _____ Dates				

Indicators of Developing Control and Comprehension

Code: M = Most of the time   S = Sometimes   N = Not yet

Talking and Listening   Code   Comments

Talking and Listening					Comments
– Communicates with others about own activities					
– Explains ideas clearly					
– Uses expanded vocabulary related to classroom activities					
– Communicates in a group setting					
– Repeats nursery rhymes, chants, poems, etc.					
– Responds to and talks about stories					
– Sings songs					
– Dictates stories, personal messages					
– Listens attentively to class activity					
– Listens and responds in community talk					
– Talks about reading and writing					

Reading

– Displays interest in books					
– Chooses to spend time with books					
– Asks for rereading of favorite stories					
– Anticipates and joins in on repetitive phrases					
– Displays sense of story					
– Understands environmental print					
– Possesses knowledge about letters					
– Pretend or memory reads					
– Recognizes some words					
– Focuses on deriving meaning from text					

Writing

Writing					
– Displays interest in print					
– Pretend writes and attaches meaning					
– Spends time writing					
– Attaches print to art work and other work					

Figure 10.7 Continued

Writing (con't)		Code			Comments
– Understands a variety of purposes and kinds of writing					
– Uses inventive spelling					
• random letters					
• some representative letters					
• phonetic spelling					
• correct spelling of high frequency words					
– Writes on own for personal communication					
– Patterns writing after literary structures					

Indicators of attitudes and social behaviors

– Is willing to be challenged					
– Is productive and involved during work periods					
– Expresses enjoyment as a result of hard work and achievement					
– Cooperates with others					
– Contributes to group work					
– Displays sensitivity and respect for others					
– Learns from watching others					

Indicators of thinking skills

– Articulates ideas clearly					
– Generates solutions and ideas to solve problems					
– Considers suitable resources					
– Differentiates between relevant and non-relevant information					
– Considers other points of view					
– Spends time reading, writing, constructing, researching, reflecting, etc.					
– Talks about information discovered					
– Explains, shows or helps others to understand learning					
– Asks worthwhile questions					
– Plans, organizes and carries through on tasks					
– Understands not all problems have simple solutions					

Figure 10.8

Developing to Independent Stages

	1st	2nd	3rd	4th
Name _____ _____ Dates				

Indicators of Developing Control and Comprehension

Code: M = Most of the time   S = Sometimes   N = Not yet

Talking and Listening	Code				Comments
– Expects what is heard to make sense					
– Monitors understanding of spoken language by asking questions, seeking clarification, etc.					
– Uses a variety of speaking patterns to adjust to audience					
– Speaks confidently before a group and within the community					
– Communicates clearly and effectively					

Reading					
– Selects reading material with confidence					
– Reads for literary experience					
– Reads to be informed					
– Reads to perform a task					
– Constructs meaning, develops interpretation and makes judgements					
– Compares and contrasts, makes application					
– Understands story features - irony, humor, organization, point of view					
– Uses a variety of strategies - prediction, rate, background, information, etc.					
– Rereads for different purposes					
– Displays an expanding vocabulary					

Writing					
– Initiates writing for specific and personal purposes					
– Incorporates models from literature					
– Participates in writing conferences by asking questions and giving comments					
– Is aware of voice, sense of audience, sense of purpose					

Figure 10.8   Continued

Writing (con't)	Code				Comments
– Displays control over mechanics					
• punctuation					
• grammatical constructions					
• spells high frequency words correctly					
– Pieces are well developed and organized					
• style					
• characters					
• setting					
• detail					
• logical progression of events					
– Informative pieces are well developed					
– Displays research skills					
– Edits and proofreads					
– Talks confidently about writing					

Indicators of attitudes and social behaviors

– Is willing to be challenged					
– Is productive and involved during work periods					
– Expresses enjoyment as a result of hard work and achievement					
– Cooperates with others					
– Contributes to group work					
– Displays sensitivity and respect for others					
– Learns from watching others					

Indicators of thinking skills

– Articulates ideas clearly					
– Generates solutions and ideas to solve problems					
– Considers suitable resources					
– Differentiates between relevant and non-relevant information					
– Considers other points of view					
– Spends time reading, writing, constructing, researching, reflecting, etc.					
– Talks about information discovered					
– Explains, shows or helps others to understand learning					
– Asks worthwhile questions					
– Plans, organizes and carries through on tasks					
– Understands not all problems have simple solutions					

The work of Don Holdaway (1980) contains important print-related learnings that could serve as a base to develop your own lists. In addition, the work of Anne Forester and Margaret Reinhard (1989) is most helpful with young students. Another recommended resource would be *The Primary Language Record* (1988), published by Centre for Language in Primary Education, London, and available in the United States through Heinemann Educational Books. Since miscue analysis and running records were discussed earlier in this book, they were not included here, although the teachers in our district do make use of these techniques.

Epilogue

Our story is far from finished; it is only beginning. Just as evaluation, assessment, and record keeping are ongoing, ever changing aspects of learning, so too, is the story of teaching. I would like to thank the teachers in our district who serve on the language arts committee and those in the river grant project for allowing me to tell some of their stories. But most of all, I am grateful to them and their students for teaching me so much about the essentials love, justice, trust, compassion, and courage. They have forged ahead with courage; they have trusted the students to learn; compassion and love abound in their rooms; and justice to children and their accomplishments can only be achieved through the constant pursuit of providing credible and viable ways to document student progress. I am convinced that through these techniques discussed here and those yet to be discovered, we will, in actuality, become more accountable to ourselves, our children, and the public we serve.

References

Atwell, N. (1987). *In the middle: Writing, reading, and learning with adolescents.* Portsmouth, NH: Boynton/Cook, Heinemann.

Cambourne, B. (1988). *The whole story: Natural learning and the acquisition of literacy in the classroom.* Auckland, NZ: Ashton Scholastic.

Cambourne, B. & Turbill, J. (1990). Assessment in whole language classrooms: Theory into practice. *The Elementary School Journal, 90,* (3), 337–49.

Dillon, D. (1990, March). Editorial for *Language Arts, 67,* (3), 237–39.

Forester, A. & Reinhard, M. (1989). *The learner's way.* Winnipeg: Peguis Publishers.

Goodman, Y. (1989). Evaluation of students. In K. Goodman, Y. Goodman, & J.W. Hood (Eds.), *The whole language evaluation book.* Portsmouth, NH: Heinemann.

Graves, D. (1982). *Writing: Teachers and children at work.* Portsmouth, NH: Heinemann.

Hansen, J. (1987). *When writers read*. Portsmouth, NH: Heinemann.

Harste, J., Short, K.B., & Burke, C. (1988). *Creating classrooms for authors*. Portsmouth, NH: Heinemann.

Holdaway, D. (1980). *Independence in reading*. Toronto: Ashton Scholastic.

Taylor, D. (1990). Teaching without testing: Assessing the complexity of children's literacy learning. *English Education*, February, 4–74.

Chapter 11

A Principal's View on Reporting Progress to Students, Parents, and Administrators

Ron Hutchison

In our effort to keep new ideas alive and improve upon today's learning/ teaching strategies in our classrooms, we must always ask ourselves.

How can I improve on today's lesson? What did I do today that can be improved upon tomorrow? How can I provide pertinent feedback to each student? What does this newly gained information mean to me in terms of the growth and development for each child?

Then the question arises, "How can I report the growth and development in a manner that is meaningful and reflects the whole child?" These are questions that have haunted teachers and administrators for years and have caused countless hours of sleeplessness. It is with this attitude that we keep development and innovation alive in our classrooms and schools. This sort of reflection is the impetus for change, but the process of change is lengthy, frustrating, and not without criticism. When we entertain the thought of change in education, we also must think about the cultural, social, and political histories of our education system. It is our personal backgrounds and experiences that serve as a base for the many varying opinions about what should and should not be taught in our classrooms. As we embark on the change of a system that is steeped in tradition, controversy, success, and failures, one thing soon becomes very obvious if we are to success-fully change the opinions and ideas of our students, parents, and administrators. It won't be an easy transition from our traditional methods to a new way of thinking about the learning/teaching/evaluation process.

Teachers all across the United States and around the world are challenged by questions that require them to examine their instructional practices, evaluation techniques, and the means of recording and reporting student progress. Some of the questions facing whole language teachers today are,

> How do you report student progress? How do whole language students measure up? How will whole language students perfom on standardized tests? Why are we using reporting systems that do not reflect current research and methodology? How can we have a more clear understanding of what growth or progress the students are making in our classrooms? How do we clearly communicate our understandings to our students, parents, and administrators?

Before we can address these questions to various levels of satisfaction, we must first focus, for a minute, on the purposes of reporting student progress and the various audiences that receive the information. The first objective is to communi-cate to the diverse groups the "how" and "what" each student has learned during a specified period of time. Several other objectives are of no less importance:

- To improve teaching strategies and evaluate various materials used in the process of teaching
- To assess the goals of our curriculum
- To evaluate what we know about the developmental process of learning.

These objectives are often obscured by the belief that we are in the business of fixing the student rather than fixing the curriculum. The assessment/evaluation process should always provide students with valuable feedback and insight about their own personal learning and progress, just as reflective teachers do when they ask themselves, "How can I improve on today's lesson?" Then we start adjusting the curriculum to meet the child's needs rather than adjusting the child. This is only true to the point of a school system being founded on the philosophy of recognizing all children as unique individuals arriving with varied backgrounds, experiences, attitudes, and abilities. These beliefs make it very clear that no single system of letter grades, number scores, or percentiles will be able to convey to students, parents, teachers, and administrators all the necessary information about an individual's personal growth.

When we focus on the task of creating meaningful reporting systems about student progress, we must first work together for the elimination of competitive-ness between states, school districts, classrooms, and students. We must always remember that the primary purpose of gathering information is to better understand the whole child and to create appropriate teaching/learning strategies that meet the child's needs, interests, and abilities. A secondary purpose is to inform the creation of philosophies, programs, budgets, and policy that will support the children in our classrooms. However, we often forget that the objective of education is to foster in each child the innate desire to learn and create. This is not an easy task for a society and school system whose purpose for two centuries has been to produce industrious, obedient students and citizens that will contribute to keeping our nation strong and fostering an attitude of getting ahead and staying ahead.

Reporting Progress to Students

We seek feedback about ourselves constantly whether in the form of a critique in front of a mirror, a glance at the scales, or asking a colleague what they thought of a particular lesson. Throughout each day, principals and teachers are constantly reflecting on their previous experiences and making decisions based on the knowledge and information gained from those past experiences. This is a process of self-evaluation. Students need to be active participants in the evaluation process as well. Self-evaluation provides the teacher with valuable insight about how students perceive their abilities and growth. During the process, students gain the ability to think critically, reason, and express themselves in relation to what they have learned and how they feel.

We ask students the following questions:

- What have you learned in . . .?
- What would you like to learn next?
- What materials, resources and/or books do you need?
- What help would you like me to provide?

In so doing we provide students the opportunity to reflect on and evaluate their progress. When we invite students to participate in the evaluation process and be involved in making decisions about their learning, they become students with high self-esteem and self-motivation.

Throughout the teacher/student dialogue, teachers need to provide students with specific feedback about what they have successfully accomplished rather than their failures. This greatly enhances the child's self-esteem and fosters a trusting relationship. Later in this chapter, we will take a closer look at the impact many current reporting systems have on the self-esteem of students.

I believe that when a student's insight is solicited and valued by the teacher then learning and evaluation become natural life long processes. Isn't that our goal as educators? Various means for organizing and collecting meaningful insight about how students perceive themselves in the learning process already exist. They range from inventories to asking open-ended questions during student-teacher conferences. Teachers that have used questionnaires, self-rating scales, and journals to gain information from students are constantly revising their strategies. This revision process reflects the teacher's growth as he or she gains more insight into self-evaluation. Shirley Grenshaw has used a weekly evaluation form, shown in figure 11.1, that was developed by the students in her reading classes. (Watson, 1987)

Figure 11.1

Self-Evaluation

Grade

Name_____

Sustained Silent Reading   _____

_____

_____

Writing Activities   _____

_____

_____

Content-Area Reading   _____

_____

_____

Special Assignments   _____

_____

Work Attempted   _____

_____

Work Completed   _____

_____

_____

This week I learned:

_____

_____

_____

Whatever the means used for self-evaluation, the process of communication between students and teachers is most important. Teachers use this information to better plan projects, experiments, and other related learning experiences with children. When students are actively involved they perceive themselves as capable learners and valuable contributors to the community of learners in their classroom.

A kindergarten teacher that I know acquired three-ring notebooks for each of her students. Each child's notebook was to hold samples of student work, notes from the teacher, art work collected periodically, and other samples collected throughout the school year. The notebooks were kept on a shelf within reach of the students so they could place a valuable paper into the notebook when ever they chose or when directed by the teacher. During free reading, the teacher observed several students electing to look at and share their notebooks with other students in the class. The teacher then overheard students talking about how their writing had improved compared to the beginning of the year. These kindergarten students freely choose to read, evaluate, and comment to others about their progress since the start of the school year! The teacher and I knew the classroom had become a place where students were truly the center of the curriculum, where each student viewed him or her self as a capable person succeeding in school. The teacher had no established or preset criteria or number for items to include in each child's notebook. She judged what pieces of work provided the best evidence or benchmarks in an individual child's growth over a period of time. Each item was dated and often included the teacher's notes about the child's current progress. The interaction and reflection (evaluation) that took place between these kindergarten students is not possible if students are standing at the teacher's desk peering into the teacher's grade book or waiting for a report card to come home. When self-evaluation is part of the evaluation/reporting system of a classroom, it boosts student self-esteem because students are not always being judged by an outside set of standards

Julie Craig uses student feedback and self-evaluation in her first grade class to determine how students perceive themselves in the learning process. The students are asked to write or comment about their writing. Some of the comments to "How has your writing improved?" were:

- I am staying on the lines and I am writing smaller, too.
- Smaller spaces, spelling better, making better y's and p's.
- Smaller letters than before, I don't have to erase as much. I don't have to double my letters. I put caps instead of smalls. I'm dotting my i's.
- When we started dictation my writing was gross, but now my writing is a little better because I leave spaces and stay on the lines.
- My writing is neater.

These comments from students provide us with valuable information about how and what they observe in their own writing.

When the teacher and her classroom aide sit down at the end of the school year to interview each child, more valuable information was gained about how he or she perceived their learning in the areas of writing, reading, and math. The teacher also thought this would be a good opportunity to ask about friends and what they thought about school. Her only regret was that she didn't have this type of interview at the beginning and during the school year. I think you will agree the following anecdotes provide us with more insight than a number or letter grade, especially when you add this information to other pieces of data collected throughout the school year.

ALEXIS: Self-Evaluation, June 7, 1989

Writing: Writing just came to me. I used to write real sloppy, with no straight lines, and no spaces between my words. Now I do it a lot nicer. I get my ideas to write about from things that really happen to me. Other times I just like to make things up in my head. It's kind of like dreaming things, and then putting them down on paper in a story.

Reading: I couldn't read any of the books in Mrs. Craig's class when I came to school. I could read a few at home that my Mom would read to me. I guess I really learned with my Mom, so it was fun when Mrs. Craig did it the same way. She would read to us and we would read to her.

Math: I could count by fives, but not by tens when I first came. I really wanted to count by tens, and now I can.

Friends: I make more friends now. I felt shy before but after awhile I got used to new people. Sometimes that's hard. Learning things in the first grade has helped me make new friends.

School: I will like going to second grade. I want to learn how to write in cursive, and how to put periods in my writing.

I would like to draw words more than draw pictures. Drawing is fun, but I like drawing words a lot more.

I like to make up stories. When I do that, it makes me feel special.

I would like to tell Mrs. Craig that I always felt that I could ask her anything, and she would tell me about it. That made me feel good about learning. If I needed help, she would always tell me what I wanted to know.

BREEZY: Self-Evaluation, June, 1989

Writing: I learned how to write here. I didn't even know about it at all until I got in first grade. Writing in my journal helps me. I can put my thoughts down for other people to read. Then they will know me.

Reading: I learned in Kindergarten. Reading books here, Krissy really helped me a lot. We did a play "The Bears Picnic," and I could just read. Krissy told me I could, and she was right.

Math: I learned my math in the first grade. I do subtraction better now than at my other school. My art work helps me with my math. I don't know how, it just does.

Friends: When I came here, everyone else had been here so they all knew each other. I felt real shy. Now I play with them because they are my friends, and I know it. I'm a good friend to them, and play on the swings, and slide with them.

School: I like school, Yeah! In second grade I want to learn to write cursive. I can write my name in it now, and I think it looks real pretty. I feel good about what I've done in the first grade, and feel pretty special sometimes. Mostly when I write. When I write, I can say things that I might be too shy just to say right out, so I think writing is real important.

JAMIE: Self-Evaluation, June, 1989

Writing: I knew a little how to write from home. My big brother writes a lot and I would watch him. I paid good attention. Reading books helps me write, and gives me ideas. It makes me remember how to spell words when I write them down. I can remember how to spell something if I read it in a book. Writing in my journal has helped too.

Reading: I learned how to read here in first grade. I had a friend who used to read to me, and I could read some words from books that she read me. I like to read a lot, and if you like to do something, you just can. I read big books at home a lot. We have a lot of books at home. I've read about 15 big books. My brother helps me when I don't know a word or two.

Math: I'm good at math. I learned most of my math here in first grade with Mrs. Craig. She helps me when she explains things and writes them on the board. Usually if I can see something written down I can understand better than if someone just tries to tell me how to do something. My brain likes to read.

Friends: School was big when I first came here, but now not so big. Actually I guess the school is the same size, but I'm seeing it different than before. I try to be nice to people, and talk to them if we're having a problem with each other. I like to help people when they need help. I think I make a good friend.

School: I like going to school here. Sometimes in the morning, I just wake up and think, "Today I get to go to school," and it makes me feel happy, and I want to get up and get going. Next year in second grade, I want to learn how to write punctuation and how to make sentences happen like they do in books. I feel good about what I've done in first grade.

Mike Jenson had this to say about his reading.

I can read now, too. I couldn't before. I read with Mom, and she helps a lot. I read to her, and she reads to me. I really like to read. Writing helps me read too. And when you read you can write better. It just happens. One day you can't read a book, but maybe the next day you can. You just have to keep trying.

Writing helps you read and reading helps you write and you just have to keep trying. The whole process is summed up by a first grader!

In Jessica Groffy's reflection about the school year, she said this about sharing things:

Sometimes some things are just too special to share. I might draw a picture, but I won't want to show it to anyone until just the right time. When I write things or read sometimes I just don't want to share it with anyone, it's just too special.

Evaluation is an integral part of the teaching/learning process and should not be confused with grading. Parents and students need to know specific strengths and weaknesses. Grades, percentiles, smiley faces, scores, stickers, and remarks of "good job" or "excellent" do not tell students or parents how a child is performing. People, and students are people, need to have specific feedback about what and how the teacher perceives them doing in the learning process. Using specific feedback provides the child with a true affirmation by focusing attention on their capabilities. "I really like the way you described the setting in the opening paragraph." This kind of feedback provides the student with a clear understanding of what you like and assists in establishing a trusting relationship between the teacher and student. When teachers receive feedback from their principals about an observed lesson or their teaching performance over the course of a school year, they would be insulted if they received a grade, smiley face, or just the word "excellent" written in the corner of their evaluation along with a notice for a contract renewal. You would probably wonder what your supervisor really thought about your growth or performance during the school year. I believe students are no different in seeking feedback about their performance. We perform best and feel best when we know specifically how someone views our performance and progress. The suggestion here is that it's not positive feedback that improves a student's self-concept, but specific reinforcement about what you observed about a student's successful performance and your suggestions for improvement that enhance a student's self-concept. Let's also not forget to involve students by listening to their ideas and perceptions about their performance, as in the interviews in Julie Craig's first grade class.

Reporting Progress to Parents

As mentioned in reporting progress to students, self-esteem is of the utmost concern when we inform parents how their child has or has not grown during a specific period of time. Let's examine self-esteem and what the reporting systems have done to foster poor self-esteem in our students. The Natonal Association of Elementary School Principals in 1989 published a two page article entitled, "Report to Parents: Reducing Report Card Stress." The opening paragraph stated:

> For many children, report cards are terrifying documents. Here is a child's total effort and achievement of a single marking period, all summed up by a row of letters and a brief comment by one or another teacher. On top of that, it has to be carefully read, understood, and signed by parents.

The article went on to provide tips in helping your child experience as little report card stress as possible.

- Talk about your child's progress throughout the year.
- Put report cards in perspective.
- Avoid blame, punishment, and harmful labels.
- Find out the real reason for any low grade.
- Be constructive.
- Don't take your child's achievement for granted.
- Make allowances for setbacks.
- Accentuate the positive.

What is the purpose of report cards when the NAESP feels the need to write a "Report to Parents" on how to reduce the stress that accompanies report cards? If the intent of the report card is to convey to parents individual progress in various areas of learning during the school year, they we need to refocus on what the child has accomplished rather than on what has not been accomplished. The reporting system should also provide teachers and parents insights about an individual child's style, abilities, and interests.

Several school districts are examining the purposes and styles of their report cards. One such school district in their pursuit to communicate to parents established such as system that was met with mixed reviews by parents. The philosophy statement in Figure 11.2 recognizes that effective communication between school and parents about their child's progress is essential in creating successful home-school partnerships and that the report card is only one means of communicating individual progress and growth.

The school district's philosophy statement also recognized five beliefs.

- Each child is unique and arrives at school with varied backgrounds, experiences, and abilities.
- Each child learns best in a supportive, child-centered environment.
- Each child needs to experience success in his or her own learning and growth.

- Each child learns best when she or he is an active participant in the learning process.
- Each child progresses through the developmental stages at his or her own rate.

Figure 11.2

REPORT CARD PHILOSOPHY STATEMENT

Grades 1–5

Effective communication with parents regarding their child's progress in school is essential in fostering successful home-school partnerships.

The report card is one means of reporting individual student progress and growth. In additon, the District promotes the use of conferences, notes, phone calls, newsletters, and so forth to further strengthen home-school communication. Each method of communication needs to be clear and concise to avoid possible misunderstandings and confusion.

Communications which focus on what the child can do, rather than what he or she cannot do, will enhance student self-esteem. Our report card reflects our philosophy of teaching the whole child to prepare him or her to function in a rapidly changing world. It is self confidence and the ability to locate, process, and make effective use of information that will enable our students to be productive members of the society they will live in.

(Lincoln County School District, Oregon, 1988, p. 1)

It is upon this base that we will build successful learners. As I had mentioned, the more narrative report card in Figure 11.3 met with mixed reviews from parents because many felt that students would be less motivated to learn if they did not receive a letter grade. But, rather than shelve the more holistic effort to communicate with parents, the school district provided parents with the option to choose letter grades or a more narrative progress report on the card.

The development of this report card took a full year of meetings, discussions, and input from teachers throughout the school district. The various elementary schools and their parents were all at different stages of understanding about the whole language process, which created frustration and caused rejection of the report card. The parent unrest just reaffirms for me that we have a long way to go in redirecting the manner and purpose in which we communicate student progress and growth to parents.

In contrast, the Cajon Valley Union School District, El Cajon, California, a whole language team successfully developed the Whole Language Progress Report in Figure 11.4 to replace their more skills-based report card. This was

Figure 11.3

LINCOLN COUNTY SCHOOL DISTRICT

L|C
S|D

Student Name_____ Grade_____ Year_____

School Name _____ Teacher _____

GRADES 1-5 REPORT FORM "A"

ATTENDANCE	1	2	3	4	TOTAL
Days Present					
Days Absent					
Days Tardy					

If the "IEP" following the section title is circled, that section reflects the student's progress on an Individualized Educational Plan.

MARKING CODE	
S	Steady Growth
I	Improvement Needed
X	Doesn't apply at this time

SOCIAL DEVELOPMENT	EP	Quarter 1	2	3	4
Follows rules and routines					
Accepts responsibility for own behavior					
Works cooperatively with others					
Responds favorably to correction or guidance					
Respects rights, feelings and property of others					

READING DEVELOPMENT (✓ Check One) — IEP

Beginning to acquire expected skills				
Developing the expected skills				
Independently performs expected skills				

READING SKILLS — IEP

Reads fluently				
Reads with understanding				

SPELLING DEVELOPMENT (✓ Check One) — IEP

Beginning to acquire expected skills				
Developing the expected skills				
Independently performs expected skills				

WRITING — IEP

Expresses ideas				
Revises for ideas and organization				
Edits grammar and usage				
Spelling				

HANDWRITING — IEP

Writes legibly				

SPEAKING — IEP

Expresses ideas clearly				
Contributes to discussions				

REFERENCE SKILLS

Selects appropriate resources				
Makes appropriate use of reference materials				

TEACHER COMMENTS:

WORK STUDY SKILLS	EP	Quarter 1	2	3	4
Is prepared for class					
Uses time efficiently					
Works for quality					
Seeks help when needed					
Listens in a group					
Effort					

MATHEMATICS (Expected Skills & Concepts) — IEP

Place value, number and numeration				
Geometry				
Measurement				
Graphing, statistics, probability				
Problem-solving				
Patterns, relationships				
Explains math processes				
Computation + − × ÷				

HEALTH

SCIENCE

SOCIAL STUDIES

PHYSICAL EDUCATION — IEP

ART

MUSIC

GRADES 1-2 REPORT FORM "B"

Grade_____ Year_____

MARKING CODE	
O	Outstanding Progress
S	Steady Growth
I	Improvement Needed
X	Doesn't apply at this time

GRADES 3-5 REPORT FORM "C"

Grade_____ Year_____

MARKING CODE	
A	Outstanding
B	Above Average
C	Average
D	Below Average
F	Unsatisfactory
X	Doesn't apply at this time

Figure 11.4

Whole Language Profile for Primary Listening, Speaking, and Reading	Whole Language Profile for Primary Listening, Speaking, and Writing
Conventions of Print	**Fluency**
1. Handles Book for Reading	1. Attitude
A. Left to right	2. Quantity
B. Top to bottom	**Writing as A Process**
C. Return sweep	1. Uses pre-writing strategies
D. One to one correspondence (finger/word)	(illustrating, brainstorming, observing, tapping personal
E. Separates print from picture	experiences, clustering, mapping, diagraming (Venn),
2. Pretend reads	listing, discussing)
3. Uses title page	2. Completes Draft(s)
4. Uses table of contents	A. Writes from personal experience
5. Uses index	B. Uses elements from literature
6. Uses glossary	C. Uses knowledge from across the curriculum
Print Knowledge	**Print Awareness**
1. Identifies & matches upper & lower case letters	1. Left to right
2. Frames or reads words, sentences, and/or paragraphs	2. Top to bottom
3. Points to & defines usage of capital letters (beg. sentences, proper nouns)	3. Spaces between words
4. Points to & defines usage of period, question mark, exclamation, quotation	**Language Level**
Story Knowledge/Comprehension	1. Matches word strip to own story
1. Orally predicts repetitive language patterns during shared reading	2. Copies own story under model
2. Makes specific predictions about storyline during reading	3. Fills in key word, missing letters on words in own story
3. Shows observable personal reaction to humor and other emotions	4. Uses Magic Writing (scribble writing)
4. Describes characters in own words using own impressions	5. Uses inventive spelling
5. Orally retells story in sequence	A. Consonants only
6. States main idea of story	B. Vowels and consonants
7. Interprets story using own experience	6. Uses standard spelling
8. Evaluates story using personal observations/reactions/experiences	7. Attempts writing sentences independently
9. Evaluates story by referring to text	8. Writes with meaning (complete thoughts)
10. Responds to story orally, pictorially, in writing, dramatically & through other performances (movement, rhythm, dance, clapping)	
11. Actively participates orally in story innovations	
12. Reads with expression (voice quality, intonation, matching voice to word meaning)	
13. Voluntarily reads for enjoyment	
Integration of Reading Cue Systems	
1. Uses picture cues to interpret text	
2. Reads for meaning using semantic cues	
3. Uses knowledge of language structure to interpret text (syntactic cues)	
4. Uses sound/symbol relationship to interpret text (graphophonic cues)	
5. Uses all cue systems to self-correct reading miscues	

the result of a long process of professional development and working together in the creation of a whole language school. (Richman, 1990)

Why is it that we openly recognize the individual differences in the learning abilities of our students, but continue to judge individual achievement, growth, and progress with a system that compares the student with the advancement of others at grade level? At the 1986 Oregon Reading Association Conference, Pat Kippman said, "God didn't create kids at grade level." So, why are we continuing to use grade levels to convey to parents and students where their child ranks? We continue the grading practice regardless of the fact that performance and readiness in any elementary classroom will have a range of more than plus or minus two years. I think we all agree that children's success is fundamental to achievement and their reaching their fullest potential. In whole language classrooms, we provide students the reading, writing, and learning activities they can do successfully. The dilemma that many teachers face is how to report the child's successes and achievements in a meaningful manner. In many schools, teachers are required to keep grade books and some school districts even keep grade books in the school's archives for years after the students leave. I would recommend that teachers supplement the district requirements by keeping the parent and student abreast of progress in a holistic fashion. This can be done in several ways mentioned throughout this book. When high grades become the students primary objective then the time objective of real learning is lost and the student becomes the real loser.

Most of the assessment/evaluation time in our classrooms is spent on test taking and marks on papers that provide the student very little feedback as to what he or she has learned during the teaching/learning process throughout the school year. Most often teachers or publishers have established the criteria that the student is trying to figure out to obtain a high score.

An exercise in one 5th grade classroom might shed a little light on what we have trained students to believe. The students were heterogeneously placed into three reading groups. The students were to read the same passage from a basal reader and then discuss the main idea of the passage within their particular groups. The students were to reach a conclusion in each of the groups about the main idea of the story. It probably doesn't come as any surprise that each group came up with a different main idea. After some discussion about the varying views and opinions, the students asked the teacher to tell them the correct answer from the teacher's guide. When the teacher explained to the students that each group supported their thoughts very well and each group was correct, the students left for home perplexed and frustrated. This experience shows that we have trained students to seek affirmation through correct answers and good grades. What are we going to do with the students that don't arrive at your door "on grade level?"

We continue to affirm to them that they are not as capable as others, with a high probability of ending up in a special class, or at risk of failing. The student's self-image is greatly enhanced by what we educators tell them through our grades, scores, ability groups, our responses, questions, and even our body language. In whole language classrooms, teachers are utilizing a broader range of assessment devices, techniques, and strategies than what the small slice of post-testing provides.

When we report progress to parents we also accept the responsibility to share with them the new views about reading, writing, problem solving, and learning. However, we have trained parents to expect the *status quo* in report cards and other progress reports, saying simply that the child is missing such and such assignments and is in danger of failing. Many school districts are now realizing that you cannot build effective school programs without a strong commitment from the parents. The active involvement and support of parents in our schools is essential. One of the major ways a school establishes support is by inviting parents to participate in the reading and writing process in the classroom. The principal and teachers had to maintain an open door policy and dialogue with parents about the changes in strategies. When you build trusting relationships with the parents, staff, and students you build a successful school. A relationship is not built by the principal staying in the office, but by being active in the classrooms and working with teachers and children. Our schools are people places and a principal has to be among the people to establish rapport and trust. If we are going to be effective in the change process, we must meet our responsibility to communicate with parents about the latest research in education and the new methods we are implementing in our classrooms. One way is to invite parents to attend an "Author's Tea" to celebrate their children as authors. The parents will start to see the connection between the writing-reading and reading-writing process. When I did this in my own school, many of the parents were surprised to see their children freely choosing to write and create stories. One student remarked to her mother that she now thought in stories. Parents were surprised to have their children request books for gifts rather than simply candy that would be gone in a few days, or toys that might be broken. When the students are in control of their learning, they truly become empowered. These learners will seek answers to problems and not wait for the correct answer from a teacher's guide.

All too often in a parent-teacher conference the report card or grade book or missing assignments become the focus of attention rather than the child. The focus should instead be on what the people involved in the conference know and understand about the child. Teachers must start using all means of communication available to them to share with parents the happenings in the classroom and individual progress: students' portfolios, profiles, newsletters, phone calls, parent-teacher conferences, fairs, projects, visitations, video and audio tapes, all mentioned in earlier chapters. Parents should become involved in classroom projects either at school in the classroom, or by taking home projects that will assist in the success of the classroom. If parents can't come to school and volunteer their time and talents in the classroom, they can be sent materials to make blank books for students or other home projects that will benefit the child and school. These kinds of activities can be coordinated by the school's parent organization, room parents, foster grandparents or the classroom teacher. Schools and classrooms don't operate in isolation just as students don't learn in isolation.

The systems the teacher uses for reporting progress to parents depends somewhat on what methods the teacher has worked out in the classroom for gathering pertinent information or data. Teachers throughout this country are adapting and adopting various means of data collection for better reporting to parents. One teacher has been using a small note pad and sticking her daily observations on a sheet to place in the child's running record of observations and interactions. The teacher usually conferences with six students each day about their reading and dates each of her observations before placing notes into the file. This creates a log on each child's progress over time. The log then assists the teacher in reporting to parents about growth made throughout the school year. If we expand such a reporting system across the curriculum we start to form a true image of the whole child in the learning process. Through this kind of evaluation process we understand more about each student and how they perceive themselves as learners. parents will have a better understanding of their child's specific strengths and weaknesses that, with guidance from the teacher, will assist parents in better working with their child at home.

The goal of the teacher is to create life long learners. In pursuit of this goal, the teacher is always in a mode of self-examination. This examination utilizes all the bits of collected information we have about a student, (teacher-student conferences, anecdotal records, profiles, student self-evaluation, portfolios, district and/or state required tests, collected works, projects, and so forth). As educators, we use all of this information as a road map to facilitate daily successful learning experiences for students.

Reporting Progress to Administrators

What informational data do administrators need about student progress in order to support the teaching/learning process? When we start to examine the role of standardized testing in our schools and classrooms and how the tests impact the learning process, I think we all agree that the greater the emphasis we put on raising test scores the greater the impact on the curriculum. This is not sound cause for conducting a testing program but a reality of life. When newspapers, school boards, administrators, and others compare schools and classes solely by standardized test scores, the more are teachers apt to respond to testing. As stated earlier, the test becomes the center of the curriculum, not the child.

Some schools even test kindergarten students prior to the first day of school for ability grouping. What kind of message does this practice give our students, teachers, and parents? Rather than focusing on the whole child and accepting learning as a process, the school is categorizing children and teaching to a preconceived ability level. I am fully aware of the many decisions teachers, administrators, and school boards must make to ensure children the right to a free and appropriate education. However, we must always be mindful that test scores represent only a small piece of the whole information picture that should be considered very carefully before qualified decisions are made. Whether that decision is for an individual education plan, school plan, district, state, or at the national level, the decision makers should take a holistic view. Different audiences obviously need to make different kinds of decisions. Therefore, this necessitates different kinds of information. Teachers must make daily instructional decisions based on the feedback of the child and the classroom. Principals will make decisions based on feedback from staff, students, communities, and supervisors, while still complying with local policy, state, and federal laws. I believe all of these decision making bodies can strike a commonality in the categories of types of information they must have recorded and reported in order to establish a comprehensive profile of a student, building, or school district. Terry Johnson's book on evaluation, *The Quad* (1988), provides an excellent format that could be applied at all levels of the school system.

- Observation of Process
  Information gathered from observation of a student, school, or district. This could be in the form of interviews, written observations, or other information gathered in the process.
- Observation of Product
  This is a review of gathered products of students, a school, or district. Collected works, logs, folders, and inventories all serve as products to provide evaluative information.
- Contextualized Measures
  Information gathered through informal assessment. Checklists, portfolios, surveys, and questionaires all serve to provide contextualized information.
- Decontextualized Measures
  This is information gathered by using standardized tests or other tests developed outside of the school.

All four areas of information should be represented and reported prior to decision making at the the various levels in a school system. This approach to reporting progress requires a change of our conception of the standardized testing issue and forces us to ask some very serious questions about trust, competition, and how to convey real learning to students, parents, teachers, and administrators. We need to spend more time, energy, and money to develop better means of evaluation and determine how the information gathered will be used. (Mayher & Brause, 1986) Two of ten administrators have become overly concerned about test scores. The change to a more holistic means of evaluation is going to be difficult for all those involved. We are venturing into some new territory and that means we are leaving the security of skill exercises, drills, and workbooks behind. Administrators, teachers, parents, and even the students will, at times (in the beginning), be anxious because it is going to mean looking at school and the teaching/learning process differently. Teachers and administrators must work together with common negotiated goals for the continued improvement of child-centered classrooms and schools. Students will have to work harder and become more responsible for their own learning. They will no longer have the security of the correct answer from the teacher's guide, but will be seeking answers to open ended questions and problem solving exercises in preparation for global problems they will encounter as adults.

Summary

As we embark on this process of change in our schools, teachers will be the key public relations specialists and educators of the public. As classrooms adapt a more integrated approach to learning, teachers will have to teach parents, school boards, administrators, and the media that there is a better way to achieve the goal of improved learning. Teachers must reflect the attitude of being researchers in their classroom. They must stay abreast of current educational happenings across the continent and around the world. They need to collect data in their classrooms that will validate the fact that students are making significant accomplishments in school. When this has been shared, teachers will start to regain to professional respect they so well deserve.

Time, energy, and money—we have too little of all three items but they are necessary to refocus our direction in standardized testing. The process currently underway is outcome-based, measuring outcome or mastered objective by a particular group of human beings around the school district, state, or even nation—and compared to one another. No other nation is like ours and our students are like none others that came before them. George Madaus said, "You've got live kids and live teachers with all kinds of different backgrounds interacting in social situations with a lot of variables over which the teacher and the kids have no control." (Brandt, 1989) When administrators emphasize test scores, the test becomes the curriculum, not the student. In America, we seem to be moving faster and faster in a world of ever increasing knowledge and information. We live in a high tech world of computers, fax machines, satellite communication, jet travel, and fast food. Getting the machine-scored test results back quickly has been a selling point for many companies. Where does the human being we call a student become involved? Too much emphasis has been placed on test results and not on the care, understanding, and attention we should give to our students. We need to invest in a better way to evaluate our students, classrooms, and schools. Our objective should be a change of attitude from the "best scores are the best schools" to an attitude of care and understanding for each human being in the classroom.

References

Brandt, R. (1989). On misuse of testing: A conversation with George Madaus, *Educational Leadership*, *46*, (7), 26–29.

Johnson, T. (1988). *Evaluation: A perspective for change.* Crystal Lake, IL: Rigby

Lincoln County School District (1988). Teachers guide to the report card. Newport, OR: Lincoln County School District.

Mayher, J. & Brause, R. (1986). Learning though teacher: Is testing crippling integrated language education?" *Language Arts*, *63*(4), 390–396.

National Association of Elementary School Principals (1989). Reducing Report Card Stress. *Report to Parents*. Alexandria, VA: NAEP.

Richman, C. (1990). Evaluating the whole language learner. *The California Reader*, *23*(4), 4–5.

Watson, D. (1987). Shared Evaluation—ideas and insights. *Language arts in the elementary school*, pp. 218–219.

Chapter 12

A Vision for the Future of Assessment in Whole Language Classrooms

Jerome C. Harste and William P. Bintz

Language Story #1: Who's Testing Who?

Lynn is an elementary school teacher in Detroit. The Detroit school system uses the old "Draw a Man" test as part of its entrance requirements to kindergarten. To make themselves look modern, Detroit has updated the test. It's now called the "Draw a Person" test.

Recently, Lynn was giving the new "Draw a Person" test to an entering kindergarten student. As per the directions, the little girl was told to draw a person and put in as many details as possible. Based on how "the subject" draws the person—whether it is a tadpole person with arms and legs coming out of the head or a more normal looking creature—the tester supposedly is able to determine the child's current state of emotional and cognitive development.

In this instance, the little girl picked up her pencil and rapidly sketched a head with arms and legs coming out of it. She then added another lump on each side of the head. "Ears," she said. Pausing a bit she added two dots for eyes, a loop for the nose and a half moon for the mouth, naming each as she added them. Scanning her composition, she added curlicues for hair and then paused, thinking what else she might do.

Assuming the stance of "The Thinker," she dramatically put one hand to her brow. With the eraser end of the pencil resting on the corner of her bottom lip, she though a while and then reflected, "Hmm, I'm not sure where the pancreas goes!"

***

Language Story #2: Who's Testing What?

Ferris is a first grader, and the daughter of one of the authors. One day after school, she rushed into the kitchen, zipped open her backpack, pulled out what appeared to be a hopelessly crinkled sheet of paper, placed it on the kitchen counter, and said to her father who was standing nearby, "Here, Daddy, you need to read this." "What is it, Ferris?" I asked. "I don't know, Daddy," she replied impatiently, "it's just something my teacher said you need to read."

After flattening out the sheet of paper several times with the palm of my hand, I finally was to decipher that it was a notice from her school principal informing parents that ISTEP, the Indiana Standardized Test of Educational Progress, would soon be administered to all first graders.

Over the next three weeks I began to notice that ISTEP was suddenly receiving increased attention in the community. General information about the test began to appear in the local newspaper, and specific information about taking the test, i.e., "making sure children get a good night's sleep, and a healthy breakfast," began to appear in the principal's weekly newsletter sent home to parents.

During the same period, I also started to notice changes in my daughter's behavior and attitude about going to school. These changes were unexpected, and contrasted sharply with her earlier positive attitudes about school. The following is a series of brief conversations between Ferris and me describing some of these changes.

7:30 AM—Three weeks before ISTEP. I am fixing breakfast, while Ferris is sitting at the kitchen table, still dressed in pajamas.

> *Bill:* "Ferris, you're still not dressed? C'mon, it's 7:30. You'll be late for school."
> *Ferris:* "Daddy, I don't want to go to school today."
> *Bill:* "Why not?"
> *Ferris:* "My teacher says something real important is coming up, and I'm afraid."
> *Bill:* "Afraid of what?"
> *Ferris:* "Uh, I don't know, Daddy, something about a test, and I'm afraid they are going to do something to me."
> *Bill:* "Ferris, they're not going to do anything to you. They are going to give you a test to see how you're doing in school. You remember that notice you brought home a few weeks ago? That's what that notice was all about."
> *Ferris:* "Daddy, I don't care. I still don't want to go to school today."
>
> *

7:00 PM—Two weeks before the test. One evening Ferris is sitting at the dining room table, preparing to do her "homework." In this instance, homework was a math worksheet requiring her to solve approximately 80 addition problems. After laying out a variety of pencils, papers, and erasers on the table, Ferris initiated the following conversation.

Ferris: "Daddy, can you come over here? You have to help me with my homework tonight."

Bill: (coming over to the table, and sitting next to her) "Okay, how can I help?"

Ferris: (holding up the worksheet, and pointing to the right hand top corner) "See? You have to time me."

Bill: (reading the phrase "58 in 5 minutes" written boldly at the top of the worksheet next to blank lines for her name and grade) "I have to time you?"

Ferris: "Yeah, with your watch."

Bill: "Why do I have to do that?"

Ferris: "I don't know. You just have to do it. My teacher says you should."

Bill: (grudgingly) "Well, okay . . . (playfully) . . . Ready, Set, Go!"

Ferris immediately went to work solving one addition problem after another with apparent enthusiasm and confidence. I watched patiently as she correctly solved the first seven addition problems. At the eighth problem ($7 + 2 = ?$), I noticed that after writing down the number 9, Ferris paused, erased the number quickly, paused again, and then wrote the number 9 again in exactly the same place she had written the first 9. Afterwards, she paused again, and then finally moved on to the next problem.

After correctly answering problems 9–13, she once again returned to the eighth problem, paused, erased the number 9, paused, methodically wrote the number 9 again in exactly the same place, and then proceeded to answer questions 14–19. However, right before moving on to problem 20, Ferris again returned to the eighth problem, paused, and repeated the whole procedure once again. By this time I was completely befuddled, and decided to interrupt.

Bill: "Ferris, what are you doing? Why do you keep going back to the eighth problem, erasing the number 9, and rewriting it again?"

Ferris: (a bit irritated at the question) "Daddy, don't you know it's not right?"

Bill: "You mean $7 + 2$ doesn't equal 9?"

Ferris: "No, silly, of course $7 + 2$ equals 9. Everybody knows that. It's the nine that's not right."

Bill: (even more confused than before) "What? I don't understand."

Ferris: "I mean it's not written right. You see, the bottom of the 9 has to be drawn like this (showing how the stem of the 9 has to be written on a right angle, not straight up and down like it was before). I was drawing it wrong. Now do you see?"

Bill: "Yeah, I see."

*

6:00 PM—The night before the test. Ferris, her mother, her sister, and I are all sitting at the dining room table having supper. While her mother and sister are talking, I noticed Ferris mumbling quietly to herself.

> *Ferris:* "The little boy's name is . . . (pause) . . . Tom. (pause) Two plus two is . . . (pause) . . . four. (pause) The tiny kitten likes . . . (pause) . . . milk . . .
> *Bill:* (curious): "Ferris, what are you doing?"
> *Ferris:* "I'm practicing my questions. My teacher said these are the types of questions that will be on the test."
> *Bill:* "What do you mean?"
> *Ferris:* "Y'know. I'm practicing for the test. I'm practicing reading questions, and then answering them. That's what I'm doing."

*

7:00 AM—The morning of the test. Ferris, her mother, and I are eating breakfast at the dining room table.

> *Ferris:* "Y'know, today is the test, Mommy and Daddy, isn't it?"
> *Bill:* "Yeah, we know, Ferris."
> *Ferris:* I have to do good today, because if I don't I'm not going to be able to go to second grade."
> *Bill:* "Ferris, that's not true."
> *Ferris:* "Uh, uh. Kids who don't do good on the test stay in first grade."

*

3:30 PM—After school the day of the test. Ferris and I are riding home in the car.

> *Bill:* "How was school today, Ferris?"
> *Ferris:* " Fine, but the test was really hard."
> *Bill:* "Was it? What was hard about it?"
> *Ferris:* "Well, the questions were easy, but the circles were hard."
> *Bill:* "The circles were hard?"
> *Ferris:* "Yeah, it was hard coloring all those circles in, y'know, not leaving any white spaces. That took a long time, Daddy."
> *Bill:* (mumbling to himself) "Good grief. What a nightmare!"
> *Ferris:* "What, Daddy?"
> *Bill:* "Oh, nothing, Ferris. Let's go get an ice cream cone."
> *Ferris:* "Yeah, chocolate."

Over the years we have learned many important lessons about literacy, literacy learning, and literacy assessment from language stories shared with us by students, teachers, administrators, and parents. We introduce this chapter with the preceding language stories because they challenge several assumptions currently driving standardized testing. These assumptions include that standardized tests are valid instruments, that standardized testing informs classroom practice, that individuals not actively and closely involved in learning can accurately assess that learning, and that standardized testing measures learning outcomes. From hearing the voices of these two children, and countless others like them, we have come to believe that these assumptions are erroneous and antiquated, and that standardized testing as a form of assessment should be abandoned.

The purpose of this chapter is not to offer an alternative to standardized testing, but rather an alternative vision for the future of assessment. This vision is based on a set of assumptions that sees literacy and literacy learning in terms of purpose, function, and social context, sees knowledge as a complex web of socially constructed understandings, and sees assessment as inquiry, a process of continuous conversation between learners about the meaning of their work. We believe these assumptions should drive the future of assessment because they not only situate learners at the center, rather than at the periphery, of the assessment process, but also create the conditions for assessment to be used as a means to hear new voices, start new conversations, and structure new social relationships in the classroom.

In this chapter we will describe this vision by first reporting on the current status of assessment practice. Then, we will describe recent attempts by educators to develop a variety of alternatives to standardized testing, focusing primarily on recent efforts by reading educators to reform reading comprehension assessment. Next, we will argue that these reform efforts, while representing steps in the right direction, are inadequate because they ignore, or at least only pay token attention to, several important assumptions driving recent reading theory. Finally, we will conclude by offering a vision for the future of assessment that is based on the best we currently know about language, reading, learning, and schooling.

Current Assessment Practice: A Status Report

Standardized testing is not rich in tradition; in fact, it is less than a century old (Guba and Lincoln, 1981). And yet, in that relatively short period of time it has rapidly become endemic, if not hegemonic, to American society. Over the years standardized testing has achieved a privilege status in education, valued for its efficiency, sophistication, and objectivity, as well as for its utility and accountability. Today, it continues to enjoy much popularity, prestige, and power, and the future looks even brighter. Recent trends indicate that in the years ahead standardized testing will not only increase, but will also expand in use, propelled by the Miss Piggy philosophy that says "more is better."

In 1986–87, for example, United States public schools spent on average at least one month of every nine month school year administering a total of 105 million standardized tests to 39.8 million students, an average of more than 2.5 standardized tests per student, per year (Harste, 1990; *Newsweek*, 1990). Today, according to Valencia, et. al., (1989), 46 of our 50 states now require state-regulated testing, and of these, all 46 require testing in reading. Most recently, the United States Congress has allocated 8 million dollars to the NAEP (National Association of Educational Progress) to conduct voluntary state-by-state comparisons in mathematics at the 8th grade level in 1990, and in mathematics and reading at the 4th grade level in 1992 (see Farstrup, 1989/90). By all accounts, these commitments to norm-referenced tests at the national level, coupled with growing numbers of criterion-referenced tests at the statewide level and teacher-made tests at the classroom level, are symptomatic of an educational system well on its way to being obsessed with and consumed by standardized testing.

Moreover, the future of standardized testing will not be limited to education. In fact, a wide range of standardized tests have already been developed for use with different populations. For instance, we now have standardized tests for use not only with students, but also with teachers, supervisors, soldiers, and police officers. In fact, it appears that, if the testing industry has its way, we will shortly become what Gardner (1988) describes as a "complete testing society . . . one that is driven by a rationale that says if something is important, it is worth testing; if it cannot be tested, it probably ought not to be valued."

Interrogating Assumptions Driving Standardized Testing

Standardized testing is theoretically-based, driven by a set of assumptions about the nature of literacy and literacy learning. Several of these assumptions include that standardized tests are valid instruments, that standardized testing informs classroom practice, that outsiders not closely involved in learning can assess that learning, and that standardized testing measures learning outcomes. Over the years these assumptions have come to represent common sense, taken-for-granted knowledge, and as a result have also come to be immune from, or at least insulated from, serious interrogation. It is high time to question these assumptions. We feel the language stories that introduced this chapter do just that.

In the first language story, the new "Draw a Person" test is virtually powerless to significantly inform classroom practice. It completely ignores what knowledge this child already possesses, particularly about human anatomy, and focuses instead on verifying to what extent she has mastered a discrete and isolated skill; in this case, to what extent she can literally draw a person. Unfortunately, it can tell us little more than that. Most importantly, it can't inform us about what this little girl already knows about her social world, or about how she came to know it. What we are left with is a test that does little more than test the mundane.

In the second language story, it is clear that Ferris, like many other young children, learns very early on many important messages about assessment, and how it gets played out in school. In the beginning she suspects that adults regard standardized testing as important ("My teacher says something real important is coming up . . ."). And yet, at the same time she really doesn't understand what this testing business is all about. For the time being she sees it as something mysterious and confusing at best ("I don't know, Daddy, something about a test."), and something imposing, intimidating, and even threatening at worst.

As time goes by, Ferris continues to learn many lessons about assessment. She learns that assessment is apparently something adults do to, not with, children ("I'm afraid they are going to do something to me . . ."), that poor performance on standardized tests has potential deleterious consequences, such as not advancing to the second grade ("I have to do good today, because if I don't I'm not going to be able to go to second grade."), and that mimicking test questions and test answers will help her do well on the test ("I'm practicing for the test. I'm practicing reading questions, and then answering them."). In the end, it is ironic that Ferris experiences considerably more difficulty at blackening in circles than she does with answering test questions.

Like Ferris, we learned many important lessons about assessment as we began to take a closer look at how she went about completing that math worksheet. For one thing, we learned not to assume that standardized tests measure what they purport they measure. This math worksheet, which is little more than a miniature standardized test, is intended to measure proficiency at solving addition problems. It assumes that Ferris will attempt to solve as many addition problems as she possibly can in five minutes. It further assumes that the total number of problems answered correctly is an accurate measure of to what extent Ferris is proficient at addition. What is problematic about these assumptions is that what Ferris actually attended to on the worksheet differed significantly from what the worksheet assumed she would attend to.

For example, after five minutes Ferris had only answered 19 (all correctly) out of a total of 80 addition problems. She went on to answer only a total of 26 (all correctly) problems in approximately 15 minutes before deciding to quit. Now to an outsider, say a teacher who assigns the worksheet as homework, an administrator who analyzes the worksheet in his or her office, or a computer that scores the worksheet, it certainly appears that Ferris has not performed particularly well on this task. In fact, if the expectation were for her to correctly answer somewhere around 58 addition problems in five minutes, as was indicated at the top of the worksheet, then, by only answering a total of 19 questions, it could easily be concluded that she is not particularly good at addition, and certainly far from mastering the skill.

To an insider, however, say someone who is in a position to observe, interpret, and interview Ferris as she went about completing this worksheet, the story is quite different. By sitting next to Ferris at the dinner table, I was able to understand that she attended to more than what the worksheet had intended or assumed she would attend to. In this instance, Ferris attended to accurately drawing her numbers in addition to solving addition problems. In essence, she used this opportunity to learn more about math than what the worksheet was originally designed to teach or to test. As a result, a disparity occurred between what learning was assumed to be going on, and what learning actually took place. Because of this disparity, actual performance on this worksheet is not an accurate measure of to what extent Ferris is already proficient at addition. In fact, outsiders looking at this worksheet would not even be aware that this disparity existed in the first place. This lack of an insider's perspective makes conclusions about her proficiency at solving addition problems at best misinformed, and at worst downright distorted.

Of course, many readers, particularly those who are staunch advocates of standardized testing, will reject this whole argument. Most likely, they will reject it on the grounds that these two language stories are simply atypical examples of what normally occurs in testing situations. We believe, however, that, while these language stories certainly represent two unique instances, they are not atypical. On the contrary, they are typical in the sense that they both reflect a form of assessment that creates the conditions in which instances such as these are allowed, indeed invited, to occur in the first place.

Thus, in our view we believe standardized testing is an anachronistic sociocultural practice that is theoretically bankrupt, given what we currently know about literacy and literacy learning. In its place, we join increasing numbers of educators who are attempting to develop alternatives that better reflect recent advances in literacy assessment. In the following section we will discuss several of these alternatives with particular emphasis on describing recent attempts to reform reading comprehension assessment.

Recent Attempts to Reform Assessment

Many educators are responding to calls for reforms in assessment by proposing a variety of alternatives to standardized testing. These proposals are diverse, controversial and include attempts to improve what standardized tests test, develop literacy portfolio approaches, combine informal literacy portfolio data with formal standardized test data, and develop holistic, classroom-based data-collection procedures.

Improving What Standardized Tests Test

Over the past two decades reading assessment has lagged behind recent advances in reading theory (Valencia and Pearson, 1987). As a result, a significant gap has developed between our current understandings of reading, and the standardized tests we use to assess reading comprehension (Valencia, Pearson, Peters, Wixson, 1989; Durkin, 1987; Johnston, 1990). Many educators believe that the most expeditious and efficacious way to close this gap is to improve what standardized tests test. Recently, reading educators in the United States and abroad have been doing just that.

In Australia, educators have developed TORCH, a test of reading comprehension. This test includes a wide variety of reading materials representing multiple genres, and assesses reading comprehension through analysis of written retellings based on a modified cloze procedure. In Great Britain, educators have developed the Effective Reading Tests, a series of tests designed purposely not to look like tests at all. Reading passages in these tests are high-interest stories, and appear in an attractively illustrated book. Students read these passages, and record their answers to specific questions in a separate booklet, looking back to the passages as needed (see Pikulski, 1990).

In the United States, educators at the national level have developed TETRA-2, the test of Early Reading Ability-2. This test was designed to specifically reflect recent advances in emergent literacy. Instead of focusing on skills-based criteria such as visual perception or auditory discrimination, this test attempts to engage children in natural reading and writing activities in order to assess, for example, their ability to recognize writing as compared to drawing, or their familiarity with the concepts of letter and word (see Pikulski, 1990).

At the statewide level, Wixson, et al. (1987) report on collaborative attempts by educators, policy makers, test developers, curriculum specialists, and researchers to reconceptualize reading and reading tests in the state of Michigan. These attempts are explicitly designed to make statewide testing more consistent with recent reading theory and research. Today, reading is defined throughout the state not as a series of sequential and hierarchical skills, but more as an interactive process where readers actively construct meaning from text.

This reconceptualization has subsequently influenced the development of prototypical standardized reading tests. They are prototypical in the sense that these tests include passages and test items designed to reflect influences on reading such as topic familiarity, readability, text variability, metacognitive knowledge and strategies, and attitude and self-perception.

Finally, researchers also report on attempts to reform statewide reading assessment in the state of Illinois (Valencia and Pearson, 1987; Pearson and Valencia, 1987; Valencia, Pearson, Peters, & Wixson, 1989). These researchers, like their Michigan counterparts, are trying to develop statewide standardized reading tests that are based on interactive, rather than skills-based models of reading. To that end, tests developed so far include multiple texts, advanced organizers such as text maps and preliminary test questions, and questions designed to activate prior knowledge and access metacognitive strategies.

Developing Literacy Portfolio Approaches

Instead of improving what standardized tests test, an increasing number of educators are developing literacy portfolio approaches as alternatives to standardized testing (Valencia, 1990). They argue that these approaches better reflect recent reading theory, since they function as tools for teachers and students to document and monitor learning over time.

Simply stated, a literacy portfolio is a "living document of change" (Krest, 1990). It consists of a chronologically sequenced collection of work that records and traces the long-term evolution of student thinking (Wolf, 1987/88). This collection is open-ended, purposely diverse, and often includes writing samples, observational notes, audio and video tapes, literature logs, ideas, half-formed thoughts, sketches, photographs, questions, issues, rough drafts, peer feedback, descriptions of reading and writing strategies, personal reactions, self-evaluations, works in progress, and so forth.

It should be noted that literacy portfolio approaches are not new to education. The Arts have used portfolios as assessment tools for many years now. In particular, art education has historically used portfolios to document and assess among other things to what extent students can formulate novel problems, engage in complex problem-solving strategies, and reflect on the quantity and quality of one's work over an extended period of time (Wolf, 1989). Art educators believe that portfolios afford students a tool for reflecting on the quality of one's work, as well as an organizational device for sharing that work with others.

Recently, much research on literacy portfolio approaches, particularly in language arts, has been directed at exploring to what extent they can be used in assessing writing proficiency. For instance, at the post-secondary level, Elbow and Belanoff (1986) report on using a portfolio approach to assess writing as an alternative to traditional proficiency exams. They argue that proficiency exams, like most standardized writing assessment instruments, send wrong messages to students about writing. Among others, these messages include that writing involves producing a single draft in a predetermined period of time, writing about a topic not of the author's own choosing, and submitting final drafts without opportunities to discuss, reflect on, or revise that writing with others.

As an alternative, they have developed a portfolio approach to assess student writing ability. In an introductory writing course, students are required in one semester to produce four pieces of writing:

1. a narrative, descriptive, or expressive piece,

2. an analysis of a prose text,

3. an essay, and

4. an in-class essay completed without benefit of peer or teacher feedback.

To pass the course, student portfolios must receive at least a C grade, not only from their instructor, but also from another writing instructor in the same department who is unfamiliar with that student.

Assessment of portfolios involves a two step process. At mid-semester writing instructors meet, and read sample papers in student portfolios in order to construct a rubric of grading criteria which will be used later to issue pass or fail evaluations. Those instructors, unfamiliar with the authors of sample papers, function as outside readers. It is understood that, while outside readers make comments on student papers, it is the responsibility of those instructors who are familiar with the authors to interpret those reader comments in class. At the end of the semester, all instructors meet again, only this time to evaluate each portfolio as a whole. Students whose portfolio does not earn at least a C must repeat the course.

Elbow and Belanoff (1986) believe that a portfolio approach ultimately benefits both students and teachers. It sends more positive messages about writing to students by giving them time, encouragement, and support to produce their best writing, and to teachers by affording them an opportunity to function as coaches and advisors to student writing.

At the secondary level, Krest (1990) reports on using portfolio approaches to combat the sometimes overwhelming teacher task of reading, responding to, and grading student writing. At different times during the year, student portfolios are reviewed and issued two grades: a portfolio grade that reflects the amount of risk-taking and revision students demonstrate on all their written work, and a paper grade that reflects the outcome of one final product.

In addition to risk-taking, grades are based on to what extent students demonstrate evidence of self-assessment, reflection on peer and teacher feedback, writing fluency, revising, editing, and experimenting with different writing modes. This portfolio approach to writing assessment helps make paper loads more manageable, encourages and supports students to produce their best writing, and increases teacher interest and motivation to read and improve student writing.

Combining Portfolio Data and Standardized Test Data as Assessment

Currently, much research is being conducted that attempts to combine literacy portfolio data with standardized test data for the purposes of constructing a more holistic assessment of student learning. Simmons (1990), for instance, recently conducted a pilot study exploring the use of portfolios for large-scale assessment in writing. This study involved a total of 27 fifth-graders, and was designed

to develop "a method of large-scale assessment of writing ability using portfolios of students' best written work in combination with timed writing samples."

Analysis of combined writing samples found that students whose portfolio
pieces reflected a broad range of modes of discourse also scored higher on the
timed tests, that timed-test and portfolio assessments produced essentially the
same rank orderings of students base on criteria such as paper length, duration
of work, mode of discourse, and so forth, and that portfolio pieces provided more
holistic profiles of the students as writers. It was concluded that student literacy
portfolios are valuable assessment tools because they provide evidence that, when
combined with standardized timed-test results, permit broader and more accurate
profiles of students to be constructed.

Along these same lines, growing numbers of educators are starting to explore
the potential of using portfolios not only to assess writing, but also to assess
reading. Mathews (1990), for instance, reports that reading educators in Orange
County, Florida are moving from a skills-based system to a portfolio approach
for assessing reading at a district-wide level. This portfolio approach includes
four core elements: a reading developmental checklist, writing samples, a list
of books read by students, and a test of reading comprehension. While implementing the first three elements has been relatively easy, developing a test of reading
comprehension has proved much more difficult. Teacher review of various com-
mercially produced standardized tests revealed a lack of authentic texts and quality
questions, two criteria district teachers were specifically looking for in a test
of reading comprehension.

Farr and Farr (1990) have developed an integrated language arts portfolio
system for classroom use that combines reading and writing in a single assessment. Two major characteristics of this system are particularly noteworthy. First,
its design allows parents, teachers, and students to include multiple sources of
assessment data. Parents include biographical data, as well as information about
student reading and writing activities outside school; teachers include classroom
data such as observational notes, anecdotal records, vignettes, impressions, interview data, test records, and audio/video tapes; and students include
autobiographic data in the form of journal and diary writing, learning logs, reflection booklets, and so forth. It is predicted that these data will provide insights
into such things as student instructional histories, current interests, and future
aspirations, so that teachers can them make more informed judgments about student work.

Second, it is also intended as an organizational and analytical device for
specifically evaluating student proficiency based on a set of prompted reading
and writing activities. There are three sets of these activities, and these may be
administered through the year. The prompts include multiple opportunities for

students to use various prewriting strategies, read and write over extended periods of time, and revise their work through ongoing teacher, peer, and self-assessment activities.

Overall, this portfolio approach consists of personal, self-selected instances of reading and writing, as well as three pieces of writing based on teacher-selected prompted activities. All personal writing in the portfolio is periodically and collaboratively reviewed by teachers and students, and graded on such things as the amount of reading and writing completed during a specified period of time, the amount of reading and writing completed across genres and topics, and the degree to which students engaged in risk-taking, particularly with respect to reading more complicated materials, experimenting with different discourse styles, and writing longer, more complex pieces.

On the other hand, all prompted writing in the portfolio is reviewed by the teacher, and numerically scored from 1–4 across three major categories: response to reading addresses the amount and accuracy of information comprehended from text; management of content assesses student ability to organize, focus, and develop information; and command of language evaluates surface features such as sentence structure, word choice, grammar, and mechanics.

An increasing number of educators believe that literacy portfolio approaches, like the ones described above, that include assessments on personal as well as prompted activities provide a highly contextualized, informative, and accurate profile of student reading and writing abilities. They also believe that portfolio approaches that combine data from informal and formal measures provide a valuable tool for not only students, teachers, and parents to use at the local level, but also as a large-scale assessment instrument for administrators, curriculum coordinators, and policymakers to use at the national level.

Developing Holistic Assessment Procedures

Lastly, an increasing number of reading educators are working on developing a holistic measure of literacy assessment, one that is based on standardized miscue analysis and "kidwatching strategies" (Goodman, 1978) popular among whole language researchers and theorists for some time now. These educators are convinced that reform in reading assessment can occur only if the criteria for assessing reading significantly changes. Therefore, their efforts are directed toward extending our current understandings of reading by exploring new criteria for reading comprehension, and by developing a classroom based, learner driven data collection procedure for documenting and assessing reading growth.

Recently, we have been involved in a collaborative research project designed to explore alternatives to traditional forms of reading comprehension assessment (Harste, et al., 1989). In this project we attempted to use recent advances in evaluating writing as a metaphor for what might be possible in assessing reading comprehension. For example, recent attempts to assess writing proficiency through such procedures as holistic scoring, writing portfolios, and primary trait scoring have done much to allow writing researchers to perceive writing differently (see Cooper and Odell, 1977). Similarly, we believe that exploring alternative procedures for assessing reading comprehension will allow reading researchers to perceive reading differently as well.

Specifically, we set out to develop a viable, classroom based, learner driven data collection procedure by holistically scoring three different types of comprehension data (in process think alouds, retellings, freewrites) collected from 20 proficient readers as they read and reacted to the reading of an intact professional article. We believe analysis of this comprehension data has provided new insights into the reading process as well as resulted in the development of several taxonomies that permit assessment far beyond standardized testing, and incorporate much of what is known about the dual processes of reading comprehension and writing given psycholinguistic (Goodman, 1967), schema (Pearson and Anderson, 1984), and socio-psycholinguistic theory (Harste, 1988, 1990; see also Kelleher, C., et al., 1989; Chandler, P., et al., 1989; Beverstock, C., 1989).

The taxonomy constructed from analysis of student freewrites is a case in point. Traditionally, freewriting has been used as a prewriting strategy for helping students generate ideas for writing (Elbow, 1983). We believe, however, that freewriting also represents a unique potential for assessing reading comprehension since it encourages and supports unedited personal responses to text. We hoped to use student responses to text as a window through which we could view not only what readers comprehended from text, but also how they went about comprehending through text.

This freewrite taxonomy reflects four major patterns characteristic of the mental trip students took as they went about reading. These patterns indicate that students engaged in

1. developing a sense of voice;
2. going beyond the text by making intertextual ties and personal links, as well as by speculating, synthesizing, extending, and analyzing;
3. taking risks by questioning, taking a position, shifting interpretive stances, and rethinking one's current position; and
4. being reflective by searching out, identifying, and working through anomalies.

From this analysis we have learned that freewriting offers an alternative way of seeing reading, and understanding reading comprehension. We believe freewriting has learning potential for identifying, understanding, and appreciating the personal meanings readers construct from text, as well as the strategic meaning-making processes readers use while comprehending text. We feel these patterns, when integrated with analytic patterns gleaned from other protocols, such as oral and written retellings, think alouds, miscue analysis, can be used holistically in developing alternative criteria for reading comprehension assessment.

Interrogating Assumptions Underlying Recent Reform Efforts

We believe recent efforts by teachers and researchers to reform assessment are steps in the right direction. Moreover, we believe that recent attempts by reading educators to reform reading comprehension assessment are positive attempts to close the gap between reading assessment and reading theory. These efforts deserve our continued support.

At the same time, we also believe that these efforts are inadequate. While they have certainly been successful at improving the form of assessment, they have not, however, been successful at changing its function. In other words, while these efforts have certainly changed the surface structure of reading assessment, they have not interrogated, much less changed, the assumptions underlying these surface changes.

For instance, each of these reform efforts, including our own work with holistic assessment, continue to see reading primarily as an individual phenomenon, a learning activity individuals do by themselves, for themselves. They advocate interactive models of reading, and yet, they continue to develop assessment instruments and procedures which narrowly define interactions as those instances that occur only between an individual reader and a single, prescribed text. They have ignored, or at best only paid lip service to, the belief that reading is a social engagement, a learning strategy where learners not only read for themselves, but also read with others, for others (Harste, Woodward, Burke, 1985).

This token attention to the social nature of reading is due in part to the fact that skills-based models of reading have historically perpetuated a single score, single text, single reader mentality in reading assessment. To their credit, recent reform efforts have successfully challenged the single score mentality by incorporating multiple measures, as well as the single text mentality by including multiple texts in alternative assessment instruments and procedures. Unfortunately, they have neither successfully challenged the single reader mentality, nor adequately addressed the use of self-selected texts in reading assessment (Newman, 1989; Cairney, 1989). We believe these issues can only be solved by developing alternatives for reading comprehension assessment which invite, encourage, and support transactions between a reader sharing multiple self-selected texts with other readers.

Moreover, each of these reform efforts continues to be rooted in what we believe is a behaviorial model of learning. Attempts to improve standardized testing by altering what it tests certainly makes us look modern, up to date, on the cutting edge of reforming reading assessment. But, by only improving standardized testing, this effort makes us appear as taking only token risks, playing it safe, protecting our backs. We all know that assessment is power. It's a tool that is often used to control, rather than reflect student learning. Our willingness to alter only the form of standardized testing is also indicative of our unwillingness to alter who is in control of learning, who is in the best position to assess learning, and who decides what learning is to be assessed. In the end, these reform efforts certainly make the assessment deck look different, but it does not alter who remains in control of all the cards.

Finally, literacy portfolio approaches, particularly those that combine portfolio data with standardized test data, are to a large extent also rooted in a behavioral model of learning. On the one hand, by including personal portfolio data, these approaches have attempted to shift, or at least share, power and control over learning and assessment to learners themselves. This is a significant step in the right direction.

On the other hand, however, these portfolio approaches, while not wanting to only standardize test data, nevertheless, still want to privilege standardized test criteria. That is, whether portfolio data or standardized test data (or both) is used to assess learning, in both cases specific assessment criteria have been predetermined and externally defined. These criteria are not individually defined based on purpose and function, but rather are uniformly applied to all students based on convention and control. In the end, literacy portfolio approaches, especially those that utilize standardized test data, end up amounting to little more than just another form for collecting, representing, and verifying the same outdated criteria used on standardized tests.

In the final analysis, literacy portfolio approaches and standardized testing represent two different assessment tools, each of which is designed to travel a different road to assessing literacy and literacy learning. What is problematic is that in each case, because the assessment criteria remains essentially externally defined and predetermined, both these roads still end up leading to the same destination. In our view, this is tantamount to an "all roads lead to Rome" mentality, and a significant step backwards in reforming literacy assessment.

Let's Get Messy with Assessment

Recently, Graves (1990) has suggested that now is a very opportune time for experimenting with, reflecting on, and getting messy with assessment. We agree.

In fact, we believe the messier the better. Learning is certainly messy business. Why should assessment be any different? But how do we begin to get messy with assessment? How do we begin to develop new images, new potentials, and new visions of literacy assessment based on what can be, rather than what is?

We belive a good first step is to recognize that standardized testing is inherently flawed (Goodman, 1986; Harste, 1990). Considerable evidence already exists that more or less indicts standardized testing as a practice that is ecologically invalid and culturally biased (Mischler, 1979); that ignores the influence of social context on learning (Barrs, 1990); that precludes an understanding of learning processes (Clay, 1990); that privileges linguistic and logical-mathematical proficiencies over other ways of knowing (Gardner, 1988); that focuses on individual weaknesses, not individual strengths (Cohen, 1988); that uses a single digit mentality to represent complex learning processes (Tierney, 1989); and that disempowers learners by preventing them from participating in self-assessment (Harmon, 1989/90).

With respect to reading, there is also much evidence to support the notion that standardized testing has little relationship to real world reading; that is, to the types of reading people do in their everyday lives. In fact, to date, no data exist which support the belief that what is being tested by standardized testing has any relationship to real world reading. On the contrary, existing data suggests that standardized testing is based on outdated assumptions about the reading process (Cambourne, 1985).

For example, skills-based models of reading currently drive standardized testing. These models assume that reading is decoding, that reading is an exact process, and that reading is made up of a sequential and hierarchical collection of subskills, such as inferencing, word recognition, and sound/symbol relationships. Recent reading theory, however, contradicts these skills-based assumptions, and supports instead socio-psycholinguistic and socio-semiotic models of reading. These models are antithetical to standardized testing because they assume that reading is a social process of constructing meaning, that reading is a flexible and selective process based on formulating predictions and making connections, that reading involves using minimal use of grapho-phonemic knowledge, and that, although there is but one reading process, it gets played out differently depending on social context (Harste, 1986).

In large part, this contradiction is due to the fact that standardized testing views reading as primarily a text based and skills driven individual activity, whereas socio-psycholinguistic and socio-semiotic models view reading as a flexible, learner-based, and strategy-driven social engagement. This contradiction also highlights why current reading assessment practices are antiquated.

Valencia and Pearson (1987) have illustrated this contradiction by identifying several assumptions that reflect recent reading theory, and then contrasting them with assumptions that currently drive reading assessment. For example, on the one hand, recent reading theory posits that prior knowledge influences reading comprehension, that inference is essential to reading comprehension, that skilled readers vary reading strategies to fit text and context, and that skilled readers are fluent. On the other hand, however, reading assessment fails to address the influence of prior knowledge by using short passages on multiple topics, uses test items that rely on literal comprehension, uses multiple choice test items that focus on single correct answers, seldom assesses metacognitive knowledge and strategies, and fails to assess fluency.

These, of course, are just a few of the contradictions that currently exist between reading theory and reading assessment. Nevertheless, this disparity raises serious questions about what standardized testing really tests. After all, if it doesn't test real world reading, then what does it test? If you ask those who wish to ban standardized testing, they will most likely answer than it has nothing at all to do with real world reading. If you ask others, many will answer that they simply don't know what standardized tests test. What they suspect is that they do little more than measure student "test wiseness"; that is, student ability to take tests.

Kemp (1985), for instance, found that students when required to answer multiple choice questions often read passages on standardized tests only as a last resort. They reported that a more successful strategy is to ignore the passage, and answer the test questions first. In most instances, this strategy is successful because test questions are factual and literal-level in nature. They add, however, that if this strategy is unsuccessful and reading the passage becomes necessary, then they will resort to skimming the text, looking specifically for discrete answers.

Given this type of mounting evidence, we take the position that standardized testing should be banned. At the same time, we also believe that it is unlikely to happen soon. In fact, if the recent trend in reading assessment over the past two decades is any indicator, then we will continue to be voracious consumers of standardized testing. This prognostication raises serious questions about who determines reading assessment practices in this country. Is it reading educators who base reading assessment decisions on what we currently know about reading and reading instruction, or is it corporate executives from the testing industry who base reading assessment decisions on the best they know about how to develop and market standardized tests? We suspect the latter.

A second step is to recognize that whole language is based on a different view of literacy and literacy learning than the behavioral view which drives standardized testing. Whole language sees literacy and literacy learning in terms of function, purpose, and social context, whereas standardized testing sees them in terms of convention and control. Furthermore, standardized testing focuses on using externally defined criteria for cross evaluation purposes, whereas whole language focuses on internally defined assessment criteria that emerges from insider perspectives within a particular social context. Lastly, standardized testing views assessment as verification, whereas whole language views assessment as inquiry, as "thoughtfulness" (Brown, 1987), a critical process of open ended questioning to which no one knows the answers, and of presenting problems to which there may be many possible solutions.

A third step is to recognize that whole language has not been dragging its feet when it comes to literacy assessments. On the contrary, it has made significant advances in literacy assessment by developing a methodology based on the best we currently know about literacy and literacy learning. Teale, et al., (1987), for instance, have developed a set of principles which suggest that assessment is part of instruction, that assessment should involve a variety of methods and instruments, that assessment focus on multiple dimensions of a literacy, that assessment is ubiquitous, that assessment is context-specific, and that assessment is sensitive to cultural background.

Similarly, Goodman (1989) has developed an assessment methodology for use in whole language classrooms. This methodology is based on the notion that assessment is a continuous process of observation, interaction, and analysis. These interrelated processes can occur formally through systematic record keeping, as well as informally through natural contact between teachers and students. These processes can also occur incidentally, for instance, when teachers have a professional hunch or intuitive judgment predicting that specific activities may yield important insights about student learning.

Likewise, whole language advocates have been busy developing a variety of observation and interview-based, kidwatching, strategies (Goodman, 1978) for use in assessing student learning. These strategies include systematic observation, periodic sampling of student reading and writing, peer conferencing, formal and informal interview, standardized miscue analysis, retrospective miscue analysis, anecdotal record keeping, and developing cumulative records such as writing folders, literacy portfolios, and so on (Barrs, 1990; see also Goodman, Goodman & Hood, 1989).

A final step is to recognize that much current debate tends to focus on seeing literacy assessment as primarily a methodological issue. And, of course, to a large extent it is. But, it is also an epistemological and philosophical issue. We believe that if whole language advocates are to play a major role in shaping the future of assessment, then we also need to start developing a model of assessment that is firmly based on the best that what we currently know about language, learning, knowledge, and schooling.

Assessment as a Theory of Language

Language is an open ended system of symbols. This system functions as a tool for individuals to understand, name, and reflect on their social worlds. Language is both generative and representational in nature. That is, it is a means by which individuals generate meaning in their lives, as well as a way to communicate that meaning to others.

Whole language is based on a theory of language that sees reading as an instance of language use (Burke, 1990). In other words, what we believe about language also holds true for what we believe about reading. In fact, what we believe about language also holds true for what we believe about any communication system, whether it be reading, writing, speaking, listening, art, drama, math, and so forth. Assessment is no exception. Although it is clearly uncharted territory, we are starting to make connections between what we believe about language and what we believe about assessment.

Standardized testing, however, treats language as a closed, rather than open, symbol system. Evidence of this can be found by examining the nature of reading passages which appear on these tests. Instead of authentic texts, these passages are more like nontexts, or what Harste (1990) describes as "textoids," short, poorly structured pieces of writing which are nothing like the reading individuals encounter in their daily lives. These inauthentic texts reduce potential for personal meaning-making because they do not allow personal experience to come into play, and therefore restrict the connections readers can make with past experiences. This potential is further reduced when these passages are used with multiple-choice, question-answer formats that assume that one right answer exists. These passages reflect a form of assessment that violates the best we currently know about language, ignores personal experience, and reduces reading to a process of finding single answers.

Assessment as Theory of Knowledge

Along these same lines, what we believe about language is also a reflection of what we believe about knowledge. Whole language has demonstrated that knowledge is socially constructed, that knowledge is historically and culturally rooted, that knowledge is deeply embedded in the social context in which it is learned, and that knowledge is connected knowing, conceptualized as a complex web of current understandings influenced by prior knowledge, past experience, current interests, and future aspirations. It has also demonstrated that learners extend these understandings through meaningful conversation with other learners in supportive learning environments.

Standardized testing, however, assumes that knowledge is a commodity, a collection of skills and content that can be directly transmitted from an expert, one who knows (a teacher), to a novice, one who doesn't know (a student). This model sees knowledge in hierarchical terms; that is, it sees knowledge getting passed down from above through what Friere (1973) calls "communiques" rather than conversations. These communiques are disempowering because they systematically take control over learning out of the hands of learners. As a result, learners are marginalized, conversation shuts down, and silence soon follows.

Assessment as A Theory of Learning

Whole language assumes that learning is a process of outgrowing our present selves. Learners can't do that by answering other people's questions; they can only do that by asking their own. It is this notion of learning as a question-asking process which makes the difference between educative and miseducative experiences (Dewey, 1938). Educative experiences propel learning forward and outward; miseducative experiences keep learning at rest.

Standardized testing, however, is based on a behavioral model of learning because it sees literacy and literacy learning in terms of convention and control, not purpose, function, and self-selection. It assumes that a one-to-one correspondence exists between teaching and learning; that is, it assumes that what gets taught is what gets learned. Standardized testing seeks answers, not questions, from students. It privileges its own questions over those that individuals can generate themselves.

Assessment as a Theory of Schooling

Whole language believes that schooling is the practice of freedom. It seeks to create classroom contexts that are democratic, that value diversity, and that recognize teachers and students as collaborators in the learning process. These contexts function, not to transmit knowledge, but to actively construct social worlds.

Standardized testing, however, is based on a transmission model of schooling. This model sees schooling as a means to transmit specific knowledge necessary for individuals to compete in a free market society, achieve social mobility, and perpetuate our democratic heritage. In our view, this model is anything but democratic. It holds a uniform view of human development, views knowledge as static, uses standardized testing to verify knowledge, and in general creates the conditions for unquestioned, authoritarian teaching and assessment practices to be used in classrooms.

A Vision for the Future of Literacy Assessment

Although neither one of us claim to be clairvoyant, we are confident in predicting that, if education in this country is ever to be more than just a practice in mediocrity, then the future of literacy assessment must look significantly different than it does today. We believe that the future must be driven by the best' we currently know about language, learning, knowledge, and schooling. We also believe that conversation must play a central role.

We do not see conversation as assessment in hierarchical terms. On the contrary, we agree with Friere (1973) who reminds us that "At the point of encounter (dialogue), there are neither ignoramuses, nor perfect sages; there are only men (and women) who are attempting, together, to learn more than they now know." Rather, we see conversation as inquiry, a potential for starting new conversations where none existed before, for hearing new voices where only silence existed before, and for altering social relationships where only hierarchical ones existed before.

Through conversation, we see assessment not as a matter of teachers verifying student learning, but as a process where learners collaborate with other learners in generating and answering their own questions. The process is generative in the sense that through conversation, assessment can ask learners to ask themselves "What have I learned?", "How did I learn it?", and "What do I now want to know more about?" It is this ongoing question-asking process that affords learners opportunities to use themselves as a research instrument, and to use assessment as a tool for outgrowing their present selves.

We see assessment through conversation as an opportunity for learners to not only engage in learning, but to reflect on that learning as well. We believe it is taking a reflective stance that really puts an edge on learning, that really pushes us to make public what we currently know in order to move to what we don't know.

Finally, we don't claim that this vision is the answer to the problems facing assessment today. We do claim that we have some very high standards about assessment, that this vision is a good starting point for asking more questions about what we want the future of assessment to look like, and that we look forward to continually assessing these standards through conversations with others.

References

Barrs, M. (1990). The primary language record: Reflection of issues in evaluation. *Language Arts, 67,* (3), 244–53.

Beverstock, C., Bintz, W., Copenhaver, J., & Farley, T. (1989, December 1). *Exploring freewrites as assessment: Insights and patterns.* Paper presented at the National Reading Conference, Austin, Texas.

Brown, R. (1987). Thoughtfulness, *Phi Delta Kappan, (69)1, 49#52.*

Cairney, T. (personal correspondence), 1989.

Cambourne, B. (1985). Assessment in reading: The drunkard's search. In L. Unsworth (Ed.), *Reading: An Australian perspective* (pp. 165-72). Melbourne, Australia: Thomas Nelson.

Chandler, P., Poling, N., Ono, N. & Mustapha, Z. (1989, December 1). *Exploring retellings as assessment: Insights and patterns.* Paper presented at the National Reading Conference, Austin, Texas.

Clay, M. (1990). Research currents: What is and what might be in evaluation. *Language Arts, 67,* (3), 288-98.

Cohen, A.S. (1988). *Tests: Marked for life?* New York: Scholastic.

Cooper, C.R. & Odell, L. (1977). Evaluating writing: Describing, measuring, judging. Urbana, IL: National Council of Teachers of English.

Durkin, D. (1987). Testing in the kindergarten. *The Reading Teacher, 40,* (8), 766-70.

Elbow, P. (1983). *Writing without teachers.* New York: Oxford University Press.

Elbow, P. & Belanoff, P. (1986). Portfolios as a substitute for proficiency examination. *College Composition and Communication, 37,* (3), 336-39.

Farr, R. & Farr, B. Personal correspondence.

Farstrup, A. (1989, December 1990, January). Point/counterpoint: State-by-state comparisons on national assessments. *Reading Today, 7,* (3), 1, 11-15.

Gardner, H. (1988). *Assessment in context: The alternative to standardized testing.* Cambridge, MA: Harvard Project Zero, Unpublished paper.

Goodman, K. (1967). Reading: The psycholinguistic guessing game. *Journal of the Reading Specialist, 4,* May, 126-35.

Goodman, K. (1986). *What's whole in whole language?* Portsmouth, NH: Heinemann.

Goodman, K., Goodman, Y., & Hood, W. (Eds.). (1989). The whole language evaluation book. Portsmouth, NH: Heinemann.

Goodman, Y. (1989). In K. Goodman, Y. Goodman, and J.W. Hood, (Eds.). *The whole language evaluation book.* Portsmouth, NH: Heinemann.

Goodman, Y. (1978). Kid watching: An alternative to testing. *Journal of National Elementary School Principals, 57,* (4), 41-45.

Graves, D. (1990, May). Presentation made at International Reading Conference, Atlanta, Georgia.

Guba, E. & Lincoln, Y. (1981). *Effective evaluation.* Beverly Hills: Sage.

Harmon, S. (1989/90). The tests: Trivial or toxic? *Teachers networking: The whole language newsletter, 9,* (1).

Harste, J., Woodward, V., & Burke, C. (1985). *Language stories and literacy lessons.* Portsmouth, NH: Heinemann.

Harste, J., Bintz, W., Beverstock, A., Copenhaver, J., Farley, T., Kelleher, S., Chase, M., Tseng, Yueh-Hung, Meng, A., Alwasilah, C., Chandler, P., Poling, N., Ono, N., Mustapha, Z. (1989, December). Symposium presented at the National Reading Conference, Austin, Texas.

Harste, J. (1989, December, 1990, January). Point/counterpoint: State-by-state comparisons on national assessments. *Reading Today, 7,* (3), 12-13.

Harste, J. (1989) *New policy guidelines for reading: Connecting research and practice.* Urbana, IL: National Council of Teachers of English.

Harste, J. (1986). What it means to be strategic: Good readers as informants. *Reading-Canada-Lecture, 6,* (1), 1–17.

Kelleher, C., Chase, M., Tseng, Y., Meng, A., & Alwasilah, C. (1989, December 1). *Exploring think-alouds as assessment: Insights and patterns.* Paper presented at the National Reading Conference, Austin, Texas.

Kemp, M. (1985). Standardized tests and reading-for-not-reading. In L. Unsworth, (Ed.). *Reading: An Australian perspective.* Melbourne, Australia: Thomas Nelson.

Krest, M. (1990). Adapting the portfolio to meet student needs. *English Journal, 79,* February, 29–34.

Johnston, P. (1987). Teachers as evaluation experts, *The Reading Teacher, 40,* (8), 744–48.

Mathews, J.K. (1990). From computer management to portfolio assessment. *The Reading Teacher, 43,* (6), 420–1.

Mishler, E. (1979). Meaning in context: Is there any other kind? *Harvard Educational Review, 49,* (1), 1–19.

Newman, J. (1989). Personal corresopndence.

Not as easy as a,b, or c. (1990, January 8). *Newsweek,* 56–58.

Pearson, P.D. & Valencia, S. (1989). Assessment, accountability, and professional perogative. *Research in Literacy: Meaning perspectives.* Thirty-sixth Yearbook, National Reading Conference.

Pikulski, J. (1990, May). The role of tests in a literacy assessment program. *The Reading Teacher, 43*(9), 686–88.

Simmons, J. (1990). Portfolios as large-scale assessment. *Language Arts, 67,* (3), 262–68.

Teale, W., Hiebert, E., & Chittenden, E. (1987). Assessing young children's literacy development. *The Reading Teacher, 40*(8), 722–77.

Valencia, S. (1990). A portfolio approach to classroom reading assessment: The whys, whats, and hows. *The Reading Teacher 43,* (4), 338–40.

Valencia, S. & Pearson, P.D. (1987). Reading assessment: Time for a change. *The Reading Teacher, 40,* (8), 726–32.

Valencia, S., Pearson, P.D., Peters, C., & Wixson, K. (1989, April). Theory and practice in statewide reading assessment: Closing the gap. *Educational Leadership, 46*(7), 57–63.

Wixson, K., Peters, C., Weber, E., & Roeber, E. (1987). New directions in statewise reading assessment. *The Reading Teacher, 40,* (8), 749–54.

Wolf, D. (1989, April). Portfolio assessment: Sampling student work. *Educational Leadership, 47*(7), 35–39.

Wolf, D. (1987, December, 1988, January). Opening up assessment. *Educational Leadership, 45*(4), 24–29.

Contributors

Bill Harp is currently Coordinator of Graduate Studies in the Center for Excellence in Education at Northern Arizona University. He received his Ph.D. from the University of Oregon. Drawing on his experience as an alementary school teacher, a principal, and university professor, he authored the popular "When the Principal Asks" column for *The Reading Teacher* (1988–1989). He is coauthor, with Dr. Jo Ann Brewer, of *Reading and Writing: Teaching for the Connections* (1991), published by Harcourt Brace Jovanovich.

John E. Bertrand received his Ph.D. from The Ohio State University. He is currently Research Specialist at the Center of Excellence for Basic Skills at Tennessee State University.

William Bintz is a doctoral student in the Language Education Department at Indiana University. He has taught language arts at the junior and senior high school levels in the United States and Puerto Rico as well as in Saudi Arabia. He is currently teaching elementary and secondary reading courses.

Maggie Castillo   holds her M.A. in reading education. She currently teaches kindergarten in the Flagstaff Public Schools. She is particularly interested in implementing a literature-based curriculum at the kindergarten level.

C. Jean Church   is the Elementary Curriculum Coordinator for the Vigo County School District in Terre Haute, Indiana. She received her Ph.D. from Indiana State University. She is currently investigating the process of change in teachers and principals and also spends a great deal of time in classrooms with teachers observing literacy development.

Ward Cockrum   received his Ph.D. in curriculum and instruction. He currently teaches elementary education methods courses at Northern Arizona University. His current interests include children's literature and methods of literacy development.

Jerome C. Harste   Professor of Language Education at Indiana University, has been an elementary school teacher, a Peace Corps Volunteer, and a Board Member of the International Reading Association (1988–1990). He has also chaired NCTE's Commission on Reading and has served as President of the National Reading Conference and the National Conference on Research in English.

Janice Henson is a doctoral candidate at the University of Missouri at Columbia. She has taught in the elementary grades as well as at the college level.

Ron Hutchison has been a school administrator since 1975. He is currently principal at Jackson Elementary School in the Hillsboro School District, Oregon. In 1988 The Oregon Reading Association named him Administrator of the Year for his outstanding contributions to reading and literacy.

Dorothy F. King is a Senior Research Associate for Research and Training Associates, Inc., and serves as a field-based consultant for Rural Technical Assistance Center, Office of Indian Education Programs. She received her Ed.D. from the University of Missouri.

S. Jeanne Reardon teaches primary grades in the Montgomery County Public Schools, Maryland. She received her A.B. from Oberlin College and has done graduate work at George Peabody College, Vanderbilt University and the University of Maryland. Her areas of special interest include writing, children's literature and classroom research.

Yvonne Siu-Runyan is Assistant Professor of Reading at the University of Northern Colorado. She received her Ph.D. from the University of Toledo. Her special interest areas include children's and adolescent literature, teacher as researcher, and the development of writing and its relationship to reading.

Hilary M. Sumner received her M.S. in Special Education from the University of Oregon. She is currently Learning Disabilities Specialist in the Beaverton, Oregon schools.

Dorothy J. Watson is Professor of Education at the University of Missouri at Columbia. She is President of the Whole Language Umbrella and has authored or coauthored several books, including *Ideas and Insights* (NCTE, 1987) and *Whole Language: Inquiring Voices* (Scholastic, 1988).

Index